KEEPING HOPE ALIVE

Stirrings in Christian Theology

DERMOT A. LANE

Gill & Macmillan

Gill & Macmillan Ltd
Goldenbridge
Dublin 8
with associated companies throughout the world

0 7171 2460 6

Index compiled by Helen Litton
Typeset by Kenneth J. Burnley at Irby, Wirral, Cheshire
Printed in the USA

A Cataloguing-in-Publication record of this book is available from
the British Library.

2 4 5 3 1

Dedicated to my sister,
Henrietta Lane,
who died on 30 July 1995,
while this book on hope was being completed

CONTENTS

ACKNOWLEDGMENTS

THIS BOOK OWES ITS ORIGINS to a generous invitation issued by Professors Enda McDonagh and Sean Freyne in 1987 to contribute a text on eschatology to a series of books by Irish theologians under the general title of *Theology of a Pilgrim People*. This series got off to an excellent start with three significant volumes in the late 1980s. Thereafter the series was abandoned for various reasons but individual volumes have continued to appear independently. As happens all too often with theological projects of this kind eschatology arrives late!

I am also very grateful to many different theological institutions at home and abroad that provided teaching opportunities to explore my thoughts on the theology of hope. At home these included Mater Dei Institute of Education, Holy Cross College and Milltown Institute of Philosophy and Theology. Abroad I received gracious hospitality from St Michael's College, Vermont, Seton Hall University, New Jersey, and the Pontifical College Josephenium, Ohio. From the staff and students of these colleges I benefited from many lively and fruitful theological conversations.

Many friends and colleagues have encouraged me along the way in writing this book and more recently I have the enjoyed the support of the people and priests of Balally Parish – to all of them unnamed I express my sincere thanks.

I am particularly indebted to several colleagues who took time to read parts of the manuscript and offer valuable criticisms: Bernard Boran, Paul Couture, Elizabeth Lovatt-Dolan, Anne Thurston and Terence Tilley.

I also wish to record my personal thanks to Phyllis Divilly, Maura Mitchell and Maura Purcell who patiently typed and edited various versions of the text.

Finally, I am grateful to Michael Gill of Gill & Macmillan for pursuing me to complete the text when at times I was tempted to put it aside.

INTRODUCTION

GIVEN THE AMAZING NUMBER of books published in theology on Jesus, the Church and the Trinity over the last thirty years, it is quite extraordinary that so little has been written on eschatology, that part of theology which deals with 'hope seeking understanding'. Apart from monographs by John Hick, Hans Kung, Zachary Hayes, Jurgen Moltmann, Peter Phan, Karl Rahner and Anton van der Walle, very little has appeared on eschatology. It might be argued that it is not surprising that so little has been published on this subject because there is very little that can be known about eschatology, and so we might be better off, in the words of Ludwig Wittegenstein 'Whereof one cannot speak, whereof one must be silent.' I have some sympathy with this point of view. However, it must be acknowledged that a negative theology is more a point of arrival than a point of departure. We need to arrive at a stage of 'learned ignorance' *(docta ignorantia)* in most matters theological and this is particularly the case in eschatology. Thus one of the purposes of this book is to lead people to an informed state of ignorance about eschatology in contrast to the simplistic dismissals that generally greet the subject. It could be argued at the very least that it is better to struggle with the questions of eschatology than simply to ignore them.

Another reason for attempting to write a book on eschatology is that classical eschatology appears to claim too much and seems far too certain on matters of detail. This is perhaps less the fault of the classical tradition – which is often more sophisticated and nuanced than we acknowledge – and much more a problem with our literal appropriation of that tradition and our twentieth-century blunting of the symbolic imagination.

A third reason for addressing eschatology is that we live in a world and a Church that has lost its way in the welter of cultural change, scientific paradigm shifts and mounting pluralism. Both Church and society desperately need a vision of hope, and one of the aims of this book is to keep hope alive – not just hope in the next life but especially hope in this life; not just individual hope but also communal hope. Growing cynicism with politics and increasing apathy with religion are widespread phenomena as we approach the end of the second millennium – attitudes that exist in stark contrast to the debates surrounding the end of the first millennium.

A fourth reason for addressing this subject is that eschatology is still seen by so many people as something about 'life after death' and therefore need not detain us in our pragmatic approach to this life. The underlying thesis of this book is that eschatology is at least as much about life before death as it is about the so-called 'next world'.

One of the most distinctive features of contemporary culture is its failure to discuss death and to take dying seriously. Modern science and technology have marginalised or 'anaesthetised' the realities of death and dying. A death-denying culture is ultimately a life-denying culture as we claim in Chapter 4.

This book begins by looking at the changed context in which eschatology, 'hope seeking understanding', must give an account of itself. Questions arising from the Marxist critique of Christianity, the nuclear threat, the ecological crisis and the apparent emptiness of so much post-modern thinking are addressed in Chapter 1. An appropriate starting-point for any discussion about hope in the future is surely a re-examination of what it means to be human and this is explored in Chapter 3. Against this background a case is made in Chapter 5 for the possibility of hope in the present and the future. The presence of hope in the history of Judaism and the life of Jesus is then examined in Chapter 6.

The central thesis of the book in Chapter 7 is that the shape of the future for humanity, society and the world is prefigured in the Cross of Christ. The reality of the crucified and risen Christ as the Hope of the world is explored at length in Chapters 8 and 11. Only in the light of the advent of the end of time (the *Eschaton)* in Christ can consideration be given to secondary questions about the last things (the *eschata*) and different disputed questions which are addressed respectively in Chapters 9 and 10. The concluding chapter emphasises the need to keep the memory of Christ alive through the celebration of the Eucharist as an important source of Christian hope.

The purpose of this book is not to offer a finished text or a complete eschatology; the purpose is far more modest: to initiate a debate about the ultimate questions of living and dying, to bring back eschatology to the centre of theological discussions, to show how political praxis presupposes an eschatological vision, to unify perspectives about the present and the future, to reconnect heaven and earth, to link up history and creation, and to re-establish a relationship between the Eucharist and eschatology.

If any one of these purposes is realised or if any one of the above reasons for daring to write about eschatology is fulfilled, then the author will be more than satisfied.

Dermot A. Lane
1 February 1996 (St Brigid's Day)

ABBREVIATIONS

The 1966 Walter M. Abbot edition and translation of the documents of the Second Vatican Council have been used and are abbreviated as follows:

A.G.   *Ad gentes:* Decree on the Church's Missionary Activity
C.D.   *Christus Dominus:* Decree on the Bishops' Pastoral Office in the Church
D.H.   *Dignitatis Humanae:* Declaration on Religious Freedom
D.V.   *Dei Verbum:* Dogmatic Constitution on Divine Revelation
G.S.   *Gaudium et spes:* Pastoral Constitution on the Church in the Modern World
L.G.   *Lumen gentium:* Dogmatic Constitution on the Church
N.A.   *Nostra aetate:* Declaration on the Relationship of the Church to Non-Christian Religions
O.T.   *Optatam totius:* Decree on the training of priests
P.O.   *Presbyterorum ordinis:* Decree on the ministry and life of priests
S.C.   *Sacrosanctum Concilium:* Constitution on the Sacred Liturgy
U.R.   *Unitatis redintegratio:* Decree on Ecumenism

Other abbreviations include:
C.C.C.   *Catechism of the Catholic Church,* Dublin: Veritas, 1994
C.D.F.   The Sacred Congregation for the Doctrine of the Faith, Rome
G.C.D.   *The General Catechetical Directory,* Rome, 1971
I.T.C.   International Theological Commission, Rome
N.J.B.C.   *The New Jerome Biblical Commentary,* edited by Raymond E. Brown, Joseph A. Fitzmyer and Roland E. Murphy, New Jersey: Prentice Hall, 1990
S.T.   *Summa theologiae,* Thomas Aquinas

Scripture quotations are taken, unless otherwise stated, from the *New Revised Standard Version,* 1989.

1

Reclaiming Eschatology

As Czeslaw Milosz has observed, no intelligent contemporary is spared the pressure exerted in our world by the void, the absurd, the anti-meaning, all of which are part of the intellectual atmosphere we subsist in; and yet Milosz notices this negative pressure only to protest against a whole strain of modern literature which has conceded victory to it.

(Seamus Heaney, 1995)

THE CLASSICAL DESCRIPTION of theology has been faith seeking understanding or, as many would prefer to say today, faith seeking understanding in human experience. The trouble with this perception of theology is that the faith in question has lost contact with hope. Most theologians agree that faith, hope and love are all of a piece and that you cannot fully appreciate one without reference to the other. In practice, however, we know that all too often these three different but complementary approaches go their own respective ways giving us three distinct disciplines that rarely interact with one another: morality, theology and eschatology. By far the most neglected of these three is hope, and so eschatology – which is really about hope seeking under-standing in human experience – has fallen on bad times.

FROM THE MARGINS TO THE CENTRE

Eschatology has been criticised by Karl Barth as a harmless tract coming at the end of theology, and Johann Baptist Metz talks about the presence of a 'bland Christian eschatology' promoting empty time; by this he means 'an eschatology without apocalyptic sting'.[1] By and large escha-tology has been marginalised within theology to the detriment of the whole of theology. What is left to the end is all too quickly forgotten whereas one of the important functions of eschatology is to enable us to remember throughout the whole of theology not only the past but also the future.

The neglect of eschatology has been damaging to theology in general and a contemporary understanding of hope in particular. To theology in general, because the absence of eschatology is partly responsible for the inflation of different theological claims in areas such as revelation, christology and ecclesiology. Within theology, eschatology serves as a powerful reminder that all theological claims are subject to the qualifications and reservations that come from the promise of an open eschatological future. Eschatology is a protest against the premature closure of our understanding of the present and a plea for openness towards the future. Like theology itself, eschatology has an important role to play as 'the guardian of the *docta ignorantia futuri'*.[2] Eschatology also has a critical and constructive function to play *vis à vis* the rest of theology.[3]

Eschatology is critical insofar as it questions the self-sufficiency of the secular order, and is constructive insofar as it sustains people in hope, empowering them to create a future from within the present. On the other hand eschatology itself has become impoverished through lack of contact with the rest of theology, especially the historical claims of revelation, christology and ecclesiology. The relationship between theology and eschatology should be one that is mutually critical and enriching.

Eschatology has been usually described as the study of the four last things: death, judgment, heaven and hell which have become known as the *eschata*. However, this classical account of eschatology is not without its own particular prejudice. For one thing this description seems to confine eschatology simply to these particular items, whereas a fuller account would focus on the advent of the end of time (the *Eschaton*) in Christ. It is only in the light of our understanding of the appearance of the end of time in the crucified and risen Christ that we can develop a Christian theology of death, judgment, heaven, hell, purgatory and the second coming. The primary emphasis in New Testament eschatology is on the significance of the appearance of the *Eschaton* in Christ which shapes our understanding of the present and the future. Over the centuries, however, the emphasis has fallen on a treatment of the individual *eschata* to the neglect of the *Eschaton* in Christ. Something of a separation has taken place between our understanding of the *Eschaton* in Christ and its relationship to the individual *eschata*. Today there is a recovery of the biblical emphasis on the close relationship that exists between the Christ-event and its implications for living and dying in the present and the future.

Furthermore, the classical description of eschatology as the study of death, heaven, hell, purgatory and the second coming could give the impression that eschatology is concerned exclusively with events in the future. Consequently eschatology appears removed from the theology of present-day realities like the Church and the world, the Eucharist and social justice, faith and ecology. This impression is confirmed by the Marxist critique of Christianity, namely that religion is the opium of the people, distracting them from their political responsibilities to improve the historical and social conditions of the present world.

In contrast, a renewal of classical eschatology seeks to address present-day historical and social issues as well as dealing with the future, keeping a critical eye on the significance of the present for the future and of the future for the present. In particular, contemporary eschatology will seek to keep alive the creative biblical tension that exists between the 'already' and the 'not yet' of the Christ-event, between Johannine realised eschatology and Pauline futurist eschatology. Furthermore, it is remarkable how the eschatology of Vatican II in principle takes account of the Marxist critique by emphasising the creative interplay that obtains between present responsibilities and future promises in Christian self-understanding.[4]

An additional challenge for a renewed eschatology will be the over-coming of the many dualisms that have plagued classical eschatology. This challenge concerns especially the dualism of body and soul, spirit and matter, heaven and earth. These dualisms can only be transformed by addressing the contemporary understanding of what it means to be a human being – an issue we will address in Chapter 3.

A further point about classical eschatology is its concern almost exclusively with individual destiny, i.e. a preoccupation with 'my destiny', and the salvation of 'my soul'. This preoccupation with individual salvation reflects more the influence of Hellenistic culture on the Christian message in contrast to the biblical perspectives which are more inclusive and wholistic. It is now clear, however, that the destiny of the individual is bound up with the destiny of the whole of humanity and the cosmos. As the Second Vatican Council points out 'the destiny of the human community has become all of a piece, where once various groups of men had a kind of private destiny of their own'.[5]

If these shifts from the *eschata* to the *Eschaton*, from the future to the present *and* the future, from an individualist approach to a more inclusive one, are to be effective then eschatology must move to the centre of theology. Some awareness of this centrality of eschatology to the rest of theology was expressed at the First Vatican Council in its *Dogmatic Constitution on the Catholic Faith, Dei Filius* (1870). This document pointed out that 'reason illuminated by faith understands the Christian mysteries' from the analogy with the objects of its natural knowledge and from the connection of these mysteries with one another and *with man's ultimate end*.[6] Contemporary theology is characterised by the quest to recover the interconnectedness of all the Christian mysteries[7] and this includes in a special way the neglected centrality of eschatology. Under the impact of biblical studies and the work of Johann Weiss we find K. Barth pointing out that 'If Christianity be not altogether a thorough-going eschatology, there remains in it no relationship whatever with Christ.'[8] In a similar fashion Jurgen Moltmann is insistent on the importance of this move of eschatology to the centre of theology:

> The eschatological is not one element of Christianity, but it is the medium of Christian faith as such, the key in which everything in it is set, the glow that suffuses everything here in the dawn of an expected new day. For Christian faith lives by the raising of the crucified Christ, and strains after the promises of the universal future of Christ. Eschatology is the passionate suffering and passionate longing kindled by the Messiah. Hence eschatology can not really be only a part of Christian doctrine. Rather, the eschatological outlook is characteristic of all Christian proclamation, of every Christian existence and of the whole church.[9]

Likewise for Karl Rahner, eschatology is at the centre of the theological enterprise.[10] This importance of eschatology becomes most evident in Rahner when he comes to draw up three brief credal statements on the meaning and content of Christian faith. One of these credal statements is explicitly eschatology:

> Christianity is the religion which keeps open the question about the absolute future which wills to give itself in its own reality by self communication, and which has established this will as eschatologically irreversible in Jesus Christ, and this future is called God.[11]

What this means in effect is that eschatology as hope seeking understanding in human experience must complement the efforts of faith and love seeking understanding, and vice versa. What these theologians were trying to do with eschatology in this century was twofold. On the one hand they were seeking to overcome the marginalisation of classical eschatology, and on the other they were also attempting to retrieve the centrality of eschatology found in the biblical and patristic traditions.[12]

In spite of these efforts by Barth, Moltmann and Rahner, and indeed other theologians like Wolfhart Pannenberg and Joseph Ratzinger, eschatology has remained around the margins of theology. Indeed, it must be stated – and this is one of the theses of this book – that eschatology is the missing link in much contemporary theology. For example, liberation theology would benefit significantly from a more explicitly developed eschatological orientation.[13] Catholic social teaching would take on a new urgency if it were given a more explicitly eschatological foundation.[14] Many theologies of creation have very little to say about eschatology in spite of the natural affinity that exists between origins and destinies as well as the Christian understanding of first creation and the New Creation.[15] It is Johann Baptist Metz more than most theologians who is acutely aware of the demise of eschatology and its need of restructuring.

CHANGES IN THEOLOGY AFFECTING ESCHATOLOGY

In any reconstruction of eschatology account must be taken of the changes that have occurred in the rest of theology in the twentieth century. A number of important shifts have occurred in contemporary theology which as yet have not been fully appropriated by eschatology. Indeed the development of eschatology in this century has fallen behind the advances that have taken place in the rest of theology. For example one of the most significant changes in theology is the turn to modernity, i.e. full recognition of the advent of the modern world. The challenge of modernity is something that began with the scientific revolution of the seventeenth century, continued in the eighteenth century by the philosophical revolution of the Enlightenment, progressed in the nineteenth century through the social and industrial revolutions, and has continued in the twentieth century through ongoing scientific and technological developments. There is a need for eschatology to face modernity and to come to grips with the full implications of modernity in the way that the rest of theology has done in this century.

Within this turn to modernity there has been a change from a classical culture to an historical consciousness, that is to say a shift from fixed essences, timeless truths and immutable substances to an open, malleable and historical culture. The discovery that natural, social and political realities are not fixed and static, not closed or divinely pre-ordained, but rather are being continually changed by the progress of modern science is part of the challenge facing eschatology today. This insight highlights the ever-increasing role that human beings play in shaping the future. This in turn has far-reaching consequences for the way we see the role of eschatology in understanding the world today. Indeed this insight is the basis upon which we will begin to highlight the importance of a this-worldly eschatology alongside an other-worldly eschatology – something that was recognised at the Second Vatican Council.[16] For many, and in particular for Hegel, it was the French Revolution that symbolised the moment in history in which humanity became aware and conscious of itself as responsible for the shape and structure of social life. Gradually it became apparent that the social and political *status quo* was not something divinely preordained. Instead the *status quo* was the outcome of human, often fallible and sometimes very self-centred, decisions. This advent of historical consciousness has signalled a new awareness within humanity of its responsibility to shape and structure the world that we inhabit.

The challenge of modernity is something that was formally recognised by the Catholic Church at the Second Vatican Council. Indeed the drama of Vatican II was about coming to grips with modernity. It sought to do this in a variety of different ways, particularly through the *Pastoral Constitution on the Church in the Modern World*.[17] A number of significant shifts took place at the Second Vatican Council which enable us to understand the implications of the emergence of historical consciousness today. These shifts embrace the turn to the human subject, the recognition of human autonomy and the importance of religious freedom.[18] Another equally important shift was the turn to human experience and the recognition that experience plays an important role in theology.[19] A third shift was the turn to hermeneutics,[20] which we will address in Chapter 2.

Another major change affecting theology today which must be recognised by eschatology concerns the crisis of modernity itself, i.e. the growing realisation that modernity itself is an ambiguous enterprise and that in many respects the inflated claims of modernity relating to the promise of progress, the promotion of endless growth and development have become bankrupt. In the light of this, many commentators talk about a move from modernity to post-modernity. The problem with this particular shift is that the concept of post-modernity is itself unclear; quite often it is more a way of signalling dissatisfaction with the modern world than actually having a grasp of a clear alternative – a symptom that is not without its own eschatological significance. Post-modernity is one of those elusive terms that is used in many difference senses, some of which are extremely negative and nihilistic. The negative sense of post-modernity is about a programme of deconstruction coming from French philosophers without any effort at reconstruction; a reduction of life to a meaningless series of images without any reality behind them. Post-modernity of this kind puts an end to theology and eschatology by eliminating all patterns of meaning and relationships within community. Everything is atomised and there is no dance or order or poetry or meaning left to life; just chaos, empty time and vacuous space remain. This perception of post-modernity marks the end of all the great narratives about the meaning of life, and all that is left are small individualised narratives, i.e. privatised interpretations without any coherence or centre. Within this perspective the dancer is removed from the dance of life, the orchestra eliminated from the sound of music, the composer removed from the orchestra, and all relationships are reduced to chance contacts and new forms of emptiness.

On the other hand a more positive understanding of post-modernity is being proposed among some North American thinkers seeking to reconstruct the meaning of life and reality according to the emergence of a new paradigm: inclusive, processive, organic, wholistic. This new post-modern paradigm is coming to birth under the impact of the converging influences of feminism, ecology, the new physics and process thought.[21]

Some have seen the crisis within modernity as an excuse to by-pass the challenge of modernity and to leapfrog over modernity altogether into a kind of pre-modern post-modernity. This kind of move forgets that theology and eschatology must be able to address the demands of the present as well as live out of the wisdom of the past. There is no escaping the fire of modernity. It is only in and through the crucible of modernity that we can move on to the more positive aspects of post-modernity, which include an ethical resistance to more of the same, a concern for difference, and a deep interest in otherness.

FORMULATING THE QUESTION OF
ESCHATOLOGY FOR TODAY

In the light of these changes in theology and their effect on eschatology, and in the light of the move of eschatology from the margins to the centre, we can now begin to formulate the tasks of eschatology for the late twentieth century. Any formulation of the eschatological question must take account of the presence of new pressures on eschatology. These include the existence of so much mass death in the Third World, the permanency of the nuclear threat, the ongoing ecological crisis, and a new awareness of the finiteness of our small blue planet. How then do we formulate the question of eschatology for today?

In the first place we must recognise the urgent need for a renewed eschatology, a need that has been brought home to us as much by developments in the world as by demands from within theology itself. These needs from within and from outside theology must be kept in mind in formulating the question of eschatology for today.

One of the outstanding characteristics of the twentieth century is the ever-increasing consciousness of the existence of mass death since the First World War. The difference between the Black Death of the fourteenth century and the presence of so much death today is that in the fourteenth century mass death came from uncontrollable natural forces whereas in the twentieth century so much death is caused directly or indirectly by the inhumanity of humans to humans: war, poverty, hunger, violence. This reality of mass death is something that continues in the Third World countries through the presence of so much hunger and starvation. Even more recently the increasing AIDS epidemic is a further expression of the reality of mass death in the twentieth century.

Over and above the obvious question about the meaning of life in the face of so much death, the existence of mass death raises questions about the destiny of the whole human species. Mass death forces us to go beyond questions about my individual death, enabling us to realise that individual destiny is bound up with the destiny of the whole human race. In other words mass death seems to suggest that questions about the destiny of the whole human race are as important as questions about individual death. Closely linked to the issue of mass death is the meaning of the Jewish holocaust, a reality which continues to haunt the memory of Christian Europe and at the same time raises searching questions about the presence of God in the face of such death.

A second pressure is the nuclear threat. Though the nuclear threat has been considerably reduced by the ending of the cold war it is still a reality. As *Time* magazine sums up: 'Though the cold war is over, the world has become a more, rather than less, dangerous place . . . More than twenty-five countries have developed or may be developing the arms of mass destruction.'[22] The reality of the nuclear threat highlights the human potential for global destruction; it also highlights the need for greater vigilance in making the world a safer rather than a more dangerous place in which to live. The nuclear threat demands the development of a this-worldly eschatology alongside an other-worldly eschatology. The nuclear threat raises both secular and theological questions. As Jonathan Schell observes:

> By threatening life in its totality, the nuclear peril creates new connections between the elements of existence – a new mingling of the public and the private, the political and the emotional, the spiritual and the biological.[23]

At the same time the nuclear reality also raises questions about human power and divine power. As the American bishops point out in their Pastoral on Peace: 'We are the first generation since Genesis with the power to virtually destroy God's creation.'[24] What was once reserved to God, namely the gathering together of the human family in a final act of redemption in the fullness of time, now appears as something that can be thwarted by human action.[25]

A third issue for eschatology concerns the ecological question. We are reliably informed by scientists that if humanity continues to live by a consumerist ethic of 'more', i.e. to live as if the resources of the earth were unlimited, then we will end up destroying the earth. Many hold that the ecological issue is as serious as, if not more insidious than, the nuclear threat because the destruction of the planet earth is more gradual and therefore less dramatic in comparison to the nuclear issue. Indeed some would hold that we are in danger of invisibly crossing over a threshold that is irreversible in terms of the gradual destruction of the earth we inhabit. The message issued to the world from the Earth Summit in Rio de Janeiro in 1992 was that we are heading for the ecological collapse of the earth's vital life-support systems unless there is a radical change of direction in the personal lifestyle of people and the corporate mores of industry and technology. Like the nuclear issue, ecology concentrates attention on saving the earth in the present for the future and also highlights the need for developing a this-worldly eschatology.

Turning to the demands within theology itself, one is struck immediately by the existence of a crisis of language within eschatology. There are at least two levels to this crisis. In the first place we have to ask what it means to talk about heaven and hell and purgatory. Whatever else it might mean, it does not mean positing places in the next world in the way we posit places in this life. Yet the popular imagination all too often interprets these realities in the same way as it thinks about this-worldly realities.

More specifically there is a crisis of language concerning expressions like 'life after death', 'eternal rest', 'saving my soul', 'the immortality of the soul', and 'the resurrection of the body'. Each of these expressions becomes problematic if they are not presented in a manner that is symbolically and analogically sensitive. For example, in talking about 'life after death' the impression is often given that eternal life is a continuation of this life, or in the words of Rahner as if it was merely a matter of 'changing horses'.[26] This careless use of language does little to advance the credibility of eschatology. Further, the image of 'life after death' for many seems to play down the importance of life *before* death, forgetting that it is only in virtue of God's love for us in this life and our response to that gracious love that we can justify the possibility of hope for eternal communion with God in the future. This crisis of language in eschatology highlights the need to draw up careful guidelines for interpreting the symbolic meaning and importance of eschatological statements.

In the light of these pressures coming from without and within theology we can now attempt some formulation of the eschatological question for today. Clearly there is no one particular formulation of the question but rather a series of different questions that point us in the general direction of eschatology. This series of questions can be captured in a variety of ways.

One particular expression of the eschatological question can be found in the *Pastoral Constitution of the Church in the Modern World* – that document of Vatican II which grappled so honestly with the challenges coming from modernity:

> . . . in the face of the modern development of the world, an ever-increasing number of people are raising the most basic questions or recognising them with a new sharpness: What is man? What is this sense of sorrow, of evil, of death, which continues to exist despite so much progress . . . What follows this earthly life?[27]

The value of this particular formulation of the question of eschatology is that it highlights the importance of beginning with the issue of what it means to be human: what is human identity? Anthropology, the issue of human self-understanding, must surely be our point of departure in trying to retrieve and reconstruct eschatology for today. No sooner have we faced anthropology than it becomes necessary to face the question of death. These two issues of anthropology and death as highlighted by the Second Vatican Council will set the agenda for the approach to eschatology that follows in Chapters 3 and 4 respectively.

A second expression of the eschatological question are the following imaginary questions from a child to its mother:

'Where did the world come from?'
'Where is the world going?'
'How long did it take to make the world?'
'How does our planet relate to other planets?'
'Does our world have a destiny?'
'Where is grandma now?'

Of course, everyone knows that these are not just the questions of a child. They are also the questions of every adult; they are the kind of questions whose answers determine the shape of eschatology. The significance of these questions coming from the child is that they tease the deadened imagination of adults. Yet the imagination of adults in recent years, in the light of a new understanding of cosmic and human origins coming from cosmology, has been stirred once again. A recent issue of *National Geographic* magazine formulates the same question with daunting deliberation:

> And so many stars. And yet we have learned also that the universe is mostly emptiness. Cold, sometimes flickering with explosive energy, this universe taunts us with mysteries. When did it begin? How will it end? What laws of nature governed its creation and evolution? Are there other universes? If so, are they like ours? Time and again since humans first acquired a sense of wonder, we have asked such questions.[28]

Another expression of the eschatological question can be found in the following words of Bertrand Russell:

> That man is the product of causes which had no prevision of the end they were achieving; that his origin, his growth, his hopes and fears, his loves and beliefs, are but the outcome of accidental collocations of atoms; that no fire, no heroism, no intensity of thought and feeling, can preserve an individual life beyond the grave; that all the labours of the ages, all the devotion, all the inspiration, all the noonday brightness of human genius are destined to extinction in the vast depth of the solar system; and the whole temple of man's achievement must inevitably be buried beneath the debris of the universe in ruins – all these things, if not quite beyond dispute, are yet so nearly certain, that no philosophy which rejects them can hope to stand.[29]

These observations of Russell force us to ask the question that is unavoidable for every human being: Is it possible that the human is merely a spark in the evolutionary spiral of progress that one day will burn out and become an empty ash on the rubbish heap of civilisation? A more modern version of Russell's thesis can be found in Jacques Monod's observation: 'Man knows at last that he is alone in the universe's unfeeling immensity out of which he emerged only by chance.'[30]

A fourth expression of the eschatological question can be found from the developments that have been taking place in contemporary science, and in particular in the new cosmic story about the origins of the universe in which we live. Will the earth ultimately burn out? Will the universe gradually move from a Big Bang to a big crunch? This particular challenge coming from the world of science is one that has been recognised in a very significant address by John Paul II to scientists in 1988 in which he singles out eschatology for particular mention:

> Contemporary developments in science challenge theology far more deeply than did the introduction of Aristotle into Western Europe in the thirteenth century . . . What, if any, are the eschatological implications of contemporary cosmology, especially in the light of the vast future of our universe?[31]

A final expression of the eschatological question can be found in the story, available in the opening pages in the Dutch Catechism, about the seventh-century monk Paulinus who visited King Edwin in northern England to persuade him to accept Christianity. The King summoned his advisers, discussions took place, and one of the King's advisers addressed the assembly:

> Your Majesty . . . In the winter when the fire burns warm and bright and the storm is howling outside bringing snow and rain, it happens . . . that a little bird flies into the hall. It comes in one door and flies out through the other. For the few moments it is inside the hall, it doesn't feel the cold but as soon as it leaves your sight, it returns to the dark. It seems to me that the life of man is much the same. We do not know what went before and we do not know where he is going. If the new doctrine can speak to us of these things, it is well for us to follow it.[32]

An important part of the appeal of Christianity is its vision of what has gone before and what follows.

What is significant about these different expressions of the eschatological question is that in one way or another they focus on beginnings and endings, on origins and destinies. This highlights the need for eschatology to concern itself with our understanding of creation. We can hardly talk about where we are going unless we have some sense of where we have come from. Further, knowledge of where we have come from and where we are going will surely influence the steps we take in our historical journey. Consequently it is imperative at some stage in one's eschatology to work out what I call a creation-based-eschatology – a challenge we will take up in Chapter 11. The bringing together of creation and the New Creation, of origins and destiny is one of the most urgent issues facing eschatology today. A credible eschatology, therefore, must be able to chart a course that contains some degree of continuity between past, present and future while at the same time leaving room for the important elements of change and transformation. According to one commentator the conjunction of Genesis and Apocalypse 'may yet prove to be a decisive way for a theological recovery of the Bible and for the rebirth of theology itself'.[33] If this coming together of Genesis and Apocalypse is to succeed, then account must be taken of the contemporary understanding of the world in which we live. One of the reasons why so much eschatology has become incredible today is that it is constructed out of a picture of the world quite different from the findings of contemporary science. As one commentator puts it concerning classical Christian doctrine, and we can take it that eschatology is included in these observations:

> It was a picture based largely on the physics and sociology of Aristotle (fourth century BC) which was later elaborated into the medieval model. In that picture heaven was completely separated from the earth . . . things in heaven were not only made of a different substance from those on earth but they obeyed different physical laws. Man and the earth were central to the whole scheme of things; heaven was above man's head and hell was beneath his feet. Every detail of what man did and thought was closely watched over by God and his angels.[34]

A renewed eschatology, if it is to be credible in the twentieth century, must take account of the findings of contemporary science concerning our understanding of the world today. This does not mean that eschatology will take over the findings of contemporary science, but it does require at least that eschatology should not be in contradiction with those findings.

2

THEOLOGICAL SUPPOSITIONS
OF ESCHATOLOGY

*We are struggling for a discipline that stops me taking myself for granted
as the fixed centre of a little universe, and allows me to find and lose and
refind myself constantly in the interweaving patterns of a world I did not
make and do not control*

(Rowan Williams, 1994)

IN SEEKING TO RETRIEVE eschatology for the next century it becomes
necessary to assume certain theological principles. Without these
principles eschatology will never get off the ground. Among these
theological suppositions we must include as given the existence of the
religious dimension of human experience, the christomorphic character
of eschatology, and the presence of the Spirit of God as active in the
world and the Christian community. Although these are theological
suppositions, which we will be invoking in the following chapters, they
require some preliminary introduction.

EXPERIENCE AND HERMENEUTICS

The turn to human experience, so characteristic of twentieth-century
theology, must be applied to eschatology.[1] At the same time, however,
this turn to experience must be accompanied by an equally important
emphasis on the understanding and interpretation of human experience
through the science of hermeneutics.

Eschatology is a particular interpretation of human experience, an
interpretation that attends closely to the promise and potential latent
within human experience. Eschatology therefore is an approach to the
future based on our understanding of present human experience, especially insofar as this experience is influenced and illuminated by the
Christ-event. Eschatology articulates a hope about the possible fulfilment of the present experience in the future. Following Karl Rahner it

can be said that eschatology entails the transposition of present experiences of salvation from a mode of beginning into a mode of consummation.[2] Eschatology therefore is not some kind of esoteric, privileged knowledge available to a select few, nor is it some idle speculation about the future, nor is it a kind of reporting of what goes on in the afterlife. Instead eschatology must be understood as a particular interpretation and understanding of what is going on in present human and Christian experience in terms of its significance for creating hope in the future.

It is important to emphasise the link between human experience and Christian eschatology because in this way we can begin to understand why certain forms of traditional eschatology have fallen on hard times today. Traditional theologies about heaven and hell, judgment and Purgatory, have collapsed not because they are untrue or false but because they have become derailed from contemporary human experience and the interpretation of that experience as informed by both the Christ-event and our understanding of the world in which we live. Once religious symbols become detached from contemporary experience they begin to take on a life of their own, assuming an ontological status that goes beyond the warrants of faith seeking understanding in experience. When this happens these religious symbols can become more ideological than theological. We should remember in this context that theology is partly about the conceptualisation of religious experience. Alfred Whitehead has remarked we 'cannot think without abstractions'[3] and then goes on to point out that 'a civilisation which cannot burst through its current abstractions is doomed to sterility after a limited period of progress'.[4] Eschatology at present needs to break through some of its old cultural abstractions, especially in the light of ecology, feminism, cosmology and the new physics. It will be necessary, therefore, to take account of these new impulses in the retrieval and reconstruction of eschatology.

It might well be asked at this stage what kind of human experiences does eschatology deal with? Clearly there is a broad range of human experiences that are of particular interest to eschatology. Among these reference must be made to the positive experience of becoming, an experience that is a fundamental characteristic of what it is to be human. The innate capacity to become, the potential to grow and to develop, carries within it a promise of fulfilment, the seeds of a future. It is these particular experiences that open up the possibility of eschatology. A second, negative range of experience is the realisation and awareness of the limitations and incompleteness of the human condition, especially in terms of human vulnerability and finiteness. Such experiences highlight the need for completion, for healing and for wholeness. It is these needs

15

that human eschatology seeks to address. A third significant human experience for eschatology is the quest for justice, i.e. the concern to right the wrongs of life, to balance out the ills and evils with the goodness and justice done out of love. It is this quest for justice that lies at the origins of apocalyptic eschatology in the Hebrew Scriptures.

A further experience that eschatology interprets are those moments in life when we move beyond what David Tracy calls our lacklustre selves, moments when we step outside the temporal, when we rub shoulders with another dimension in life, whether in good conversation, in relationships, in listening to music or being absorbed by the needs of others.[5] An additional important experience for eschatology is the experience of enjoyment and love, each of which cries out for fulfilment. Frederick Nietzsche suggests 'that every enjoyment seeks to be eternal'. A further significant human experience is the experience of friendship and love which gives us a glimpse of human potential, a hint of who we are, and the life of communion we are called to live. As Gabriel Marcel points out, to say 'I love you' means 'I believe you will live for ever.' The experience of love awakens hope in the human heart. A final experience that eschatology must address is the experience of human suffering and death. C. S. Lewis in one of his books tells the story of the death of his friend Charles and remarks 'when my idea of death met my idea of Charles it was my idea of death that changed'.

It is these experiences and many others that are the basis and foundation of theological eschatology. In seeking to interpret these experiences eschatology will focus on elements of continuity and transformation. On the one hand there will be a line of continuity between the present and the future, between being and becoming, between beginnings and endings. At the same time there will be an equally important line of discontinuity and transformation wherein the emphasis will be on newness, recreation and the possibility of being surprised by joy.

While the link between experience and eschatology is important, it must be said that the interpretation of human experience is equally significant. Indeed we need to avoid the temptation of separating experience from interpretation. There is no such thing as pure experience or an uninterpretative experience. This does not mean that there cannot be new interpretations of human experience or indeed new experiences seeking interpretation. To the contrary there will always be a need for renewed interpretation of eschatological experiences because the interpreter is always situated in a particular time frame and place which are socially and culturally conditioned. In view of this, past interpretations and present experiences will mutually enrich and critique each other.

This means that our hermeneutics will be shaped by Paul Tillich's method of correlation and its refinement by David Tracy in terms of requiring a mutually critical correlation between experience and tradition, between the Christian message and the contemporary situation.[6]

If a critical correlation is to take place between human experience and eschatology then account must be taken of some of the criticisms that have been made of eschatology down through the centuries. By far the most outstanding criticism is that of Karl Marx who claimed that Christianity is the opium of the people. Lying behind this criticism is a particular eschatology, one which suggests that belief in the next life is responsible for people neglecting their human, social and political responsibilities in this life. If this criticism is to inform our retrieval of eschatology, then we must draw up certain criteria that will take account of Marx's criticism. These criteria will include the following points:

1. Eschatological interpretations of experience should give a particular depth and urgency to the meaning of present existence. Eschatology therefore ought to be life-enhancing in its affirmations and not a distraction from the challenges of life in this world and our responsibilities for constructing a better world in the present.
2. Eschatology should open up possibilities in this life that would otherwise remain closed or absent. Eschatology should enable people to go beyond cynicism, fatalism and apathy concerning the possibility of improving the quality of life in this world. Eschatology therefore must affirm the value of human actions and social praxis both for this life and the next life.
3. Eschatology should generate a particular energy for the work of justice, especially in relation to those who exist on the margins of life, as well as empowering people to care for the well-being of the earth in the present and the future. Eschatological statements, therefore, should have an emancipatory thrust to them.

These three criteria are simply a way of spelling out the observation made at the Second Vatican Council that 'the expectation of a new earth must not weaken but rather stimulate our concern for cultivating this one'.[7] This particular emphasis could be said to be new or at least a development in the teaching of the Catholic Church.

A second principle guiding the eschatological interpretation of experience is the acknowledgment that all eschatological statements are symbolic. It is essential to good theology and in particular to eschatology to remember that the language of faith and hope is symbolic, dialectical and analogical. Most controversies in the history of theology have been caused by the neglect of the symbolical significance of theological statements. Eschatology is a prime example of this neglect. Indeed the demise of eschatology in this century has been caused by the failure to keep alive the symbolical, sacramental and analogical imagination. The death of metaphor in post-modern consciousness is one of the most serious obstacles to a reconstruction of eschatology. Unless we have some sense of inhabiting a universe that carries symbolic meaning and is ultimately sacramental it will be extremely difficult to retrieve the eschatological interpretation of experience.

Religious symbols point beyond themselves to a dimension in life that is not immediately available to experience. The symbol is not the reality symbolised and yet the reality symbolised is only present through the mediating power of the symbol. Symbols introduce us to different levels of reality: they bring to light the hidden meaning of life and embody in a concrete way what cannot be grasped directly. A religious symbol effects a union between a sensible image and a reality that cannot be fully contained within the limits of language. Part of the crisis in eschatology today has been caused by the collapse of the dialectical relationship that exists between image and reality, between the concrete and the ultimate, between the human and the divine. When this happens new images need to be created and reconfigured.

Equally important within the realm of the symbolic and analogical imagination is the recognition of the limitations attaching to eschatological statements. Like all theological languages, eschatology is significantly limited in its final import. The little we do know about matters eschatological is given to us more by way of negation than by affirmation. The words of the Fourth Lateran Council in 1215 about the relationship between the creator and the creature are particularly applicable to the relationship that exists between human experience and eschatology: 'No similitude can be expressed without implying a greater dissimilitude' (D.S. 806). What Aquinas had to say about the mystery of God is also equally valid to the mystery of the *Eschaton*: 'The ultimate of man's cognition of God is to know that he does not know God' (*De Potentia* q. 7, 5, ad. 14). Similarly what Augustine says about God also applies to the *Eschaton*: If we think we have fully understood the reality of God then it is not God.

THE CHRISTOMORPHIC CHARACTER OF ESCHATOLOGY

Eschatology from beginning to end ought to be christological in focus. What happened in the life, death and resurrection of Jesus is understood to have absolute significance for the future of humanity, history and creation. The Christ-event opens up new possibilities and promises for the world in both the present and the future and it is precisely these possibilities and promises that constitute the heart of Christian eschatology. This christological focus of eschatology is prominent in Paul who tells us God

> had made known to us in all wisdom and insight the mystery of his will, according to his purpose which he set forth in Christ as a plan for the fullness of time, to unite all things in him, things in heaven and things on earth.[8]

The person of Jesus reveals who God is, who we are, and what we are called to become in the future. In particular the person of the crucified and risen Christ is the focus, or better the paradigm, for interpreting eschatological statements. The Christ-event, the story of salvation in Christ, gives us a preview of the future, a teaser of what is to come, embracing not only individuals but society and the whole of creation. It was precisely this focus on the primacy of the work of Christ that got lost in some of the classical statements about the particular *eschata*.

Given the centrality of the Christ-event we can say that eschatology is about the application of christology to the self, society, history and creation in a mode of fulfilment. In particular the Paschal Mystery of the crucified and risen Christ is the hinge or paradigm for understanding eschatological statements. We must take account of the Cross as apocalyptic as well as highlighting the importance of the resurrection as eschatological. Some contemporary eschatologies, especially those of the 1960s and 1970s, did not take sufficient account of the Cross; in retrospect some of these eschatologies now appear too sunny and optimistic – they did not face realistically the elements of tragedy and failure, suffering and death that are an intrinsic part of the human condition.

In giving eschatology a christocentric focus, we must avoid Barthian-like traces of christological monism or exclusivism. Eschatology is not simply a continuation of christology, nor is it merely a reproduction of christology. We must remember that christology is based primarily on the first coming of Christ which has given rise to the claim that something new has been established in principle in history. At the same time however, christology recognises that the first coming of Christ is from one point of view unfinished and so there is an important claim about the second coming of Christ as the *terminus ad quem* and the completion of the work of Christ. Eschatology mediates this twofold element of 'the already' and 'the not yet' of the Christ-event; it embraces both the presence and absence of Christ in the world; it acts as a control and a check on christology as well as the rest of theology. Traces of this understanding of eschatology can be found in the writings of contemporary theologians and the documents of Vatican II. This does not mean that the Second Vatican Council provided in any sense a worked-out eschatology. At most there are merely statements about eschatology in the Council documents that have not been developed or elaborated. What is significant however is that the eschatological vision of the Second Vatican Council is one that centres primarily not on the *eschata* but on the *Eschaton* as realised in the life of Jesus, emphasising not only the future but also the present, not only individual destiny but also a social destiny.[9] For example the *Pastoral Constitution of the Church in the Modern World* points out that Christ: 'is the goal of human history, the focal point of the longings of history and of civilisation . . .'.[10]

Many contemporary theologians have emphasised a close relationship between christology and eschatology. For example Karl Barth, writing over fifty years ago, could say in his *Epistle to the Romans*: 'If Christianity be not altogether a thoroughgoing eschatology, there remains in it no relationship with Christ.'[11]

In 1960 Karl Rahner pointed out that 'Eschatology is the view of the future which man needs for . . . his faith. It derives from the situation in the history of salvation brought about by the event of Christ.'[12]

Like Rahner, Walter Kasper refers to Christ as 'the hermeneutic principle of all eschatological statements'.[13] What is important here is that Christ, in particular the crucified and risen Christ, is the form and shape of the future. The Paschal Christ gives us in embryo a glimpse of that which is to come.

ESCHATOLOGY AS THE OUTCOME OF THE GRACIOUS SPIRIT OF GOD IN THE WORLD AND IN THE CHURCH

The image, or images, of God with which we operate in eschatology are by far the single most influential element in the construction of eschatology. After all, eschatology is about the work of God in this world as well as the completion of that work in eternity.

If we operate with an image of God as absolutely transcendent, then our eschatology will tend to be other-worldly. Likewise if we understand the mystery of God solely as immanent, then our eschatology will be principally this-worldly in orientation. Part of the challenge facing any reconstruction of eschatology is to move beyond these two extremes in the light of God's revelation in Judaism and Christianity. What is distinctive about Christian eschatology ought to be its capacity to unite the elements of transcendence and immanence.

For too long the God of Christian faith has been viewed philosophically in linear fashion as the logical outcome of rational reflection on the world. Within this perspective God appears as an inference of reasoning or a conclusion to syllogism. This kind of God, however, appears as an outsider God, arriving too late, seeming to be detached from the world, and available only when called upon. God comes and goes – the word most frequently used is 'intervenes' – in mysterious ways for strange reasons. This kind of God, who is still prominent in the consciousness of many believers, gives rise to an other-worldly, highly transcendent eschatology. For example this is the God we hope to meet in 'life after death', forgetting however that the Christian God of hope is the God we meet and know and love in this life. The trouble with the God who 'intervenes' only when difficulties arise or who is present only in dramatic or inexplicable moments of life quickly becomes a God who is absent in the ordinary and everyday affairs of life wherein most mortals live out their lives.

In contrast to this traditional image of God I suggest an alternative, an image that is more in keeping with the omnipresent God of classical theology and reflects more closely the God of the Judaeo-Christian revelation. This alternative image of God sees God as immanent and present in the world from the beginning of time. Such a God is the Creator-Spirit-God of Genesis who broods over the waters of chaos from the very beginning of life. This God is discovered as co-present in the ordinary everyday experiences. We come to this God not as a conclusion to a syllogism but as a dimension implicit in the whole of human experience *ab initio*. This God is discovered as one who enfolds the world and everything in the world in God's love; this God is 'always already there' ahead of us whether we recognise God or not; this God is co-known and co-experienced in our everyday knowledge and experience of creation, history and human beings. In a word this God is 'God with us' or, to use biblical language, this God is the God of creation, covenant and incarnation.

In more contemporary language we might say that God is in the world and the world is in God without however identifying God with the world. This particular formulation of the presence of God is often referred to as pan-en-theism in order to differentiate this position from pantheism which identifies God with the world, and from classical theism which separates God from the world and denies that there is any real relationship between God and the world.

This alternative image of the presence of God in the world is found in different authors down through the Christian centuries. Augustine talks

about the God who is more intimate to the soul than the soul is to itself;
he refers to God as the light of the intellect (*lumen intellectus*) and invokes
the image of the sun as co-present in the human act of seeing as a way of
symbolising the permanent co-presence of God in the life of the individual. Aquinas talks about the God who is implicit in everything we know
and understand because the intelligibility of things in the world is a participation in the intelligible nature of God.[14] Pascal tells us we would not
be seeking God if we had not already found God.[15] Frederick Von Hugel
argues that God is much more present in human experience than we will
ever fully know or understand.[16] Carl Jung, over his retreat house in
Switzerland, has the motto: 'Whether called upon or not God will be
present'. T. S. Eliot reminds us that the intellectual journey is about
discovering what we are already familiar with although we have not
fully recognised it:

> We shall not cease from exploration,
> and the end of all our exploration
> will be to arrive
> where we started
> and to know the place for the first time.[17]

The theologian who has done most to retrieve the co-presence of God
in the world in the twentieth century in contrast to the God of interventions is Karl Rahner who, looking back on his life, tells us in a remarkably
frank manner that:

> My ultimate purpose, in all that I have written, is but to say this one
> simple thing to my readers – whether they know it or not, whether
> they reflect on it or not, human beings are always and everywhere, in
> all times and places, oriented and directed to that ineffable mystery we
> call God.[18]

Elsewhere Rahner argues persuasively that the mystery of God: 'is the
inexplicit and unexpressed horizon which always encircles and upholds
a small area of our everyday experience of knowing and acting, our
knowledge of reality and free action'.[19]

What is important about this image concerning the omnipresence of
God in the world is that it lays the foundations for the development of an
eschatology that is both this-worldly and other-worldly, both immanent
and transcendent. If God is ultimately bound up with the world in its
present existence, then we have a basis for taking this world seriously as

well as hoping for the completion and transformation of this world by God into a New Creation in the future. Eschatology, therefore, is something that begins with this life, not in some 'life after death'. Eschatology is grounded in the God who loved us into existence in the first instance, that is the God in whom we live and move and have our being in this life of present existence.

Another way of expressing this important theological point of departure for eschatology is the Christian doctrine of individual and social grace. According to the doctrine of grace every human being comes into the world graced by God: all are called by God to communion with God. This graced relationship with God from the very beginning is wounded by the reality of sin that surrounds human existence. Yet we must not lose sight of the fundamental theological truth that the individual is born into the world graced with a basic orientation towards God. The documents of the Second Vatican Council clearly affirm that 'from the very circumstances of his origin, man is already invited to converse with God'.[20] This grace, which the early Fathers of the Church called first grace,[21] is one of the important foundations of eschatology. Because the individual is graced by God from the very beginning of existence, there is hope for the future. In the words of John: 'We love because he first loved us.'[22] This grace given in creation is the seed of glory sown in the life of every individual.[23] For Aquinas there is a very close relationship between the life of grace and glory to come; the life of grace in present existence is inchoate glory because, according to Aquinas, there can be no further gift of the Holy Spirit short of its ultimate consummation.[24] As Newman puts it, the historical life of grace is glory in exile. The Second Vatican Council picks up on this theme by pointing out that the individual 'bears in himself an eternal seed which cannot be reduced to sheer matter'.[25] It is this gift of grace first in the life of the individual from the moment of creation onwards that is the point of departure for eschatology. This point of departure demands that we see eschatological fulfilment not as something extrinsic to human nature, nor as something subsequently added on to life, but rather as the culmination and consummation of that which God has already set in motion in and through the gift of creation.

This God who is omnipresent in the world as grace is the gift of the Spirit of God, the third person of the Triune God, poured out over the whole of creation from the beginning of time. Eschatology is the fruit of the work of the gracious Spirit of God alive and active in creation, the history of the people of Israel, the life of Jesus, the new community of the people of God and the world today. This same Spirit of God is described as the creative source of life: defined by the Nicene Creed as the giver of life (*Vivivicantum*) and referred to by the Second Vatican Council as the one in whom 'we journey towards the consummation of human history'.[26]

This Spirit of God fills the whole world and is present in all things. Theology talks more and more about the indwelling of the Spirit of God in creation, in history, in human beings and in the Christian community. This is the Spirit that encircles the world, upholding the universe: inspiring and empowering cosmic, biological, human and cultural evolution. At the same time this Spirit of God is the one who renews the face of the earth,[27] active and creative, not just in the past but in the present, not just at the beginning of the world but in the unfolding evolution of creation. This Spirit of God completes her work in the world by making all things new.[28] This is the Spirit that not only initiates and sustains but also completes and transforms God's creation.[29]

The Scriptures talk about the Spirit of God in a variety of images. One particular image that is instructive here is the image of the Spirit as water. Cyril of Jerusalem, explaining why Christ called the Spirit water, talks about the same Spirit which makes water 'white in the lily, red in the rose, purple in the violets and hyacinths, different and varied in each species. It is one thing in the palm tree yet another in the vine, and yet all in all things.'[30] It is this creative activity of the Spirit of God in the world that enables us to hope that the selfsame Spirit will transform creation into a New Creation that is white, red, purple, different and varied beyond human imagination.

One scientist compares the creative activity of the Spirit in the world to the choreographer of an ongoing dance, or the composer of an unfinished symphony.[31] Thus we find the documents of the Second Vatican Council pointing out that: 'Enlivened and united in his Spirit, we journey towards the consummation of human history.'[32] It is this omnipresent gift of God, the gracious Spirit of God poured out over the whole of creation and within human history that constitutes the essential point of departure and underlying assumption of eschatology. In brief the Spirit of God active in creation, in history, and the Christian community is God's eschatological gift to the world in the present.

3

THE SELF IN CRISIS: THE DEMISE OF ESCHATOLOGY

Persons . . . are constituted by their mutual relation to one another. 'I' exist only as one element in the complex 'You and I'. We have to discover how this ultimate fact can be adequately thought, that is to say, symbolised in reflection.

(John Macmurray, 1961)

ANTHROPOLOGY IS A KEY CATEGORY in Christian theology. The major moral and doctrinal questions facing Christianity today concern the nature of the human self and the meaning of what is involved in being a person fully alive. Twentieth-century Catholic theology has seen a significant shift in the appreciation of the primacy of the human and this is reflected quite formally in the *Pastoral Constitution of the Church in the Modern World*.[1] Karl Rahner has been particularly eloquent in highlighting the link between anthropology and theology,[2] giving special emphasis to the intrinsic connection that should exist between anthropology and eschatology.[3] Most commentators today would agree on the indissoluble bond that exists between anthropology and eschatology.[4] Thereafter however, agreement seems to end. In spite of the success of what is often called the anthropological conversion in Rahner and others, serious difficulties persist in understanding the human. The self is under critical scrutiny in contemporary thought from a variety of sources: feminism, ecology and cosmology. These difficulties with anthropology in turn are inhibiting contemporary efforts to reconstruct a viable eschatology. For example, classical dualist anthropologies of the body and soul as well as modern anthropologies of the independent self-sufficient subject are perceived to be antithetical to the development of a social eschatology. On the other hand, collectivist anthropologies of the Marxist type or other utopian visions lose sight of the dignity of the individual and the possibility of a personal eschatological destiny. Is there a way forward out of this seeming impasse? Is it possible to discern the outline of an alternative anthropology? How might a renewed anthropology relate to eschatology? The purpose of this chapter is to review the dissatisfaction with modern anthropologies, to propose an alternative, 'post-modern' anthropology,[5] and to outline *in nuce* how this renewed anthropology might help in the reconstruction of eschatology.

CRITIQUES OF MODERN ANTHROPOLOGY

Many commentators associate the present crisis in modern anthropology with the ambiguous legacy of modernity generated by the philosophers of the Enlightenment.[6] It is as well to remember, however, that modern anthropology with its emphasis on the independent, self-sufficient, punctual, substantial subject is a relatively recent invention of not more than a few hundred years. Its most powerful and influential expression is to be found in Descartes' (in)famous dictum 'I think, therefore I am.' Prior to the Enlightenment, namely the classical pre-modern period, the individual was understood to belong to a larger social and cosmic order, and as such lived life in a world that was organic and hierarchical. With Descartes there is the separation of the self from the world, the introduction of a subject–object split, and a consequent disenchantment of the universe. From now on, the individual subject is set over and against 'the objective world' which is reduced to mechanistic laws of the physical sciences. These developments, of course, did not happen all at once and it is probably unreasonable to lay all the blame on Descartes. Nevertheless it is true to say that Descartes sowed the seeds of what is called today the modern subject-centred anthropology of independent self-consciousness.

Over a period of time, this subject-centred self-consciousness became wrapped up in its own self-importance and lost contact with the immanence of God in the world. Though Descartes himself believed in God, the logic of his move towards the affirmation of the primacy of human self led in time to a denial of the divine. In effect what took place during the Enlightenment was a dramatic shift from the interior self of Augustine to the isolated ego of Descartes, 'a secularisation of Christian interiority' as Charles Davis calls it.[7] Whereas the interior self saw itself as related to God, the isolated ego sees itself only in relation to itself.[8] In this way, the birth of an iron-clad, autonomous, disengaged, independent self of modern anthropology evolved. This separate self was so strong, so confident and so independent that it became the ground of its own being: self-sufficient and self-defining without reference to any other reality, be it natural, historical or divine. The rise of the self-sufficient subject of modern anthropology has issued in the creation during this century of a new culture of individualism.

A variant of this modern anthropology can be found in certain forms of modern psychology, which go to great lengths to promote the illusion of self-sufficiency, self-realisation, self-determination and self-fulfilment – symptoms of an increasingly Pelagian culture in the latter half of the twentieth-century Western world.

It must be pointed out that this outline of the rise of modern anthropology with its focus on the individual self is, of course, only one side of the story of modernity. There is another important aspect, a more positive one, to the modern experiment which must not be forgotten. This is the story of the hard-won recognition of the primacy of human reason, the place of human rights, the centrality of individual freedoms, and the importance of justice. These gains over the last two hundred years must not be jettisoned simply because of excesses in the struggle to understand human identity. Instead the positive fruits of modernity must be preserved in the quest for a more inclusive and wholistic anthropology that goes beyond the lost and lonely self of modernity.

One of the most significant critiques of the modern self has come from the feminist movement. With the rise of feminism in its many forms (radical, liberal, reformist), women have been quick to point out that the image of the autonomous, self-sufficient and independent subject is largely the creation of patriarchy and the outcome of a particular type of sexual stereotyping within culture. Further, women claim that their experience and understanding of human identity is quite different from that of the existence of an independent and isolated self. Even more significant is the suggestion by women that the illusion of the self-sufficient subject is responsible for the pervasive presence of so much sexism in society and the cultural exploitation of womanhood.

In contrast, therefore, to the separate self of modern anthropology, feminism argues for the existence of a radically relational, processive and multi-polar self.[9] Within women's experience, it is noted that there is a strong sense of interdependence and interconnectedness. It is suggested that women do not define themselves as persons over and against other persons in the way the self-sufficient male subject of modern anthropology does. Instead, women in the light of their particular experience tend to define themselves in mutual relation to other persons. Further, many feminists argue that the illusion of the separate self is bound up with the existence of many other dichotomies in the world: the separation of human and ecological relationships, the fragmentation of social connectedness and political interdependence. A link is seen to exist between the male quest for separation alongside the passion to conquer and divide, symbolised by the ancient figure of the warrior hero and the modern phenomenon of the war-lord. In brief, the women's movement in its great variety of expression coheres in a shared perception of the human self as relational, organic, inclusive, processive and multi-polar.

Another equally impressive critique of the self-sufficient subject of modernity can be found in the ecological movement.[10] According to many ecologists, the critical condition of the earth has been caused in part at least by an excessive anthropocentricism in recent centuries. Man (*sic*) since the time of the Enlightenment has situated himself at the centre of the earth. The relation between man and the earth has been one of domination and exploitation. The earth has been perceived to exist solely in the service of man and his needs. Nature and her resources have been regarded as 'lifeless' matter since the Enlightenment and in consequence have become 'the object' of exploitive manipulation by modern science and technology.

A further critique of modern anthropology comes from post-modern cosmologies.[11] These new cosmologies complain about the removal of the human from the natural world of creation. Cosmology within the experiment of modernity was reduced to the level of inert, objective matter. The cosmos was interpreted as mechanistic with no intrinsic value or worth in itself, beyond serving the needs of man. This divorce between the human and the natural, between the self and the earth, between creation and history has resulted in an exaggerated sense of human independence, self-sufficiency and autonomy of the human subject. In contrast, these post-modern cosmologies are calling for the relocation of the human within the context of a new cosmic story, that is, within the long history of some 15 billion years of cosmic evolution that has resulted in the relatively recent advent of the human. Within this larger picture an intimate relationship is perceived to exist between the universe, the earth and the human. The human person, according to Tom Berry, is the earth in a mode of self-consciousness: 'that being in whom this grand diversity of the universe celebrates itself in conscious awareness'.[12] There is also an important sense in which it is true to say 'we bear the universe in our beings as the universe bears us in its being'.[13] Because of this organic relationship between the human and the universe, between anthropology and cosmology, new responsibilities follow. Instead of saying the earth belongs to humanity, we must now acknowledge that humanity belongs to the earth. The cosmological critique of modern anthropology is effecting an important shift in self-consciousness, inviting us to move from living in a man-centred world to an organically inter-related universe in which the human person has a new role to play in creating a sustainable universe of life.

An extreme critique of the independent self-centred subject of modernity can be found among a small group of thinkers who are united in their reduction of the human individual to a mere blob in the landscape of life. This group would include such diverse and otherwise different movements as particular expressions of the New Age, some strains of feminism, totalitarian forms of socialism and 'post-modern' deconstructionism. These movements have one thing in common, namely the elimination of the status of the 'I' to that of a fiction. The uniqueness of the individual self is flattened out into ambivalence, ambiguity and anonymous multiplicity. The one is sacrificed absolutely to the many. Certain restricted forms of feminism talk about humanity being molecular rather than atomic. Totalitarian socialism in its extreme forms reduces the individual to the level of a mere cog in the service and sacrifice of an historically driven socio-economic machine. The deconstructionist, Richard Rorty, refers to 'the human self as a centreless web of historically conditioned beliefs and desires'.[14] These different movements end up with the liquidation of the human self. Clearly, these diverse views are an extreme reaction against exaggerated representations of the existence of the independent substantial and essentialist self. In their excess, these movements highlight the need to construct an alternative conception of the self to that of self-sufficient subject of modern anthropology. One must ask, however, whether the reduction of the self to a social blob in this manner does justice to the lived experience of human beings, whether such anonymous multiplicity is able to conduct a human conversation, to make promises and pledge loyalty, to enter relationships and engage in meaningful action for others, not to mention the capacity to issue such unified and consistent statements about the nihilism of the self.[15]

A final critique of the independent self of modernity has come from social commentators on the contemporary culture of individualism and consumerism. Robert Bellah and his colleagues in their collection of papers entitled *Habits of the Heart* observe how North American society is driven by extreme forms of individualism. The individual knows only the needs of the self with little or no attention given to the needs of others in society: 'the individual has (become) a primary reality whereas society is a second order, a derived or artificial construct'.[16] Bellah and his co-authors 'are concerned that this individualism may have grown cancerous – that it may be destroying those social integuments that Tocqueville saw as moderating its more destructive potentialities, that it may be threatening the survival of freedom itself'.[17]

TOWARDS AN ALTERNATIVE ANTHROPOLOGY

What begins to emerge from these critiques of modern anthropology is the need to construct an alternative way of looking at what it means to be human. Without a renewed anthropology it would be very difficult to reconstruct eschatology. Calls 'to re-invent the human',[18] 'to replace a narrow anthropocentric sensibility',[19] to rethink the 'modern notion of the self'[20] and to develop a more 'chastened anthropocentricity'[21] are the order of the day. This alternative anthropology will seek to take account of female *and* male experience as well as wrestle with the challenges coming from ecology, cosmology and deconstructionism as outlined above. At the same time, this alternative understanding of the self will also aim to be open to the possibility of human, social and cosmic fulfilment in the future.

The obvious temptation in constructing an alternative anthropology is simply to react to the limitations of modern anthropology. This would involve moving from the separate self to a connected self, from individualism to communitarianism, from autonomy to interdependence. This reaction should be resisted for at least two reasons. On the one hand it runs the risk of reversing the distortions of modern anthropology. Secondly, yielding to this temptation ends up perpetuating male and female stereotypes. For example, to concentrate, as modern anthropology does, simply on the advancement of the self-sufficiency and strength of the human subject is to promote a male stereotype. To focus exclusively on the self as connected and relational is likewise the promotion of a female stereotype.

Stereotyping is a major part of the problem of modern anthropology with its pretension to making the male experience normative for all human beings. It needs to be acknowledged clearly that male and female stereotypes are the outcome of truncated anthropologies. Further, it must be pointed out that sexual stereotyping ignores a substantial body of contemporary medical and psychological evidence which holds that all human beings embody both male and female experiences, qualities and characteristics in different degrees. What is important from our point of view is that an alternative anthropology should seek to include both female and male experiences in a manner that affirms equality and values difference. As to what extent male and female experiences are shaped by gender or biology or both is a matter beyond the scope of this Chapter.[22]

The first step in moving towards an alternative anthropology is to affirm the primacy of relationality regarding human identity. There is no self without relationships, no self apart from other selves, no self without being constituted by the actions of other human subjects. This primary principle coming from feminism and process thought applies with equal weight to the female and male self. Further, this vision of relationality is confirmed by contemporary ecologies and certain reconstructed post-modern cosmologies which tell us that everything in the world is organically related, inter-connected and inter-dependent.[23] Relationality is a primary category, a fundamental characteristic of all beings in the world and not just human beings.

However, no sooner have we made this affirmation about the primacy of relationality in describing what it means to be human than we need to follow it immediately with a statement about individuality. Individuality arises in and through human relationality. It becomes necessary to state that relationality and individuality, attachment and autonomy, connectedness and independence co-exist in varying degrees within every human identity. To exist individually is always to co-exist, to be is always to be in relationship. In other words, it is relational existence that begets individual existence.

Chronologically speaking, the human self evolves and emerges out of a particular configuration of relationships among others; the human self is derivative biologically, psychologically and theologically. It is the human other that generates and calls into being as it were out of a radical relationality the development of the human self: 'Selves are beings who become aware of their status as selves only by being addressed by others.'[24]

On the other hand, once the self is constituted and individuated, there is an important sense in which it is continuously necessary for the human self to go out towards other selves in order to sustain the self in process. It is here that the importance of Wolfhart Pannenberg's principle of exocentricism comes into play, namely that true human freedom emerges out of the ability of the self to exist *ad extra* in relationality.[25] It is only in and through the movement out towards others that the self maintains itself in existence and that self-consciousness is expanded to embrace a deepened co-awareness of a transcendent, divine dimension within the human and the natural world.

We are seeking here to keep a necessary but creative tension in existence between relationality and individuality, between autonomy and mutuality. It is out of relationality, the relationality between husband and wife and more specifically the relationality between a parent and child that individuality emerges and this individuality in turn realises itself through ongoing relationality with others. It is necessary to express human identity in this way in order to avoid the impression, so strong in modern anthropology, that somehow an individual, already constituted, substantial 'I' pre-exists relationships of action and knowledge with others. In contrast, we are proposing that the individual existence comes forth as a result of being addressed and summoned in loving relationality by others in the first place.

It is necessary to express human identity in this complex twofold fashion in order to highlight the suggestion that once individuality is awakened, it is open to continuous development through relational engagement with other selves. The human subject is always in-process-of-becoming more fully personal throughout historical existence, through relationships and actions with others. This process-of-becoming only reaches finality at death. The human subject, or more accurately the subject in-process-of-becoming, perdures throughout life but it only realises itself historically through ongoing relational encounters and actions with others.

There is a need to transform the fixity and rigidity of the independent substantial self belonging to modern anthropology. The human self is radically relational, always in-process-of-becoming and to that extent has within itself a certain flexibility of development. At the same time, we must insist on an underlying continuity within the development of the human self: '. . . it is necessary to see the self as a continuous, even if continuously changing, centre of purpose and power'.[26]

Another way of describing this alternative understanding of human identity is to invoke the Teilhard de Chardin principle that 'union differentiates'. For Teilhard the coming together in evolution of different parts within the whole does not obliterate or suffocate these parts but perfects and fulfils them giving them a deeper identity: 'True union does not fuse the elements it brings together; by mutual fertilisation and adaptation, it gives them a renewed vitality. It is egoism that hardens and neutralises human stuff. Union differentiates.'[27] This particular principle of evolutionary growth is applied by Teilhard with special force to the relationships of human beings: 'The more "other" they (individuals) become in conjunction, the more they find themselves as "self".'[28]

An expression of this ongoing concern with anthropology can be found in an important debate taking place in recent years about the possibility of retrieving Aquinas' understanding of the self as substantial being within a new relational framework. To the fore in this debate has been the significant work of the neo-Thomist, W. Norris Clarke, SJ. Clarke seeks to recover the classical notions of substance and relation within a more dynamic reading of Aquinas. He argues impressively that the 'We are' of interpersonal dialogue is a more appropriate starting point for metaphysics.[29] In particular, he proposes that being is dyadic: 'to be real is to be a dyadic synthesis of substance and relation; it is to be substance-in-relation'.[30] Clarke's thesis is most suggestive and gives new life to neglected aspects of Aquinas' thought. Lingering questions, however, remain: Has he given full equity and parity to substance and relation? Is the influence of relation on substance as significant as that of substance on relation? Is the substance he talks about still too self-contained and too mature?

A more attractive formulation of the issue has been put forward by Robert A. Connor who suggests that substance and relation are resonating manifestations of a deeper existential core which we call the human person.[31] According to Connor, we must go beyond the extremes of understanding human identity simply as perduring substance or as pure relationality. Instead, we must discover a new model of personal being wherein substance and relation are equally valid primordial modes of one and the same single human reality.[32]

At this stage it will be asked with justification have we reduced human identity 'to nothing more than a pattern of relationships with no subjects grounding them, or a pattern of events with no agents enacting them'.[33] Is there not a danger that the above emphasis on relationality will dissolve individuality and difference?[34] In response it must be pointed out that these charges can be avoided by affirming the equality, mutuality and reciprocity of substance and relation within the personal self. Relationality and individuality co-exist in the person, inhering in each other and as such presuppose and develop each other. Further, relationality is an important element in the emergence of individuality and difference.

There is a real difficulty here in finding an appropriate language. One possibility is to describe the human person as a historical-being-in-becoming *and* an historical-becoming-in-being. Another option is to describe human identity as the outcome of an ongoing interaction between *esse* and *actio* and *actio* and *esse*. Human action does have an enduring effect on the make-up of human identity. A third possibility is to perceive the individual as a processive self-in-continuous-relationship-with-other-selves.

It is perhaps Paul Ricoeur who provides the most coherent philosophical framework for describing the different tensions within this important first step in the construction of an alternative anthropology. According to Ricoeur in *Oneself as Another* the unity of relationality and individuality can be summed up as a 'dialectical tie between selfhood and otherness'.[35] Within this dialectic, otherness is not something simply added on to selfhood to overcome the danger of solipsism; instead otherness belongs 'to the ontological constitution of selfhood'.[36] The advantage of this dialectic 'is that it keeps the self from occupying the place of foundation'.[37] Further, this particular dialectic reminds us 'that the selfhood of oneself implies otherness to such an intimate degree that one cannot be thought of without the other'.[38] Equally important for Ricoeur is the need to keep together change and continuity within the human self. To achieve this he affirms the presence of sameness (*idem*) alongside a developing sense of selfhood (*ipse*).[39] For Ricoeur there are two fundamental dialectics in describing human identity: sameness and selfhood on the one hand and selfhood and otherness on the other hand.

In effect, within this first step of constructing an alternative anthropology, to be is to be in relation, to exist is always to co-exist, and to co-exist is to co-experience a radical relationality – a relationality reaching back to origins, embracing the present and stretching out towards the transcendence of the future.

A second step towards an alternative anthropology necessitates a rediscovery of the belongingness and solidarity of all human beings within the unity of the human race. Given what we have already outlined regarding the primacy of relationality, it should be clear that human beings belong to each other in an extraordinary degree of natural solidarity and social togetherness. This strong sense of solidarity can be seen not only at the human level but also on a wider cosmic scale in the light of the emerging common-creation story. In particular, evidence for this underlying solidarity between humans, the earth and the cosmos can be found in the so-called 'anthropic principle'. According to the findings of some post-modern cosmologies, the universe evolved the particular way it did because it was coded to support the advent of *anthropoi*. For example, Stephen Hawking points out: 'If the rate of expansion one second after the Big Bang had been smaller by even one part of a hundred thousand million million, the universe would have recollapsed before it reached its present size.'[40]

In a similar vein, Princeton physicist Freeman Dyson observes: 'The more I examine the universe and details of its architecture, the more evidence I find that the universe in some sense must have known we were coming.'[41] An extraordinary unity and solidarity is perceived to exist between the universe, the earth and humans.

A third emphasis that must inform an alternative post-modern anthropology concerns the composition of the human self. How are we to describe the reality of the human self? Do we refer to it as a soul, a spirit, matter, a body, a body-soul, spirit in matter . . . ? An adequate answer to these questions would require a revision of the received Hellenistic dualism of body and soul, the Thomistic unity of body and soul, and the spiritualism and materialism of other traditions – something beyond the purview of this chapter. Instead we will attend once again to impulses coming from feminism, ecology and cosmology as well as the biomedical sciences. These recent developments favour a recovery of Jewish perceptions of the person as an embodied reality. These more recent perspectives react negatively against any portrayal of the human self simply as a soul, or a purely spiritual entity, or a disembodied self.

Most forms of feminism, basing themselves on the appeal to human experience, emphasise the importance of the body throughout the whole of life. By and large, they strongly oppose any traces of a dualistic anthropology and positively affirm the reality of human existence as being embodied through and through. This should not be taken to mean that feminism reduces personal existence to a new form of materialism or biologism. Instead the human self is a 'bodied' reality, enfleshed and incarnate, a spiritual substance that is embodied from beginning to end.[42]

In a similar vein, ecology sees the human self as that being which bears the material reality of the world in a mode of self-consciousness. Given the relation of solidarity that obtains between the cosmos, the earth and humanity, it is argued that there is a gradation of consciousness throughout the world that reaches a high point in the human person. Human beings are, as it were, conscious children of cosmic dust. As Brian Swimme remarks with considerable poetic insight, 'The universe shivers with wonder in the depths of the human'[43] and John Polkinghorne proposes 'We are all made of the ashes of dead stars'.[44]

Likewise, the 'anthropic principle' of contemporary cosmology points in the direction of the human person as the individualised personal embodiment of cosmic energy.[45] Brian Swimme and Thomas Berry capture some of the extra-ordinary cosmic and human unity expressed and embodied in the human person in the following way: ' . . . the eye that searches the Milky Way galaxy is itself an eye shaped by the Milky Way. The mind that searches for contact with Milky Way is the very mind of the Milky Way galaxy in search of inner depths.'[46]

In the light of this focus on cosmic unity and the underlying presence of an 'anthropic principle', whether 'strong' or 'weak', the most compelling description of the human person appears to be that of *embodied self-consciousness* – an outlook that refuses to separate the senses and the spirit, the body and the soul, mind and matter.

In addition, developments in the biomedical sciences are concentrating more and more on the individual as bodied existence. The body is the key to the personal and we are informed that a better understanding of the body gives us a deeper understanding of the human spirit. This new emphasis from the biomedical sciences on the importance of the body and the significance of the person as embodied should not be dismissed as just another attack on the spiritual.[47] Instead it presents a new opportunity for anthropology to recover its rootedness in the body and to rediscover the full meaning of the medieval principle that the human is a sacred reality: *Res Sacra Homo.*

A fourth emphasis within a renewed anthropology must be a retrieval of the social and communal nature of the individual. The human is social and as we have seen the individual self sustains itself in relationships with other selves, including the divine Self. The human self therefore is at least interpersonal; but the interpersonal dimension of human existence in turn develops and expands historically into the wider domain of community. A movement takes places in the life of the human subject from being interpersonal to being inter-communitarian. The self in personal relationship develops outwards and becomes a self-in-community[48] leading to a life of communion with others.

What is significant about the shape of this alternative anthropology is that it resonates with the hidden dimensions of the more primordial experiences of humanity. Evocative descriptions and interpretations of these primary experiences can be found in Alfred N. Whitehead, Teilhard de Chardin and Alice Walker. In other words this alternative anthropology is grounded in some of the most basic experiences that humans undergo.

According to Alfred Whitehead our most primary experience is an experience of totality, a feeling of being part of and belonging to a larger continuum of past, present and future. There is within human experience a vague sense of the many which are one and of the one which includes the many. We discover within our most human experiences a feeling of the ego, of others, and totality. We are, each of us, one among others and all of us are embraced in the unity of the whole.[49]

A similar perception can be found in Teilhard de Chardin who had a strong experiential and scientific sense of the unity of humanity, history and the cosmos. Teilhard's vision of this fundamental unity is captured in the following moment of searching self-reflection:

I stepped down into the most hidden depths of my being, lamp in hand and ears alert, to discover whether, in the deepest recesses of the blackness within me, I might not see the glint of the waters of the current that flows on, whether I might not hear the murmur of their mysterious waters that rise from the uttermost depths and will burst forth no man (woman) knows whether. With terror and intoxicating emotion, *I realised that my poor trifling existence was one with the immensity of all that is and all that is still in process of becoming.*[50]

What is quite remarkable about Teilhard's vision is the way in which he unites the present with the the future of 'all that is still in process of becoming'.

A further instance of this underlying unity between humans and nature can be taken from Alice Walker in her novel *The Colour Purple*:

My first step from the old white man was trees. Then air. Then birds. Then other people. But one day when I was sitting quiet and feeling like a motherless child, which I was, it came to me: that feeling of being part of everything, not separate at all. I knew that if I cut a tree, my arm would bleed.[51]

This profound unity between humans and the cosmos is summed up strikingly in an observation attributed to Karl Rahner: 'When a child cries, the stars shudder.'[52]

Each of these authors captures imaginatively a fundamental and forgotten dimension of the experience of solidarity that exists between human beings and the universe. Neglect of this unity between human beings and the natural world arose out of the divorce that took place between anthropology and cosmology since the Enlightenment.

This outline of radical relationality within solidarity between humans and the cosmos suggests a number of key points in the reconstruction of an alternative anthropology:

- that a dialectic exists between relationality (otherness) and individuality (selfhood);
- that anthropology, to be properly understood, must embrace cosmology;
- that a profound relationship of respect, reverence and responsibility should exist between anthropology and cosmology;
- that the life and well-being of the cosmos 'is all of a piece' with the life and the well-being of the *anthropos*;
- that humans as free and self-conscious expressions of the earth have a particular responsibility for the well-being of the earth, which if not heeded will rebound to the detriment of humans;

- that solidarity suffuses the relationship that exists between humans, the earth and the cosmos;
- that the self as personal and social is embodied.

ESCHATOLOGICAL OPENINGS WITHIN
A RENEWED ANTHROPOLOGY

The purpose of this critique of modern anthropology and mapping of an alternative anthropology is to open the way for the reconstruction of eschatology in the chapters that follow. We began by noting that many current anthropologies were at least unsympathetic to eschatology, if not a major part of the present-day crisis in eschatology. To conclude this chapter we will outline some of the emerging sympathies within the above alternative anthropology towards eschatology.

The first opening can be found in the understanding that eschatology is not something additional or extrinsic to anthropology. Instead, eschatology is, as Rahner frequently points out, anthropology in a mode of fulfilment; that is, anthropology conjugated in the future.[53] Eschatology completes what is already going on in history and taking place in human experience; it is not as the early Moltmann seems to suggest simply the addition of something extra on to the individual nor imposition of something alien from outside. Instead, eschatology is the fulfilment of promises implicit in human hope and the flourishing of the innate human capacity to become. In other words, eschatology is the full realisation of something already set in motion from the very beginning, namely the gift of a graced existence in creation. As John Henry Newman reminds us: grace is glory in exile whereas glory is grace fulfilled. To this extent eschatology is about the full flowering of the gift and grace of historical existence in eternity.

A second opening within this renewed anthropology towards eschatology arises from the human capacity to be formed by relationships and to form relationships. This capacity to receive individuality through relationship puts the human subject in touch with God and humanity at the beginning of life and throughout life. The grace of existence co-conferred on the human subject by God the Creator through the act of procreation both *ab initio* and within history is the foundation of immortality.[54] As already emphasised, to exist is to co-exist and part of that co-existence includes the discovery that we are embraced by the love of God *ab initio*. It is this interaction between the divine and the human initiated by God through the grace of creation that grounds the possibility of immortality. Pannenberg's principle of exocentrism, Rahner's emphasis on the human subject as a relational self-transcending being, and Lonergan's focus on the dynamic intentionality of the human subject are each in their own incomplete way expressions of the fundamental orientation and relatedness of the human subject towards the divine mystery. An important link exists between divine–human relationality and immortality, and this link provides an opening towards eschatology.

A third opening into eschatology from a renewed anthropology arises from our emphasis on the historical and developmental dimension of the self. Any suggestion that the human subject is some kind of fixed, self-contained substantial entity seems to preclude the kind of change and transformation offered by eschatology; the enclosed self may be amenable to the continuities of Greek immortality but not to the transformations of Christian eschatology. There is a need to move away from the fixity lodged in our understanding of the self, without eliminating the importance of an underlying continuity within the development of the self. To be human is to be *en route*, even at the point of death. It is this fundamental openness of the human subject in historical life and in death that is the object of eschatological reflection. Similarly, the focus on the historical character of the human self raises questions about life, its direction and completion, that eschatology seeks to address. Because the historical self is so amenable to change, so relentless in the quest for wholeness, so irrepressible even in the face of tragedy, and so vulnerable to relationships of love, the question of human fulfilment and transformation is unavoidable and once raised puts people on track of issues that are ultimately eschatological.

A fourth aspect of the proposed alternative anthropology sympathetic to eschatology, especially a social eschatology, concerns the solidarity of the self with the whole of creation. An independent, self-sufficient, detached human subject seems out of harmony with the aspirations of the self within community. Further, a self that is cosmic and social in origins is amenable to an eschatology that is social and cosmic in conclusion. More and more it is becoming evident from the perspectives of the so-called 'hard' and 'soft' sciences that the destiny of the self is bound up with the destiny of the world. The individualism of modern anthropology and its concomitant isolation of the individual from the cosmos restricts the reconstruction of a social and cosmic eschatology. In contrast the possibility of a 'post-modern' anthropology that concentrates on the social and cosmic solidarity of the self recovers important Jewish eschatological perspectives wherein the destiny of the individual is perceived to be bound up with the destiny of the whole of Israel. This recovery of the intimate relation that exists between the self, society and the universe is important not only for understanding an eschatology of the end-time but also for an eschatology that bears directly on ethical and ecological responsibilities within present history. A renewed socio-cosmic anthropology calls into question the viability of a purely individual eschatology and paves the way for highlighting the necessity of a unified individual, social and cosmic eschatology.

A fifth eschatological opening in the above anthropology derives from the emphasis on the human subject as an embodied self. The trouble with the body–soul and spirit–matter anthropologies is that, though they may be defensible in certain forms, they run the risk of being understood dualistically. When this happens, the focus is reduced to the purely spiritual dimension and an emphasis is placed simply on spiritual survival. Christian eschatology, however, is grounded in the hope of the resurrection of the body. An anthropology that emphasises the self as an embodied self is much more available to an eschatology of bodily resurrection. The primary eschatological symbols of Christianity, namely the New Creation, the new heaven and new earth, the heavenly Jerusalem, the reign of God, and bodily resurrection are all in one way or another corporeal and embodied. What is distinctive and central about Christian eschatology is its inclusive reference to material creation and embodied existence. The arrival of the *Eschaton* is not about the survival of disembodied souls and spirits, but the transformation of enfleshed beings into a New Creation.

It is surely no mere coincidence that 'Aquinas did not believe in a self which was distinct from the body, nor did he think that disembodied souls were persons.'[55] Instead, in his commentary on the First Letter to the Corinthians Aquinas points out:

> A human being naturally desires his own salvation; but the soul, since it is part of the body of a human being, is not a whole human being, and my soul is not I; so even if a soul gains salvation in another life, that is not I or any human being.[56]

In the light of this quotation from Aquinas and his refusal to identify the disembodied soul with the historical self, it is not unreasonable to suggest that he would be sympathetic to an anthropology of the embodied self. This particular suggestion would seem to be the case especially with the later Aquinas who was more influenced by Aristotle's *De Anima* than Plato's doctrine of the immortality of the soul. What is important here is that an anthropology of the embodied self seems to have a much closer affinity to the eschatological doctrine of bodily resurrection than the distorted and dualistic anthropologies of body and soul.

A final point of convergence between a renewed anthropology and eschatology arises out of the perception of the person as ordered to life-in-community. We have seen that the self-in-personal-relations develops into a self-in-community. Self differentiation begins in relation to another person and develops more fully in the context of the self-in-community. It is more accurate to see the self as belonging to a community of selves than simply in relation to one person which always runs the risk of being reduced to what the French so aptly refer to as *un égoisme à deux*. There is something fundamentally communal about the human self in terms of identity, being and living. This communal character of the human self is fulfilled in the *Eschaton* that gathers the human and cosmic family into a new life of communion with the Christian God who is Triune. A fundamental unity exists between the historical self-in-community and the transformed self of the *Eschaton* who enters into an eternal life of communion and love in the Trinitarian God.

To sum up, we have suggested that anthropology is the key to eschatology, that modern anthropology is in need of reform, that this reform has been coming from feminism, ecology and cosmology, and that a renewed anthropology in the light of these influences does in fact have sympathetic openings for the development of and reconstruction of Christian eschatology.

4

The Permanence of Death: Reconnecting Life and Death

It is death that is spinning the globe. . . . But about the topic of my own death I am decidedly touchy.

(Annie Dillard, 1990)

DEATH IS THE QUESTION MARK that hangs over life for everyone. Death disturbs every easy answer to the meaning of life, it interrupts human hopes, and calls into question the value of human existence, it challenges most acutely the possibility of constructing a credible eschatology. In this chapter we will begin by describing the changing experience of death in this century and some of the consequences of this, such as the emergence of a death-denying culture. Against this background we will then reflect on three different accounts of death which move in the direction of reconnecting life and death without, however, addressing at this stage the particular question of what actually happens in death. In the final section we will look at different but inadequate responses to death and conclude with an outline of some of the elements that might go into constructing a more adequate response to the question of death today.

THE CHANGING EXPERIENCE OF DEATH

The question of death is an omnipresent question facing every human being. No matter how much the question is repressed or ignored, it is unavoidable either through the death of a loved one, a friend or a parent, and ultimately through the inevitability of our own death forced upon us either through illness or tragedy or old age.

The underlying issue when faced with death is the possibility of non-existence, the possibility that death is the absolute end of life, the prospect that perhaps each one of us is merely a spark in the evolutionary spiral of progress and that as sparks we will burn out at death into lifeless and dead ashes.

The question of death is one that simply will not go away. The poet Philip Larkin puts it poignantly:

> And so it stays just on the edge of vision
> A small unfocused blur,
> A standing chill
> that slows each impulse down to indecision.
> Most things may never happen: this one will,
> and realisation of it rages out
> in furnace-fear when we are caught without
> people or drink.
> Courage is no good; it means not scaring others.
> Being brave
> Lets no one off the grave.[1]

And yet in spite of the permanent presence of death many choose to ignore it, to postpone consideration of it, preferring to keep death at arm's length. This disposition towards death is further compounded by the fact that we live in a death-denying culture, a culture that covers over the reality of death. There is a conspiracy of silence surrounding death in our modern world. This denial of death can be seen in all kinds of subtle ways within our contemporary culture.

In approaching the question of death we need on the one hand to keep a balance between what could become a morbid interest in this question and on the other hand preserve a realistic grasp of the imminence of death to every human being. Those who are morbidly preoccupied with death are more often than not those who have refused to face death realistically. It is only when we have faced the question of death and accepted death in all its ambiguity that we have fully understood who God is and have come to grips fully with who we are. The issue of death ultimately raises the question of God and more particularly the task of reconciling the reality of death with the existence of a loving God.

Up to the turn of this century the average age that people died was around forty to forty-five years whereas today the average age of people before they die is somewhere around seventy-five years. Within this century there has been a dramatic increase in the life expectancy of people.

In former times death was experienced as something that came from the outside through disease, illness, natural disasters, and so-called acts of nature. Coming from the outside this experience of death was often accepted as 'the will of God' and often referred to as 'an act of God'. Today the causes of death come more frequently from the inside, that is to say from humanity who has seized control of death in and through the advances of modern medicine or through the ravages of war. In some instances death can appear almost as something 'natural', coming at the end of life as a natural development, as something that is inscribed in our genes as it were. People move, almost by right, from infancy to adolescence to adulthood and old age as a natural kind of sequence. Thus there comes a stage where death is not only natural but desirable. Today we often hear of people 'waiting to die'.

Another shift in our experience of death concerns the actual conditions and circumstances of death. The process of dying in old age has changed significantly in this century. Indeed with the advances of medicine, dying, paradoxically, has often become undignified for so many people who are reduced to the level of vegetation through the tubes of technology or the loss of the basic faculties of memory, consciousness and understanding. In this regard it must be stated quite explicitly that every person has a right to die with human dignity. This right is in danger of being lost through the mechanisation of modern medicine. The new circumstances and conditions surrounding death have often had the effect of making man appear as the master of life and death. In the past when death came from the outside it was regarded as 'an act of God', whereas now death becomes 'an act of man' through pulling the plug of a life-support mechanism.

An additional significant shift is the fact that the care of dying has been taken out of the community and put into the charge of different institutions. Nowadays people die more often than not in hospitals and institutions. Consequently people are protected from the privilege of being with people when they die. In the past death was experienced as an affair of the local community and neighbourhood: all were involved in the experience, both young and old. Today young people have very little experience of death, with the result that very often they are ill-prepared to deal with the crisis of death when it strikes later on in life. From a social point of view death has been removed from the family to institutions, from wakes to funeral parlours, and from homes to hospitals. This so-called development in the twentieth century has had the unhappy effect of putting death 'out there', removing it from human experience and consciousness.

One example of keeping death at arm's length is to be found in the kind of language that is used to describe the reality of death in our daily news bulletins. More often than not death is presented as a cold statistic in a barrage of uncontrollable information. In addition we have devised euphemisms for referring obliquely to death: grandma passed away last night, we lost Uncle Tom recently, Mary slipped away with the family around her, Tommie has gone to heaven. And then when we do come to talk about death we usually do so in hushed voices and lowered tones. It has been remarked on more than one occasion that in the past people were shy about mentioning sex but spoke freely about death; today people are shy about mentioning death but speak freely about sex.

Another instance whereby we keep death in the background is in and through the many different forms of modern psychology. Many of these popular forms of psychology deny the reality of death by placing a very strong emphasis on self-identity, self-realisation, self-fulfilment, self-emancipation and self-autonomy. The promotion of the self as independent, autonomous and detached is often an implicit denial of the reality of death. In a somewhat similar manner certain forms of modern medical practice give the illusion that life can be prolonged, that the modern technology of medicine, organ transplants and cardiac surgery for example, can keep people alive indefinitely. While the advances of medicine must be welcomed and seen as real progress in the twentieth century, they must not be allowed to obscure the existence and reality of death. Furthermore the marketing world with its strong emphasis on keep-fit programmes, health foods and life insurances can lull us into forgetting about the nearness and imminence of death.

A final shift in our experience of death concerns the particular focus of the question. Until recently the primary emphasis was on individual death, and discussion was centred around the destiny of the individual. However, in this century the focus is changing from individual death to mass death, from questions about individual death to global destiny. This shift has been brought about by a variety of influences relating to death. These include two world wars that have had to reckon with the reality of so much mass death. In addition there has been the Jewish holocaust, the nuclear threat and the possibility of the ecological collapse of our planet, the ongoing holocaust of the Third World, and more recently the ever-increasing AIDS epidemic. These issues raise in dramatic form serious questions about the future of the human species and of the planet earth. The difference between these more recent phenomena and the presence of mass death such as the Black Death in the fourteenth century is that the twentieth-century phenomenon comes from within, that is to say it arises out of the effects of human behaviour and often comes within the control of humanity. The end of the world, the conclusion of history, the termination of human existence were once seen as those aspects of life which were in the providential hand of God, that part of life which came under a divine plan and providence bringing about the *Eschaton*. Now, for the first time in the history of civilisation, the end of the world has come within the reach of humanity. What was once regarded as a divine act is now appearing more and more as a human act. Up to now the future of the human race was assured externally through the providence of God. Now it is threatened internally by so-called 'developments' in the twentieth century. One positive outcome resulting from this shift from individual death to mass death is the growing awareness that the destiny of the individual is somehow or other tied up with the destiny of the whole world and that from now on considerations about individual destiny must be connected to considerations about global destiny.

In the light of these changes the question of death for a growing number of people is no longer a disturbing issue. Death and the question of life after death is increasingly becoming a non-issue. For many the possibility of life after death and the promise of eternal life is regarded as a distraction from this life. Belief in the hereafter is perceived as an escape from our social and political responsibilities in improving this life. This particular response to the question of death has been influenced most forcefully by Karl Marx.

For others, many of the traditional images concerning the next life are no longer credible, especially the classical images of heaven and hell. Likewise, the doctrine of the immortality of the soul and/or the resurrection of the body are responses that have lost their existential grip on modern consciousness.

Others argue that the beginnings and the endings of life have now come within the control and mastery of modern medicine. They point to the existence of test-tube babies and the possibility of prolonging life indefinitely at the other end. It is only a matter of time before medicine will be able to maintain life indefinitely. In the meantime, in some parts of America, bodies can be frozen and kept in a state of readiness to avail of the new technology when it comes.

Another increasingly popular perception is the possibility of reincarnation, a belief that is now held by around twenty-five per cent of people in Europe. For others the question of immortality is sufficiently answered in terms of personal fame, either through the continuation of one's children living on in the next generation or by contributing directly or indirectly to the progress of the world somewhat in the same way that Marx lives on in Marxism or Mozart lives on in his music.

These different shifts and changes in our experience of death have had at least two immediately obvious consequences. On the one hand there is the covering over of death giving rise to a death-denying culture. This newly emerging culture has the unfortunate consequence of creating a life-denying culture. One of the more immediate consequences is that when death does strike there is unbearable grief and crisis. Because death has become the new taboo, people are all too often unprepared and ill-equipped to deal with the reality of death when it does occur.

Furthermore because the subject of death has been repressed and passed over in silence, the reality of death has taken on exaggerated proportions, becoming an object of fear and dread to such an extent that it inhibits life and living. Many pass through life with a dreadful fear of death, simply because they have never sat down to face the issue of personal death head-on. There is a strange paradox at work here, namely that a death-denying culture has life-denying consequences. On the one hand a death-denying culture exaggerates death to such an extent that it becomes an object of fear and dread. By being an object of fear, death has the effect of inhibiting life and living. On the other hand a death-denying culture inflates our understanding of life, giving life itself a false sense of its own security.

According to Lucy Bregman in *Death in the Midst of Life*,[2] these rather naturalistic views of death have very little to say about human accountability in life or about the quest for human justice. In particular this naturalistic approach to death by-passes the question of the human self: Who and what is the self? Above all, this twentieth-century individualistic approach to death ignores the possibility of the self's relation to God by ignoring the question of God which is implicit in the reality of death.[3] In the words of one commentator reflecting on the modern experience of death:

> We look to science, that great modern faith for relief, and then to the art of psychological management as skilfully deployed by grief therapists and funeral directors, and then as a last hope to law and regulation. For all that, we still lack the foundation for a peaceful death.[4]

DIFFERENT ACCOUNTS OF DEATH: TOLSTOY, HEIDEGGER AND SCIENCE

We must now look at different accounts of death: one from literature, one from philosophy, and one from the emerging view of science.

One of the classical accounts of the human phenomenon of death is to be found in Leo Tolstoy's story *The Death of Ivan Illich* written in 1886. *The Death of Ivan Illich* is a classic both in literature and in terms of reflection on the meaning and reality of death. This story captures the reluctance of most human beings to accept death by depicting in vivid detail the story of the slow death of Ivan Illich. Ivan, a member of the Court of Justice, died at forty-five years of age at the height of his career. After marriage, initially happy, he became estranged from his wife; later he experienced a small accident while standing on a ladder. This accident is followed by the onset of pain and illness. Ivan begins the round of chasing doctors, trying to find the right diagnosis. The physicians in turn treat him as just another impersonal case, just the way Ivan had treated the accused in the courts. Over a period of time there is the gradual withdrawal by Ivan from friends and from relationships with other people.

The observations by Tolstoy in this story are all too typical and extremely accurate. They include the clumsiness of people at wakes: 'the feeling uncertain, as people always do, in such circumstances, as to what would be the proper thing to do'.[5] Then there is the 'complacent feeling that "it is he who is dead and not I"'.[6] And finally there is the usual discussion about 'the price of the plot for the grave'. Gradually the reader notes that the only person that Ivan can get on with in his terrible agony is Gerassim, one of the peasant servants. Only Gerassim tells him the truth and tries to get him to face up to and accept the reality of death as part of the universal condition: 'We shall all of us die, so why should I grudge a little trouble.'[7] Yet Ivan's whole life screened him from having to face the truth about death. Gradually he comes to see that the life he had lived was 'something trivial and often nasty'. With the gradual dawning of death, there is the reappraisal of life. Life now looks different in the face of death and the only apparent comfort that he can find is to go back to his childhood days: 'And this is really how it was. In public opinion I was going up, and all the time my life was sliding away from under my feet . . . And now it's all done and I must die.'[8]

According to one commentator, the meaningfulness of life or the meaninglessness of life is not decided for Ivan by immortality. Instead Tolstoy is careful to leave open this particular question. There is, of course, a short dialogue with God:

> He wept at his own helplessness, at his terrible loneliness, at the cruelty of man, the cruelty of God, at the absence of God. Why hast thou done this? Why hast thou brought me to this? Why, why dost thou torture me so dreadfully?[9]

It is only at the third-last hour before his death that Ivan finally accepts death and then at that moment there is light: 'He searched for his former habitual fear of death and did not find it. "Where is it?" What death? There was no fear because there was no death either. In place of death there now was light.'[10] It is interesting to note that at the end of Ivan's life, having finally accepted death he picks up on his relationships with his friends.

What is so significant about the death of Ivan Illich is his continuous refusal to accept death, a refusal that is crippling in its effects; and yet the story of Ivan is particularly characteristic of the twentieth-century experience. There is of course a second layer of interpretation to this story – one that goes beyond the obvious refusal to accept death. This second layer is Ivan's failure to recognise the dying that is taking place throughout his sickness, dying to relationships and friendships with others. In other words Ivan fails to recognise the unity that exists for all of us in living and dying, and dying and living. An important insight concerning the mystery of death is that there is another kind of dying that takes place before the physical act of dying.[11]

Another equally significant account of the reality of death is given by the German philosopher Martin Heidegger in his magnum opus *Being and Time* which was written in 1927. According to Heidegger the human person is 'a being towards death' and he describes the individual as one who is 'thrown into existence'.[12] Heidegger distinguishes between 'being there' and 'the not yet' of being there. He likens 'the not yet' of being to 'the not yet' ripeness of a piece of fruit. The fruit brings itself to ripeness. But the 'not yet' ripeness is an intrinsic part of the fruit. And so for Heidegger our relationship to death is somewhat like the 'not yet' ripeness of the fruit. Nothing that we can imagine can eliminate the unripeness of the fruit. In effect, for Heidegger it is the 'not yet' of life that constitutes the 'being there' of life. We come to an awareness of death, of being towards death, through anxiety. For the most part 'being there' covers up its inmost 'being towards death'. But, says Heidegger: '*Dasein* is dying as long as it exists.'[13] And again in a typical Heideggerian sentence: 'As soon as man comes to life, he is at once old enough to die.'[14]

For Heidegger our everyday approach to death is one of postponement: 'One of these days one will die too, in the end; but right now it has nothing to do with us.'[15] According to Heidegger concealment in the face of death dominates our everyday approach to death. For example we tell the dying person that they will be OK, as if they will escape death. According to Heidegger there is 'a constant tranquillisation about death', not only for the person dying but also for those who try to console. For most people there is a reluctant acknowledgment that 'death certainly comes, but not right away'.[16]

Heidegger goes on in his analysis of death to point out that authentic existence is found in our ability to understand ourselves as beings towards death and in our ability to anticipate the end as part and parcel of 'being there'.[17] It is this peculiarly human ability to anticipate the end that frees us for living in the present. What is important for Heidegger is that we shift attention from death as a once and for all event at the end of life, i.e. from death as something external and 'out there' to something internal, being part and parcel of life. Heidegger invites us to embrace death within and among the many projects or possibilities that we face in life and therefore to include death in our appreciation and evaluation of these projects. Most of all, what is important for Heidegger is that we are able to anticipate death in a way that enables us to think about existence as a whole and a totality encompassing the reality of death. In other words, for Heidegger the acceptance of death into life can become an integrating factor within human existence. It is this integration of death into life that constitutes technically what Heidegger calls 'authentic existence'. When this happens, death is no longer seen simply and solely as an external threat to be constantly dreaded. Instead death can be integrated into life and be seen as a factor that enables and empowers life. For Heidegger the acceptance of death is something that transforms death itself and enhances life. There can be little doubt that Heidegger's approach to death is not only realistic but also provides a very important way of integrating death into life in a manner that transforms the meaning of living itself.

While there is much to recommend in Heidegger's approach, it must be pointed out that he fails to develop the relationality of individual existence. Little or no attention is given in Heidegger's presentation to the importance of creating relationships. What is missing in Heidegger's approach to death is the importance of the radical relationality of the human subject as he or she faces death. Most commentators are critical of Heidegger in this regard and accuse him of what they call 'existential solipsism'.

A third approach to the question of death is outlined by John Bowker in his book *The Meaning of Death*.[18] Having analysed the different responses of various religious traditions to the question of death Bowker notes the emergence of a relationship between death and sacrifice. This paves the way for his conclusion: death 'is . . . necessary as a means to life'.[19] This particular thesis is one that Bowker also finds present in modern physics and biology. Looking at the evolution of the universe he reminds us poetically: 'There could not be you, and there could not be a universe, without death, the death of the stars and the death of succeeding generations of organic life . . . you are a child of the stars, as well as of your parents.'[20] In the light of this Bowker goes on to state: 'It is not possible to have life on any other terms than those of death; but where you do have death, there immediately you have the possibility of life.'[21] In this way Bowker sees a certain convergence taking place between religious and secular views on death.

While there is some self-evident truth in Bowker's thesis, it can be accepted only with caution and reservation. When science begins to talk about death as necessary for life we need to alert ourselves to the danger, especially coming from the world of science, that death may be promoted in a way that could devalue the dignity and uniqueness of the gift of life itself.

In the light of these three different approaches to death we can at least conclude that there is an important convergence towards the necessity of reconnecting life and death as an important element in any approach to the mystery of death itself. As Louis Evely points out: 'In wishing to live without dying, one dies without having lived.'[22]

COMMON BUT INADEQUATE RESPONSES TO DEATH

A number of responses to the question of death have come into existence in this century that deserve close examination.[23] The first response is to be found in the classical doctrine of the immortality of the soul. The underlying assumption is that the individual is composed of a unity of body and soul. Within this context, death is described in terms of the separation of the body and the soul; it is only the body that disintegrates and dies at death; the soul survives the destruction of death and lives on in eternity. According to this perspective there is a spiritual core that overcomes death. In effect it is only the body which dies; the soul escapes the defeat of death; the soul does not suffer the fate of the body which is one of decline, disintegration and decomposition.

Many commentators today react against this understanding of death. For one thing it seems to offend against the fundamental unity of the body and soul, the perception of the human person as an indissoluble unity of spirit and matter. It is argued that whatever happens in death affects the whole person, the body and soul. As Karl Rahner points out, we must not view death simply as that which 'affects only the so-called body of man, while the so-called soul . . . (is) able to view the fate of its former partner . . . unaffected and undismayed as from above'.[24] For

Rahner, death is an event for the individual as a whole and as a spiritual person.[25] Furthermore, this dualistic approach really keeps death at arm's length, refusing to see death as an intrinsic part of life and to accept that dying is an essential part of living. Above all, this approach by-passes the darkness of death.[26]

A second response to the question of death can be found in the well-known approach of Kubler-Ross in her books *On Death and Dying* (1970) and *Death: The Final Stage of Growth* (1975). These books have been help-ful to many people in approaching the question of death. The work of Kubler-Ross is based on wide experience of dealing with terminally ill patients. There is much that is extremely valuable and insightful in her understanding of death, especially from a pastoral point of view. Kubler-Ross maps out five stages that people go through in facing death, and she argues that these stages are based on empirical research. They include (1) the denial of death's imminence; (2) anger at the prospect of death; (3) bargaining about death with one's family, friends, doctors and God; (4) the onset of depression about death; and (5) the final acceptance of death.

The first four stages are extremely painful for people. If they are not eventually resolved and passed through they can be destructive and damaging for the patient. Within these four stages, there is a gradual let-ting go, a kind of movement towards a reluctant but ultimately freeing acceptance of death. Failure to move progressively through these four stages can be crippling for the patient. Over all there is a journey from darkness to light, from denial to acceptance. The fifth stage of acceptance becomes the norm; it is the stage of psychological maturity, a moment of deep self-understanding, and ultimately 'the final stage of growth' according to Kubler-Ross.

While this understanding of death does to some extent recognise the darkness of death it nonetheless overcomes that darkness in and through a process of acceptance. However, it must be asked whether such accep-tance really removes the ultimate darkness and destruction of death, even though it may help people to face death. A further difficulty with Kubler-Ross's scheme is that it stresses the element of continuity within death, without taking sufficient account of the rupture and disintegra-tion that is death. The element of continuity is important, but equally important is the element of discontinuity which seems to be neglected by Kubler-Ross.

A third response to the question of death is to be found in the French Jesuit, Roger Troisfontaines, in his book *I Do Not Die*. According to Troisfontaines there is a double movement throughout life: the body's diminishing decline and the human spirit's upward growth. Within this movement there are moments of tearing oneself away from one's structuring environment to a more liberating environment: the human spirit moves and advances upwards by a series of separations. These begin at birth as we move from the womb and ends at death as we move from the physical body which is a kind of 'provisional womb'.[27] Troisfontaines sums up his position in the following quotation:

> As the butterfly leaves the cocoon . . . as the foetus breaks the amnion at birth, so also when we step into the final stage of our destiny we leave this body which has been the primary condition of our personal ripening.[28]

While this understanding of death has a certain attractiveness about it, like the other two approaches, it does not face the darkness of death. If anything, death according to Troisfontaines seems to be something natural giving rise to a final moment of human growth.

The value of these three approaches is that they all in one way or another highlight the sense of continuity within death. This of course is the more acceptable side of death: each approach contains a strong sense of optimism, but not much hope.

These views could be described as naturalistic understandings of death which have become extremely important and popular in this century.[29] Such approaches to death are found to be wanting insofar as they neglect the questions of personal accountability, the issue of justice, the identity of the human subject, and the mystery of God.[30]

The real difficulty with these naturalistic approaches is that they do not adequately recognise the darkness, destruction and disintegration that takes place in death. Furthermore, these approaches do not seriously face the reality of human closure, the historical finality and the temporal conclusiveness that marks death itself, and do not recognise sufficiently the elements of failure and tragedy that death can be for so many people. As Karl Rahner points out, life after death 'is not to be thought of as a self-prolongation of time, or as a further extension in time of acts and experiences following one upon another in a series arising from some neutral substantial entity which impels itself forward'.[31] Instead, Rahner argues 'death is . . . the absolute end of the temporal dimension of a being of the kind to which man belongs'.[32]

How then are we to understand the mystery of death? In particular, how are we to approach the reality of darkness and destruction that accompanies the experience of death at the end of life? At most we can merely outline some of the elements that might go into the construction of a more adequate response to the mystery of death. Let it be said immediately that there is no fully adequate response to the darkness of death. It has been the assumption of modern medicine that there is an adequate response and it is this particular assumption that has become the singular failure of so much modern medicine. The refusal to respect the limits of nature and the human condition by medicine has resulted in the dismantling of modern medicine as a vocational and pastoral option.

In approaching death it must be recognised, as Rahner puts it, that death is the 'absolute null point' and 'the absurd arch-contradiction of existence'.[33] The first element in any approach to death therefore is one of humility, that is to say an attitude that accepts the awesome, transcendent and unknown dimensions of death. The experience of death brings us up against the limits of life; the death of a friend introduces us abruptly into the terror of transience; the loss of a loved one exposes us to the strangeness, otherness and difference of death itself. In doing so it raises the question of God: God's creativity, silence, otherness and transcendence. Death evokes, even among the hardened, humility in relation to life and in relation to any consolation that might be gleaned from belief in God. As with the mystery of God we know so little and the little we know pales into insignificance in comparison with what we do not know about God. This particular theological principle of the Christian tradition must be applied with equal weight and force to the mystery of death itself.

The second element in any response to the question of death must be one of hope. Within the context of the darkness and destruction that is death, every individual is faced with the absolute finality of life itself. It must be emphasised here that hope is something which arises as much out of darkness as out of light, as much out of negative experiences as out of positive experiences, as much out of absence as out of presence. In appealing to hope, however, it must be recognised that hope itself does not remove the darkness of death or eliminate the sense of closure that accompanies death. Again as Rahner says, hope arises only when we can find no further resources within ourselves by which to achieve a higher synthesis; such hope arises out of a sense of radical powerlessness in the face of death.[34] The nature and character and structure of this hope is something that we will take up in the next chapter.

A third element in the construction of any response to the question of death concerns the need for the individual to engage in a process of decentring the self with a view to recentring the self. Over and above the response of hope there lies deep down within human experience a little voice that cries out 'What is to become of me in death?'[35] How can we answer this all-too-human question that plagues every individual as he or she contemplates the prospect of death? If we are to seek an answer to this question we must begin first of all to move into the post-modern paradigm that we have already outlined in Chapter 3. The fact that we live in a processive, organic, dynamic, relational and interdependent world gives us a clue as to how we might begin to respond to this question. The one who asks the question 'What is to become of me?' is still 'an ego that has still not quite become a self',[36] a self that has failed to recognise its indebtedness to otherness.[37] In other words every human being needs to engage in a process of decentring the self with a view to recentring the self. This involves a movement, or better a process of passing over from being a lonely, vulnerable, autonomous and isolated self to being a self in process and relationship with other human subjects. To be human we need to move beyond the isolated ego into being a radically relational and social self. No matter how painful, each one of us needs to discover that he or she is not the centre of the universe but rather a radically relational subject who is bound up with other human subjects, the earth and the universe. In the words of Brendan Kennelly 'Self knows that self is not enough' and therefore as we face death we are challenged to move beyond the illusion of the self-sufficient subject and to realise that the self is never alone in this world but always exists in solidarity with other subjects including the Triune Self of the One God.

In addition each one of us needs to become more aware of the fact that we live in a world that has been graced by God in creation and that this world has developed over millions of years in the way it did develop because it knew that humans were coming. Above all, in this movement from being an independent self to being a radically social self requires that we recognise that the whole of the universe and all its individual subjects and subjectivities are somehow sustained as gift by the gracious love of God. What this means is that each one of us needs to make a basic choice: to grasp at finite things to sustain ourselves in existence and to turn them into an extension of the self and so become an ego again; or on the other hand to pour ourselves out into the lives of other human selves wherein we may encounter the gracious existence of that Other that upholds and sustains the world around us. In the first choice we will remain a lonely frightened ego and in the second choice we will begin to experience the underlying unity of everything within the world and our radical relationality and interdependence with the world around us.[38]

Another way of describing this process of passing over is to see it in terms of moving out of the 'culture of having' (G. Marcel) which is so characteristic of the modern world in which we live, that is a world of accumulating things and consuming them within the consumerist society. We need to move from this 'culture of having' to another culture, 'the culture of being' and relationality, realising our solidarity and social connectedness with all other human beings.

The fourth and final element making up a more adequate response to the question of death is the need to rediscover the underlying unity that exists between living and dying, and dying and living. It is only within this dynamic of living and dying, and dying and living that we will be able to let go of the human self in a personal act of self-surrender to the mystery of God that takes place finally at death.

The spirit of these observations in facing the darkness and disintegration of death is summed up in the following quotation from Maurice West:

> If a man is centred upon himself, the smallest risk is too great for him because both success and failure can destroy him. If he is centred upon God, then no risk is too great, because success is already guaranteed – the successful union of Creator and creature besides which everything else is meaningless.[39]

By facing death in the present, in struggling with the experience of dying, we begin to discover that all of life is gift, that every single moment of life is pure gift. Because life is unmerited gift, something that is only gradually disclosed by the internalisation of death, then we begin to value and appreciate life differently, we begin to see how life should be celebrated in a spirit of appreciation. This shift in understanding the meaning of life and the meaning of death is captured most dramatically in the change that takes place in the liturgical journey from Lent to Easter. We begin Lent with the saying 'In the midst of life, we already taste death' and when we arrive at Easter we affirm that 'In the midst of death, we still live.' Death therefore cannot be dissected at a distance; it must be internalised and lived to be fully understood: we must die in the midst of life if we are to understand death, appreciate life, and celebrate it appropriately.

5

IN SEARCH OF HOPE

*The death of religion comes with the repression of the high hope of
adventure.*

(Alfred N. Whitehead, 1925)

IF HOPE, ULTIMATELY SPEAKING, is the only adequate response to
death, then why is it that there is so little hope in the world today? If
anything, there seems to be a loss of hope surrounding modern culture.
Let me mention four possible sources of this crisis.

In the first place we have just seen that modern culture denies the reality of death. The sidelining of death in the modern world, the covering
over of death by contemporary culture, has removed the need for hope
because it is death in its many manifestations that provokes hope.
Secondly the pervasive presence of individualism within the modern
culture with its cultivation of the idols of consumerism, growth and
progress has replaced the need for hope with optimism. Individualism is
so much more at home with optimism, whereas hope makes too many
other-centred demands, too many social demands.

A third aspect to the crisis of hope has to do with the language and
conceptuality of classical theology which is out of sympathy with the
contemporary understanding of the universe. We live in a time of deep
transitions which are effecting a paradigm change under the impact of
impulses coming from the new physics, ecology, cosmology and feminism. The issue here is not one of adopting uncritically a new language
and conceptuality which in due course will itself become the object of
further changes. Instead the challenge is one of employing a language
and conceptuality, however provisional, that is not in conflict with the
current understanding of the world in which we live; it is, in effect, an
issue of expressing the vision of Christian hope in forms that are viable

for today. This particular challenge coming especially from the world of science is one that has been recognised in a significant paper by John Paul II to scientists in 1988 in which he singles out eschatology for particular mention:

> Contemporary developments in science challenge theology far more deeply than the introduction of Aristotle into Western Europe in the thirteenth century . . . what, if any, are the eschatological implications of contemporary cosmology, especially in the light of the vast future of our universe?[1]

In articulating a theology of hope, account must be taken of the move from a geocentric world to a heliocentric universe and from a heliocentric universe to a post-modern cosmic story.

A fourth dimension to the current crisis of hope relates to the confusion over what we can hope for. When we turn to the theological community for an answer to this question we find at best ambiguity and at worst contradiction. Some say we can hope for a better world, others point to the next life, and still others talk about spiritual realities like the immortality of the soul or resurrection of the body. American theologian Michael Scanlon, in the *New Dictionary of Theology* captures this confusion quite accurately when he says that a new line of division can be found among Christians in answer to the question 'What can we hope for?' For what Scanlon calls traditional Christians, the answer is 'eternal life after death for the purified soul', and for what he unhelpfully calls progressive Christians the answer is 'Yes, ultimately eternal life, but penultimately a more just, a more peaceful order.'[2] Despite the labels that Scanlon uses, he is certainly right about the existence of a division amongst Christians on this point, and I believe this division is reflected in the churches' equivocating reception of political, liberation and feminist theologies. The basis of this equivocation is often a particular theology of hope, a theology that is so absolutely other-worldly that it relativises the burning issues of life in this world. This particular theology also seems to have a very negative, one-sided view of the capacity of human nature.

In the light of these introductory comments on the current crisis of hope we will begin this chapter with some preliminary remarks about the nature of hope and then provide a framework for discussing hope. After that we will sketch out certain anthropological aspects of hoping, and conclude with some observations about the distinctive dimensions of Christian hope.

THE LANDSCAPE OF HOPE

Hope is a universal phenomenon which is by no means the preserve of religious people or the Christian community. Hope is implicit in everything we do and is often something that exists at the pre-reflective level of human awareness and activity. Hope is essential to the human condition and is presupposed as a given within the affairs of everyday living; indeed, hope is essential to the flourishing of the human condition – it is an outlook and attitude that influences and shapes and colours all human experiences and activities. Hope is a reaction to the challenges and difficulties of life itself; in particular the existence of hope assumes the possibility of action for change and implies, as John Macquarrie points out, the existence of an empty space for action.[3] On the assumption that the world can be changed, hope is something that is tied up with human action and brings about action in the world. In contrast to faith which is more related to the intellect, hope is driven by the will and is therefore more concerned with action; yet this distinction between faith and hope should not be made too rigidly since faith also does have a practical dimension to it and hope in its turn does have an intellectual aspect to its foundations.

In many instances hope comes into being out of a sense of unease with the way the world is; hope arises out of a certain dissatisfaction or discontent about the *status quo* and therefore implies some kind of critique of the present which is creative of new dreams and visions. Hope envisions the possibility of an alternative kind of world. To this extent hope does not ignore the realities of failure, tragedy, evil, suffering and death; on the contrary, hope arises out of the presence of such negativity within our lives. Unfortunately, however, so much hope, especially religious hope, is seen by many as pulling down the blinds on the presence of evil and suffering and tragedy in our world, that is to say a kind of flight from the world (*fuga mundi*) or, as Karl Marx would have it, an opium of the people distracting them from their personal and social responsibilities in the world. In contrast to these particular distortions, hope is an active response to the negative experiences of life, refusing to allow despair to rule the day in the face of so much pain, suffering and death.

One of the most important documents to come out of the Second Vatican Council was *Gaudium et Spes*, 'Joy and Hope'. Implicit in this document is a strong theology of hope – though in retrospect that particular theology inspired by the resurrection now needs to be restrained by a strong theology of the Cross which recognises the negativities of human existence in terms of evil, suffering and death.

In any discussion of hope it is important from the outset that a distinction be made between hope and optimism on the one hand, and hope and despair on the other. Optimism is the acceptance of the law of growth and the theory of human progress; optimism tends to ignore the ambiguity of the world in which we live and the presence of so much evil within that world. Optimism is a kind of presumption that neglects the realities of pain and suffering and evil, especially the vulnerability of the human enterprise. In contrast, hope struggles with the ambiguity of existence and responds to it by taking up a particular posture of imagining new possibilities and other alternatives, inspired by the impulses of human experience. It is principally in the midst of darkness and out of darkness that one can truly struggle in hope towards the light. It is very often only in the midst of alienation and estrangement that we can move forward in hope towards wholeness and reconciliation. It is in the experience of suffering that one can reach out in hope towards the possibility of healing. As Gabriel Marcel points out: 'The truth is . . . there can be no hope except when the temptation to despair exists. Hope is the act by which this temptation is actively or victoriously overcome.'[4]

In contrast therefore to optimism, hope is that particular approach to life which confronts the ambiguities of human existence. Optimism lives out of an attitude of 'more of the same' usually informed by the law of human progress or evolutionary development. The logic of hope, therefore, is not one of inference but rather the logic of imagination. To this extent an important relationship exists between hope and imagination as we will see later on.

On the other hand, hope is to be distinguished from despair which takes over from the response of hope by allowing the elements of emptiness and futility to predominate. Despair takes place when hope is disappointed and becomes lost. In broad terms despair may be described as the anticipation of the non-fulfilment of hope. Despair occurs when a person begins to realise 'I am no longer on the way', when fulfilment in the future no longer appears to be possible, and when a person believes 'I now possess whatever has been intended for me.' In contrast, most people perceive an element of 'the not yet' as something that is built into the very structure of human existence, and as long as that element of life remains there is hope. Closely connected to despair is the breakdown of trust. Trust is an essential element in the life and activity of hope. Without trust there is no hope; it is the absence of trust that brings about despair. On the other hand it is important to make a distinction between despair and resignation. Resignation can involve an attitude of accepting circumstances without leading to despair.

In trying to work out an understanding of hope it is necessary to emphasise that it is a response to one or other of the many different experiences that people undergo. There is a cluster of positive experiences that can stimulate the response of hope within the life of the individual. For example, there is the experience of personal development and becoming which is so characteristic of the human condition and which sows the seeds of expectation in the heart and opens up horizons of hope. In addition there is the experience of joy which, as we have already seen, seeks to be eternal. In many respects the experience of joy is one that opens the heart, quickens the human spirit and ultimately brings about a movement of self-transcendence.

Equally important are experiences of meaning, however fragmentary or partial these experiences may be. Such experiences open up the possibility of absolute meaning and generate the movement of hope within the life of the individual. A further positive experience that can inspire hope in us is a sense of the worthwhileness of human existence. Many people live their lives on the assumption that human existence is worthwhile and that element of worthwhileness, which can manifest itself in personal achievement or in the experience of forgiveness, opens up the possibility of hope. Another positive experience, by far the most important, is the experience of friendship and love. For most people this experience of friendship and love is the experience that awakens hope in the lives of people; it is especially the experience of love, that is selfless love, that empowers and enables people to hope.

On the other hand there is a series of negative experiences that also have the power and capacity to provoke hope in the life of the individual. Such experiences include the awareness of human historicity and the contingency of life as well as the realities of suffering, injustice and death itself. We will return to these experiences later on in this chapter when we come to deal with the anthropological aspects of hope.

MAPPING OUT A FRAMEWORK

It is important to construct some general framework for understanding the reality of hope and to adopt within that framework a common language in which to discuss the dynamics of hope. In broad terms it is possible to talk about ordinary, everyday human and historical hopes; these are hopes with a particular aim reaching out towards that which is reasonable in terms of human achievement. Historical hopes are based on a movement of the will towards a particular objective and this objective in turn is perceived to be within the reach of human realisation – in spite of being vulnerable and susceptible to threat and even disappointment. These human and historical hopes order and integrate everything else we hold to be important. They determine our horizons, they influence our actions and they give meaning to the general direction of life. Examples of such human and historical hopes are the kind of life that one hopes for oneself, or possibly the prospect of happiness for others, or the importance of justice for all, or issues of social importance such as the care of the earth, a happy marriage, or the realisation of a vocation. Over and above these historical hopes there is another kind of hope which is frequently called 'fundamental hope' or 'primordial hope'. Primordial hope, in contrast to human hope, does not have a particular aim or specific focus; it is rather a fundamental openness of the spirit towards the future and as such it transcends all particular forms of human hope going beyond their specific aims. To this extent, primordial hope is all-inclusive and is deliberately unconditional in orientation, refusing to set limits to that which is possible in life.

Clearly there is a close relationship as well as difference between historical hopes and fundamental hope. On the one hand they are different both in their aims and focus. Historical hopes are specific whereas primordial hope is open-ended, containing a certain readiness for the unexpected and the unimagined. On the other hand there is a close relationship between historical hopes and primordial hope. Primordial hope is that which enables people to cope with the disappointment and frustration of human historical hopes. Primordial hope prevents people from falling into despair when historical hopes collapse. When things fall apart, when all appears to be lost, primordial hope keeps people going; it enables people to cope with the collapse of historical hopes; it sustains people through personal difficulties and when necessary it inspires them to start again. It is precisely the openness of primordial hope, what some perhaps may regard as its vagueness, that is its real strength and promise. The element of inclusivity and totality is precisely that which enables people to overcome disappointments and losses within human hope, and to begin again with other particular human, historical hopes. On the other hand, human hope gives concrete expression to primordial hope. Without this concrete historical embodiment of hope, primordial hope could well appear to be empty and meaningless. Historical hopes, as it were, incarnate primordial hope, without however claiming to capture the fullness or the totality of primordial hope. To this extent there is a two-way relationship between historical hope and primordial hope.

A similar kind of language is used by Karl Rahner in his account of eschatology when he talks about the existence of categorical hopes and a transcendental hope, a this-worldly future and an absolute future.[5] The same distinction between historical hope and primordial hope is reflected in the French language which distinguishes between *des espoirs* and *l'esperance*. Joseph Pieper develops this distinction and gives it considerable importance in his philosophy of hope.[6] At times, however, Pieper seems to make too sharp a dichotomy between human historical hopes and primordial–fundamental hope, giving the impression that fundamental hope arises only out of the disappointment of historical hopes whereas human historical hopes can generate absolute, fundamental hope.

Others talk about the tension that obtains today between a culture of having, that is a culture that gives priority to possessions, accumulation and consumerism, and suggest that this corresponds more or less to human and historical hopes. In contrast there is the culture of being which corresponds more closely to primordial hope. This culture of being is one that focuses on the importance of communion in contrast to the culture of having. Whereas these distinctions are helpful for understanding the different dimensions to the phenomenon of hope, they must not be allowed to become separations when we move into the Christian context. It should be readily apparent that what is important about this framework for discussing hope is the area of primordial, fundamental hope. We must now give some consideration to the genesis of such primordial, absolute hope.

ANTHROPOLOGICAL ASPECTS OF HOPING

In the light of what we have already said about the intrinsic link between hope and the human condition, it is important at this stage to show how the genesis of primordial–fundamental hope arises out of those responses to life that are integral to the anthropological make-up of the person. The aim here is to show that the response of hope is part and parcel of that which is distinctive within the constitution and composition of what it means to be human. This approach to hope is intended to stand out against any suggestions that hope is something that is dispensable or that hope is something that could conceivably be replaced at some time in the future by certain forms of cultural evolution. Within this section we will be drawing on the anthropology already outlined in Chapter 3.

A useful point of departure is that every human being experiences life as somehow lacking in wholeness and totality. This given of human experience can be found down through the centuries in some of the great

Christian thinkers. On the one hand we have Augustine reminding us that the heart is restless until it finds its rest in God. Aquinas talks about the natural desire to see God. Maurice Blondel emphasises the dynamism of the will for human action. Bernard Lonergan refers to the unrestricted desire to know and to love within the human spirit. The existentialists talk about the ongoing search for meaning within life, and the liberation theologians talk about the struggle for justice in our world. All of these different experiences in one way or another are an expression of what Rahner calls the experience of self-transcendence. The human person is a self-transcending being and the experience of self-transcendence manifests itself in a variety of different forms: human estrangement, incompleteness, and the reality of death. The act of hope is an act of trust and self-surrender to the direction implied within the experiences of self-transcendence. Hope is about allowing ourselves to be drawn in the direction of self-transcendence in the expectation that we will not be disappointed and in the belief that there is a source animating the movement of the human spirit.

Another important characteristic of the human person is his or her radically relational nature which we have seen in Chapter 3. An anthropology of the social self is a fundamental point of entry into the construction of primordial hope. It is important to realise that there are two dimensions to the movement of hope: the interior and the exterior. Hope naturally enough has to arise from within the person – but only as a result of an encounter with the exterior world of human beings. The object is something outside us, not something which is at the disposal of the one who hopes. We have already seen that for the human to exist always means to co-exist and that to be is always to be in relationship. Gabriel Marcel makes this point succinctly: 'Hope is only possible on the level of *us*, or we might say *agape* . . . it does not exist on the level of the solitary ego.'[7] In a similar fashion we find Ernst Bloch saying: 'I am. But I do not have myself. So first of all we become.'[8]

The question is, how does this movement from the interior to the exterior take place? According to a Chinese proverb most of what we see comes from behind the eyes, that is from the prison of our own little interior world. If we remain exclusively locked up in that world, that is if we absolutise the private world of the self, then we move perilously close to a situation of despair. On the other hand, if we allow the small world of the human self to be enlarged and broken up, initially through the stimuli coming from others and ultimately through the power of our own imagination activated by the stories of others, then we can begin to hope. Imagination, especially the imagination that exists in mutuality with others, is one of the important sources of primordial–fundamental hope. Hope is animated by the stories of others which enlarge our little world through the power of the imagination.[9] Once hope comes into being through the power of the imagination then it relies on memory to sustain itself in existence. It is no mere coincidence that memory plays a decisive role in sustaining the hopes of Judaism and Christianity. Both religions depend upon power of memory to evoke the foundational events and experiences of history. Significant links therefore exist between the relational self, memory and imagination in the genesis and maintenance of primordial hope.

Another way of stating this is to talk as Edward Schillebeeckx does of the many negative 'contrast-experiences' in the lives of people.[10] These experiences provoke different forms of reaction, unease, indignation and dissatisfaction with the obvious conflict that exists between what is and what might be, between the presence of so much injustice and the possibility of its reduction, between the reality of suffering and its alleviation. It is these negative experiences that can awaken action which is the beginning of hope. In a somewhat similar vein Augustine suggests that hope has two lovely daughters: anger at the way things are and the courage to change them.

It is important at this juncture to recognise the power of negative experiences in stimulating hope. Things absent as much as things present play a sigificant role in the process of birthing hope. The poet John Keats captures the significance of things absent in his poem *Ode to a Grecian Urn*:

> Heard melodies are sweet, but those unheard
> Are sweeter; therefore, ye soft pipes, play on;
> Not to the sensual ear, but more endeared,
> Pipe to the spirit ditties of no tone.

What is significant about negative experiences is that they enable the human spirit to discern most acutely what is going on in life. To invoke another poet, Theodore Roethke observes that 'In a dark time, the eye begins to see.' In a similar manner it was Hegel who pointed out 'The owl of Minerva goes out at midnight.' The darkness of life provokes hope.

Another equally important point of entry into the genesis of primordial hope is to be found, according to Ernst Bloch, in the human capacity to experience what he calls 'the not yet' of life – that sense of unrealised potential within humanity and the world. It is this experience of 'the not yet' that effects within the human condition an anticipatory consciousness. It is this peculiarly human capacity to anticipate, especially through the power of imagination, that stimulates human hope within the human heart.

Arising out of these anthropological observations on the genesis of hope is the suggestion that hope is closely related to action, that hope in fact is embodied in action and is made manifest primarily within human action. In an important sense, I do what I hope, and I hope what I do. To this extent it must be said that hope is also constituted in and through human action. It is no accident that Aquinas associates hope primarily with the will rather than the intellect. Likewise when Karl Barth discusses hope he says: 'hope takes place in the act of taking the next step; hope is action'.[11]

Perhaps even more important than this particular emphasis on human action is what liberation theologians have come to call the importance of human and social praxis, especially the praxis of liberation. The significance of the Greek term *praxis* is that it brings out the importance of emphasising the element of transformation and liberation within human action. Such elements are essential to the venture of hope.

This emphasis on hope as praxis must be linked up with our earlier comments about hope as that which arises out of the social solidarity of the individual. I am enabled to hope only because of my radical relationality to others and the support of that relationality within the story of the universe. The expression of this basic primordial hope is to be found in the human, historical hopes of the world such as the promotion of goodness, the struggle for justice, the establishment of human rights, the pursuit of happiness, the care of the earth and a commitment to social and political reform – without, however, being reduced to any one of these particular expressions.

This basic primordial hope sooner or later runs up against the limit-situations of human existence. The experience of evil, the reality of suffering and the omnipresence of death bring the individual to the limits of life. It is at this juncture that basic primordial hope can begin to assume a religious colouration by affirming the presence and existence of a transcendent dimension to life itself. This affirmation of a transcendent dimension grounds and sustains primordial hope. To talk about a transcendent dimension to primordial hope does not necessarily mean that the object of hope now suddenly transfers itself to an other-worldly domain. For example it is instructive to observe that within Judaism the object of hope was largely a this-worldly hope except for the two hundred years preceding the common era. And even then, the possibility of hope in another world complemented rather than replaced the this-worldly hopes of Judaism. Likewise within the life of Jesus there is a close interplay between this-worldly and other-worldly hopes which we shall explore later on in Chapter 6.

An additional dimension to hope flowing out of this anthropological emphasis concerns the location of hope. While it is true to say that human hope exists primarily within the history of humanity and that one of the distinctive features of Judaism and Christianity is that the God of hope has acted in such foundational events of history as the exodus and the death and resurrection of Jesus, it must be said that the act of hope must also locate itself within creation. There are several reasons prompting this shift from an exclusive emphasis on hope in history to a more inclusive recognition of hope within creation *and* history. In the first place we have seen that in the 60s and 70s hope became linked almost exclusively with history, especially the so-called progress of history. As the early Moltmann put it so succinctly:

> The call and mission of the God of hope suffers man no longer to live amid surrounding nature, and no longer in the world as his home but . . . within the horizon of history. The man who is summoned by the divine promise to the transforming of the world falls outside the sphere of Greek cosmic thinking.[12]

History within this context was perceived to be moving towards a ful-filment that would bring many benefits to humanity: an end to poverty, disease, hunger. This progress would take place through a series of trans-formations in agriculture, industry and society. Indeed it was the promise of such historical progress that legitimated the unchecked exploitation and domination of the resources of nature. These promises of historical progress have turned out to be largely empty and are now perceived as a threat to a sustainable future. The flight from nature fostered by the historical consciousness of modernity has shaken the foundations of future existence in the 1990s. Instead our current and future hope must embrace creation as well as history: as the later Molt-mann puts it, performing a perfect U-turn without any hand signals. 'If the common catastrophe of human beings and the earth is still to be avertible . . . then it is certainly only by synchronising history within the history of nature.'[13] For the later Moltmann, human history 'must be brought into harmony with . . . the rhythms of nature'.[14]

Another good reason why hope should be relocated within creation as well as history is because of the connection that exists between begin-nings and endings, between origins and destinies. Though these two opposite terms of reference do not exist on the same level, our ability to talk about the end of time must somehow be related to our ability to discuss beginnings – an issue we will address in Chapter 11.

A third reason for situating contemporary hope within creation and history is that the history of creation is so much older than the history of humans. This considerably longer history of creation – some 15,000 million years – enables us to see signs of potential and promise that have become obscured by the exploitive approach of modernity to nature. The unfolding of a new cosmic story, the discovery of a finely tuned universe, and the presence of what scientists call 'an anthropic principle' within cosmic history provide some, though by no means conclusive, grounds for hope. At the same time it must be cautioned that the turn to creation and nature does not mean abandoning human history which has its own seeds of hope, especially within the dramatic history of Judaism and the person of Jesus. This relocation of human history within the wider horizons of cosmic history has potential to reshape hope for the future.

A further reason for turning to creation in the reconstruction of hope is that without some sense of the action of God within creation as something that is sustaining as well as initiating, something present as well as past, it becomes increasingly difficult to talk about the action of God in history and at the end of time. This is not to suggest that the action of God in creation is in any sense self-evident or unambiguously clear; rather the re-emerging unity between creation and history, between nature and humanity holds out the possibility of tracing shades of divine action, purpose and promise within our world.

Perhaps the most important reason of all for relocating hope within creation is that hope in the future, especially in the face of adversity and death, arises out of a sense that the love of God who created us in the first instance is the same love of God that sustains in the present and will transform us in the future. Hope in God in the Hebrew and Christian Scriptures is closely tied up with the God of Creation. These different emphases influencing the shape of hope, especially the links between creation and history, put us in a position now to address some of the distinctive dimensions of Christian hope.

DISTINCTIVE DIMENSIONS OF CHRISTIAN HOPE

When it comes to Christian hope a number of specific elements enter into the meaning of hope. In the first place, Christian hope is founded on the preaching and praxis of Jesus concerning the reign of God. Secondly that reign of God is understood to have been established in principle through the death and resurrection of Christ. The Paschal

Mystery of the death and resurrection of Christ therefore is the centrepiece of Christian hope. It is here that the peculiar character of Christian hope emerges. By including specific reference to the historical Cross of Christ, Christian hope embraces suffering and death as intrinsic elements of Christian existence. No amount of talk about the resurrection can remove the stark realities of suffering and death. Instead, Christian hope resides in the crucified Christ, acknowledging that this historical reality includes both darkness and light, tragedy and transformation, sadness and joy, death and resurrection. The shape of Christian hope is cruciform, made up of a 'bright darkness' or a 'dazzling darkness' (H. Vaughan) or a 'ray of darkness' (Dionysius). Darkness, as it were, becomes a special kind of light within Christian hope – an emphasis captured in the Johannine christology which unites death and glory in a single moment.

Another point about Christian hope is that because it is founded on the preaching and praxis of Jesus it embraces both the present and the future, both this-worldly realities and other-worldly realities. The hope of Jesus is both imminent and transcendent, prophetic and apocalyptic. In answer therefore to Michael Scanlon's question about what can we hope for, we must reply justice, peace and the integrity of creation in this life as well as eternal life which gathers up the work of justice, peacemaking and the preservation of creation. If the world is God's creation, if the universe is God's sanctuary, if the earth is in some sense the Sacrament of God, and this does seem to be implied in the biblical doctrines of creation, covenant and incarnation, then it must be affirmed that Christian hope includes the cultivation of creation and humanity in this life as well as the transformation of humanity and creation in eternity. The separation of this-worldly and other-worldly hopes goes against the grain of the preaching and praxis of Jesus as well as the theological significance of the Paschal Mystery of his death, resurrection and the outpouring of the Spirit and the event of incarnation.

This inclusive quality of Christian hope is captured most effectively by the Irish poet Seamus Heaney:

> History says, *Don't hope*
> *on this side of the grave.*
> But then once in a lifetime
> the longed-for tidal wave
> of justice can rise up
> and hope and history rhyme.

For the Christian, the tidal wave of justice has arisen in the ministry of Jesus and from now on the followers of Jesus seek to make hope and history rhyme.

The ultimate aim of God's plan for the world is not simply a glorified kingdom of disembodied spirits contemplating God's Self but rather a new heaven and a new earth embracing the transfiguration of the cosmos as well as the transformation of humanity. Christianity is nothing if not a religion of the body and that body includes humanity, history and creation. For Christian hope, there is no heaven without earth, as the prayer of Jesus implies. A hope that abandons or neglects the well-being of this world is not fully Christian; to this extent Christian hope is human, historical and cosmic in its embrace.

A number of consequences follow from this outline of the peculiar character of Christian hope. The God of Christian hope is a God who is immanent in the world, co-present and co-active in the ordinary everyday experiences of humanity. The God of Christian hope therefore is not a God who comes and goes intermittently in some arbitrary way. Rather the God of Christian hope is the creator God who has been involved in cosmic and human history *ab initio*. This permanent involvement of God in the world has been revealed specifically in the Christ-event. The God of creation, the God of incarnation and the God of the Cross stands out in contrast to the detached Hellenistic God of omnipotence and impassibility.

The God of Christian hope revealed in the Cross of Christ is a God who has limited God's power in and through the gift of freedom to humanity. The self-emptying of God's omnipotence in creation and in particular in the Cross of Christ must be recognised as a corollary to the divine gift of human freedom. The separation of divine power, especially as omnipotent, from involvement with the reality of human freedom is one of the most serious obstacles to the praxis of Christian hope in the world today. Unqualified affirmations of divine omnipotence too easily become excuses for human passivity concerning the future of the world. To leave the future of the world simply to the omnipotent God is in fact to abandon historical existence to what St Paul calls 'the powers and principalities of this world' or what we today might call the forces of the free market.[15] Instead the theological principle that nothing happens between heaven and earth without the free response of humans must be applied to the praxis of Christian hope for the world.

A similar modification must be made concerning the impassibility of God in the context of Christian hope. One of the many arguments against Christian hope is the existence of so much evil and suffering in the world. The reality of suffering challenges faith, hope and love in God in a way that is perhaps more effective than any intellectual argument. Within this challenge the image of an indifferent and impassible God only aggravates the issue. An apathetic theology generates an apathetic people and in particular an apathetic Church – that is a people without hope. Is the reality of an impassible God compatible with the revelation of God in Judaism and on the Cross of Jesus? I submit that the God revealed in the life and death of Jesus is analogically speaking 'a suffering God' and that this same God continues to suffer in the world until God comes again. The God revealed in Jesus is a God who affects the world and is affected by the world and continues to be affected by the suffering of the world. The proposal of 'a suffering God' of course does not eliminate the problem of human suffering but it does give us a way of facing suffering in the knowledge that we do not suffer alone but with God as the fellow-sufferer who understands.[16] In particular the presence of suffering in God until God comes again gives a new foundation to the God of hope. An equally powerful foundation for hope here might be the preferred emphasis of some feminist theology on a compassionate God. Compassion carries with it not only divine solidarity with the suffering of others but also a divine energy that empowers us to do something about the suffering and that capacity to act is an important expression of Christian hope. In the end the Christian is someone who in the face of death goes into the garden of life with hope to plant a tree and knows that she does not plant in vain.

6

HOPE IN JUDAISM AND IN
THE LIFE OF JESUS

There is such a thing as an ecology of hope. There are environments in which it flourishes and others in which it dies. Hope is born and has its being in the context of family, community and religious faith.

(Jonathan Sacks, 1995)

THERE CAN BE LITTLE DOUBT that hope plays a central role in the formation of Judaism and that the hopes of Judaism are the primary context for understanding the eschatology of Jesus. Ernst Käsemann has pointed out that Jewish apocalyptic is 'the mother of Christian theology' and more recently J. Christiaan Beker argues that 'the coherent centre of Paul's Gospel is constituted by the apocalyptic interpretation of the Christ event.'[1] It is important for any appreciation of the hope of Jesus as well as Christian eschatology that we have some sense of Jewish hope and the eschatologies of the Hebrew Scriptures. Our aim here is to discover some of the Jewish background that will shed light on the New Testament eschatology; our treatment of hope in Judaism must of necessity be selective.

THE HOPES OF JUDAISM:
PROPHETIC AND APOCALYPTIC ESCHATOLOGY

It is necessary from the outset to develop a broad framework within which we might look at the hopes of Judaism; this means that we must try to draw up some kind of agreed terms of reference for discussing these hopes. Fortunately most scholars now accept that the eschatology of the Hebrew Scriptures can be divided into two distinct but closely related strands: prophetic eschatology and apocalyptic eschatology.[2] This distinction is significant not only for understanding Judaism but also for interpreting the eschatology of Jesus.

According to Paul D. Hanson in *The Dawn of Apocalyptic*, prophetic eschatology may be described as

> a religious perspective which focuses on the prophetic announce-
> ments to the nation of divine plans for Israel and the world which the
> prophet has witnessed unfolding in the Divine Counsel and which he
> translated into the terms of plain history, real politics and human
> instrumentality.[3]

For Hanson the prophet interprets for the king and the people how the plan of Divine Counsel will be effected within the context of their nation's history and the history of the world. In other words the prophet-ic eschatology of Judaism is about decisive turning-points within the history of Israel through divine interventions and to that extent may be classified as a this-worldly eschatology. Further, it should be noted that the primary function of these prophetic utterances is to bring about a conversion of the people of Israel to the plan of God. The prophets, there-fore, were not really concerned about predicting the future but were very intent upon changing the present. The invocation of the future, often in terms of gloom, punishment and destruction, was intended to effect change in the present – not to predict with any accuracy what divine interventions or judgments might come about in the future which could only be known to God. This point should be kept to the fore in understanding Jewish eschatology, and in particular in approaching the eschatology of Jesus.

Within this broad category of prophetic eschatology it is possible to detect what one commentator has called a 'rose-coloured eschatology', that is, an eschatology of good news which was a characteristic largely of pre-exile Judaism.[4] Further within pre-exilic Judaism there are strands of a nationalist eschatology. In the post-exilic period there emerged a com-bination of positive and negative prophetic eschatologies, with an ever-increasing emphasis on punishment and destruction.

An additional characteristic of prophetic eschatology is the presence of a recurring emphasis on the coming 'day of the Lord' or the 'day of Yahweh'. This particular reference which occurs most frequently among the prophets has a wide range of meaning. It covers 'that day' on which Yahweh will judge against foreign nations or 'the day' when Yahweh will restore the fortunes of Israel, gather together other nations and establish a New Creation. The 'day of the Lord', therefore, will not be simply judg-ment against foreign nations but will also include judgment against the people of Israel for violating the covenant (Amos 5:18–20; Isa. 2:11–17;

Joel 2:1–2). The origins of the 'day of the Lord' expression are associated by some (Möwinckel) with the cultic New Year Festival which celebrated the enthronement of Yahweh as King and by others (von Rad) with a Holy War tradition in which Yahweh would triumph over the enemies of Israel.

Apocalyptic eschatology, on the other hand, is about

> a religious perspective which focuses on disclosures (usually esoteric in nature) to the elect of the cosmic vision of Yahweh's sovereignty – especially as it relates to his acting to deliver his faithful – which disclosure the visionaries have largely ceased to translate into the terms of plain history, real politics and human instrumentality due to a pessimistic view of reality growing out of the bleak post-exilic condition within which those associated with the visionaries found themselves.[5]

The focus, therefore, of apocalyptic eschatology is clearly though not exclusively other-worldly and cosmic. The apocalyptic outlook assumes a certain detachment from the affairs of the world, an indifference to developments taking place within history, largely because of their decline and corruption. In some sense it can be said that apocalyptic eschatology is an extension and development of prophetic eschatology and that therefore all apocalyptic involves some eschatology, though not all eschatology involves apocalypticism.[6]

In more recent discussions about apocalyptic, commentators have been distinguishing between apocalypse, apocalyptic eschatology and apocalypticism[7] – even though the use of these terms continues to be somewhat fluid. According to John J. Collins apocalyptic is a genre of revelatory literature composed within a narrative framework in which revelation is mediated by an other-worldly being to a human being, disclosing a transcendent eschatological reality.[8] It is important here to distinguish between the literary device used in apocalyptic literature and its particular theological intention – a distinction which all too often is conflated. Apocalyptic eschatology is more than a literary phenomenon; it is an attitude of mind which aims to interpret the course of history and to reveal the end of the world.[9] This apocalyptic outlook is ultimately other-worldly and transcendent, universal and cosmic in scope, highly imaginative with an emphasis on divine intervention from outside history, having little regard for ethical issues in this life. In contrast prophetic eschatology highlights the importance of human action and personal responsibility in this life. And yet this understanding of a sharp contrast between prophetic and apocalyptic is losing ground today. Some would now hold that apocalyptic eschatology is 'prophecy in a new idiom' which although addressed to the future of the world has importance for the individual in the here and now.[10] Apocalypticism, which arises out of apocalyptic eschatology, is a social movement, some would say even an ideology, which resolves the conflict of history by recourse to divine intervention at the end of time.

Against the background of this general framework we can begin to look at the hopes of Judaism. From the beginning of Judaism up to the present it must be said that Jewish faith understands itself to be heir of divine promises reaching out into the future. The God of Israel is a God of promises. These promises unfold gradually throughout the dramatic history of Israel beginning with Abraham and the patriarchs, moving on through Moses and David and the prophets. The promises of Yahweh are the basis of Jewish hope, and the underlying structure of this faith-filled hope is one of call, promise and covenant. The historical experience of God by the people of Israel usually contains an element of promise and this promise finds its way in one form or another into the many different covenants between God and God's people: Noachic, Mosaic etc.

By far the most influential development within this historical experience of divine promises is the foundational revelatory experience of Yahweh by Moses. The centrepiece of Jewish hope-filled faith is the revelation of the name of Yahweh to Moses on Mount Sinai in the burning bush as described in Exodus 3:1–15. Within this central event of revelation there is a strong presence of promise at least at two levels. On the one hand Yahweh says: 'I have observed the misery of my people . . . I have heard their cry . . . I have come to deliver them . . . to bring them up out of the land to a good and broad land . . . I will send you to Pharaoh to bring my people, the Israelites, out of Egypt' (vv. 7–10). Clearly, promises of deliverance and liberation for the people of Israel are perceived to be part of Moses' interpretation of this experience of Yahweh. On the other hand, when Moses enquires about the identity of the God making these promises he receives the enigmatic reply: 'I am who I am' (v. 14), followed by an instruction to tell the people: 'I AM has sent me to you' (v. 14). The word translated as 'I AM' is made up of the four Hebrew letters, YHWH, known as the tetragammaton, representing the divine name of God coming from the Hebrew verb 'to be'. The translation of 'I am who I am' is considered by many commentators to be too influenced by Greek philosophy and insufficiently shaped by the more dynamic Hebrew understanding of reality. The name YHWH refers less to God's eternal being and much more to God's dynamic presence and action bringing history to fulfilment. A more faithful translation, though still far from adequate, would be: 'I will be for you what I will be' or 'I will be there for you'.[11] The divine name for God is actually a divine promise and the spirit of this promise is found in the early Jewish creed of Deuteronomy.

> We were Pharaoh's slaves in Egypt but the Lord brought us out of Egypt with a mighty hand. The Lord displayed before our eyes great and awesome signs and wonders against Egypt, against Pharaoh and all his household. He brought us out from there in order to bring us in, to give us the land that he promised on oath to our ancestors. Then the Lord commanded us to observe all these statutes, to fear the Lord our God, for our lasting good, so as to keep us alive, as is now the case. (Deut. 6:21–4)

It is surely out of this experience, however retrospective its influence may be in the redaction of Jewish history, that the prophets of Israel spoke. This does not mean that the prophets were not fired by their own quite specific religious experiences which they most surely were – but it does imply that the Mosaic experience of the name of Yahweh was the primary filter in and through which their experiences were interpreted – a filter that contained a significant element of promise and hope.

This foundational experience led to the Sinai covenant tradition which had 'a distinctive future orientation spelled out clearly in the treaty blessings and curses'.[12] Over and above this Mosaic-covenant experience there is also within Judaism the patriarchal promise tradition and the Davidic monarchical promise tradition. Whether these two traditions are separate or related to the Mosaic experience is a matter which need not detain us here. All three historical realities contain important moments of promise, generating hope, and as such are the matrix out of which the prophets spoke and developed their great variety of eschatologies: rosy and gloomy, fearful and cosmic, this-worldly and other-worldly, historical and transcendent.

From the eighth century onwards there developed the prophetic eschatologies of Amos, Hosea, Isaiah, Micah and Jeremiah and these took on many different shades and shapes. The pre-exilic prophets initially were particularly positive, promising the development of Israel as a great land and a mighty nation in the eyes of the rest of the world, thereby developing what is often referred to as a nationalist eschatology. Gradually this yielded to the emergence of a negative eschatology which arose out of a failure to live up to the demands of the covenant in terms of a concern for the poor and a commitment to justice. Particularly outspoken was Amos 5:8–11 and Jeremiah on the issue of the presence of so much injustice alongside the worship of Yahweh.

In the post-exilic period, inaugurated by the oracles of Deutero-Isaiah, chapters 40–55, there is a return to the positive eschatology of former times. The emphasis shifts to the restoration of salvation for Israel on a grandiose scale, likened symbolically to a second exodus. For example, Jeremiah talks about a time when Israel will return to the land from which they have been exiled (Jer. 23:1–8); a time of restoration, when Jerusalem will be rebuilt (31:38–40); a time when a Davidic king will rule again (23:5–6), invoking the God of exodus who will bring God's people back as before (23:7–8). However these promises, like the creation of a new heaven and a new earth (Isa. 65:25) and the re-establishment of Jerusalem with its worship, gradually began to fade. The promises, hopes and expectations, it should be noted, are still something expected to take place within the history and institutions of Israel. The non-fulfilment of these promises were simply extended out by the prophets into the future without much concern about the fact that they had not materialised in the manner expected.

It was through the wisdom literature that attention was gradually focused on the possible destiny of individuals beyond death. This gave rise in turn to discussions about the existence of an underworld called *sheol* – a place where the dead live a shadowy and an unattractive kind of existence. Eventually within late Judaism God was understood to have some power over the dead within *sheol*. During the intertestamental period the justice of God demanded differentiation among those who had entered *sheol*. The underlying insight was that communion with God in this life was something stronger than death and would therefore survive into the next life.

However, it was principally in and through apocalyptic literature, which began around the year 250 BC that another vision of the future emerged which was largely other-worldly and transcendent. Whereas the prophetic tradition had looked to a time within history when God would establish peace and justice among the nations as well as harmony with nature, apocalyptic literature looked to a time outside of history when God would grant the fullness of salvation to the people of Israel. This vision in turn is expanded beyond Judaism and eventually embraces a universal and cosmic dimension. It is within this latter context that expectations about the resurrection of the dead began to develop within late Judaism. This apocalyptic dimension is transcendent in two senses. It goes beyond the boundaries of Judaism and at the same time surpasses everything within human history. According to some commentators this apocalyptic vision developed more and more as a reaction to a history that had become increasingly dark within Judaism due to the presence of so much suffering. Much apocalyptic literature arose out of a context of corruption, evil and persecution. What is characteristic of so much of apocalyptic is a presence of a strong element of discontinuity within Jewish history.

Apocalyptic thought tends to be other-worldly and transcendent, concerned with a climactic moment within history, involving a struggle between the good and evil forces of the world, and the final victory is one that usually has universal and cosmic application. The language of apocalyptic is normally vivid and extravagant and usually there is a sharp contrast between the present order and the future, a contrast that is depicted in terms of a crisis that emerges within the present. The overall effect of apocalyptic literature is to draw a sharp contrast between this world and the new world, highlighting the elements of discontinuity within history, focusing on the presence of collapse, destruction and disintegration. What is particularly outstanding about apocalyptic thought within Judaism is its inclusive character, embracing the destiny of humanity, history and the cosmos. However, in spite of the other-worldly dimension of apocalyptic eschatology it is becoming increasingly clear among commentators that this other-worldly aspect has some practical implications for life in the present and that a more unified understanding of the present and the future is closer to the truth. Indeed for many, apocalyptic thought is as much a political statement about the corruption of the existing social order as it is an eschatological statement with transcendent implications. The political and the mystical, the prophetic and the apocalyptic may not be as exclusive or alien as was once thought to be the case.

THE PROPHETIC ESCHATOLOGY OF JESUS

It is against this background of hope within Judaism that we must situate the preaching and praxis of Jesus. Of course before looking at the life of Jesus it is necessary to acknowledge the difficulty of arriving at reliable historical data about Jesus of Nazareth. The Gospels are complex documents that took some forty to seventy years to come into the final form we have today and we know that during that period they underwent a process of theological, ecclesial and cultural interpretation, adaptation and development within the Christian community. Within this complex process there is a visible line of evolution from the historical reality of Jesus to the faith confession of Jesus as the Christ, the Son of God, the Word made flesh.[13] This line of evolution can be traced through the careful use of historical, social and literary criticism of the Gospel material.

The catalyst inspiring this remarkable development concerning Jesus of Nazareth is complex: the preaching and praxis of Jesus, the apocalyptic experience of the Cross, the eschatological realities of Easter and the outpouring of the Spirit. Indeed, neglect of the eschatological factor in the interpretation of the Gospel is partly responsible for some of the incomplete and reductionist pictures of Jesus appearing today in biblical research. It must be remembered that in the life, death and resurrection of Jesus the disciples had experienced the advent of the *Eschaton* as already intimated in Chapter 2. Christology and eschatology cannot really be separated into two distinct realms; instead they represent different expressions of one and the same experience of Jesus as the bringer and bearer of God's salvation.

In trying to discover some sense of the eschatology of Jesus we must at least refer to the many quests of the historical Jesus now known as the 'old quest', the 'new quest' and the 'third quest' of the 1990s. The 'old quest' grew out of the historical consciousness of the Enlightenment which gave rise to the development of historical research in the nineteenth century which issued in a series of liberal lives of Jesus. The 'old quest', however, came to a head with the publication of Albert Schweitzer's book *The Quest of the Historical Jesus: A Critical Study of its Progress from Reimarus to Wrede* which pointed out that 'each epoch . . . found its reflection in Jesus; each individual created Him in accordance with his own character'.[14] Whatever we might say about Schweitzer's work, and much could be said critically, he sought to recover with some success the centrality of eschatology in the life of Jesus. Historical scepticism emerged after Schweitzer about the possibility of ever reaching the Jesus of history and this found influential expression in the work of Rudolph Bultmann.

In 1953 a significant essay was written by Ernst Käsemann entitled 'The Quest of the Historical Jesus'. Käsemann argued that the historical Jesus is important for a balanced understanding of the Christ of faith at the centre of the Kerygma. It is hardly just a coincidence that Käsemann around the same time was one who pointed out that 'apocalyptic was the mother of all Christian theology'[15] – though this cryptic observation has not always received the attention it deserves.

The 'third quest' of the historical Jesus came in the late 1980s and was sparked off predominantly by social and literary approaches to the Gospel which did not always recognise the importance of locating these approaches within a community of faith. Further, the 'third quest' among some gives as much attention to non-canonical sources such as Q and the Gospel of Thomas as it does to the canonical Gospels. These approaches in their extreme form have produced a picture of Jesus merely as a wisdom teacher or, as some say, 'a cynic sage' comparable to other cynic sages of the Mediterranean world. Among some authors like Marcus Borg, Burton Mack and John Dominic Crossan there is an attempt to strip away all the eschatological elements within the message of Jesus.

In retrospect it is instructive to note how eschatology either positively or negatively has been an area of constant debate in all quests of the historical Jesus. Indeed one might say that the subtext to the quests of the historical Jesus has been the place and role of eschatology in the life of Jesus. Did Jesus have an eschatology? Was Jesus mistaken about the advent of the *Eschaton*? Did Jesus die disillusioned in despair concerning the coming reign of God? Is eschatology simply the creation of the disappointed disciple of Jesus?

In trying to answer these different questions it is possible to discern within the old, new and third quests of the historical Jesus at least four different positions concerning the eschatology of Jesus. Around the turn of this century Johannes Weiss and Albert Schweitzer in reaction to the liberal lives of Jesus sought to recover the eschatological element within the preaching of Jesus. They argued that the future was the all-determining horizon within the message of Jesus and that in the end Jesus turned out to be a failed prophet because the kingdom of God did not arrive as he had expected. This particular view has become known as the 'thoroughgoing' or 'consistent' model of eschatology in the life of Jesus. In response to this thesis C. H. Dodd suggested that Jesus preached the presence of the reign of God within his own ministry. Dodd referred to texts like Mark 1:15 and Matthew 12:28 which focus on the existence of the reign of God in the present, appealing above all to the overall thrust of John's Gospel. Dodd's view has been known as the model of 'realised' eschatology. As one might expect a number of scholars have reacted to both of these extreme positions, pointing out that Jesus presented the reign of God as both present and future. These reactions have become known as the model of 'proleptic eschatology' or better 'inaugurated eschatology'.

A fourth approach emerges within the 'third quest' for the historical Jesus *vis-à-vis* eschatology in the life of Jesus. Our comments must be confined to 'third quest' principally insofar as it throws light on the eschatology of Jesus. Among the 'third questers' of the historical Jesus there is no uniform position or consensus about the existence of eschatology in the life of Jesus. Indeed there is considerable diversity among the 'third questers' about the place of eschatology in the life of Jesus. One can detect at least three different positions concerning eschatology in the life of Jesus.

The first position sets out to dismiss as inauthentic those words and deeds of Jesus that deal with eschatology. This extreme position is assumed by the (in)famous Jesus seminar in North America. One of their so-called seven pillars of wisdom, number five, posits a Jesus free of eschatology.[16] Examples of this approach can be found in the work of Burton Mack and John Dominic Crossan who seek to strip away the presence of eschatology by reducing Jesus to the level of a teacher of wisdom or as they say 'Cynic Sage' similar to the cynic sages of the ancient Greco-Roman world.[17] They do this by giving almost as much weight to the non-canonical sources as they give to the four Gospels about Jesus and by focusing on the Q document. There is undeniable evidence that Jesus was a teacher of wisdom and that many of his sayings are counter-cultural. However, the recovery of this important aspect can hardly justify the complete neglect of the rest of the New Testament material relating to eschatology. Further, Mack and Crossan seem to assume that Jesus as a teacher of wisdom excludes Jesus with a vision for the future of the human community. A false antithesis between the sapiential tradition and the apocalyptical tradition seems to be implied in their positions – an antithesis quite alien to Judaism, the life of Jesus, and the early Church.

A second position within the 'third quest' of the historical Jesus is represented in the work of the American scholar Marcus Borg who presents what he calls a 'more temperate case for a non eschatological Jesus'.[18] According to Borg the presumed consensus about the eschatological element within the preaching of Jesus has collapsed. He suggests that the Son of Man sayings have been discredited, that a refinement of the meaning of apocalyptic has been taking place, and that a reassessment of the meaning of the reign of God is under way.[19] Borg also argues that there is considerable confusion concerning the word 'eschatology'. When he rejects the eschatological Jesus he claims to be rejecting 'an-end-of-world-figure'.[20] More specifically Borg rejects an eschatological Jesus because such detracts from the importance of the socio-political significance of Jesus. Eschatology, he argues, results in an 'existential interpretation' that individualises and internalises the message of Jesus, producing an 'apolitical reading' of the Gospels that leads 'to a growing sense of the theological irrelevance of the historical Jesus'.[21] An 'end-of-the-world' Jesus is responsible for the presentation 'of early Christianity as an-end-of-world-movement'.[22]

Borg's thesis should not be dismissed too quickly. His concern for the neglect of the social and political significance of Jesus is important. Whether it is necessary, however, to eliminate eschatology altogether from the life of Jesus to recover the socio-political import of the preaching and praxis of Jesus is quite another question. Might it not be argued that the presence of eschatology in the life of Jesus would give greater significance to the socio-political implications of Jesus' preaching and praxis. After all, the social and political significance of the preaching and praxis of Jesus raises eschatological questions about the enduring value of such activities. Borg's case to date comes close to a rejection of eschatology by a narrow definition of the word. On the other hand it must be acknowledged that Borg's position continues to be nuanced and refined. For example, in *The Anchor Bible Dictionary* he says:

> At issue is not whether Jesus had an eschatology. He apparently affirmed an after life . . . spoke of banqueting in the kingdom . . . the issue, however, is whether he thought all this (judgment, resurrection, messianic banquet) was to appear soon.[23]

Further, in a later article entitled 'Jesus and Eschatology: Current Reflections' Borg concludes his analysis in the following way:

> I think that Jesus probably had some eschatological beliefs . . . I think Jesus was concerned about 'the future' . . . I think there is an urgency in the Jesus traditions . . . A non-eschatological Jesus need not be imagined as an enlightened master living in a timeless present or as a radically individualistic Hellenistic Cynic Sage unconcerned with the future of his people.[24]

More recently Borg points out:

> I do not think the eschatological debate is over; there are signs that news of the change is provoking (as it should) further examination of the question. Precision of terminology will be an important part of the continuing discussion.[25]

A third position within the 'third quest' of the historical Jesus affirms the presence and importance of eschatology in the life of Jesus. This position is presented in varying degrees by different authors. For example E. P. Sanders in *The Historical Figure of Jesus* argues the case for Jesus as an eschatological prophet who believed that promises to Israel would be fulfilled in the near future. For Sanders the emphasis is on an imminent eschatology in the life of Jesus with little or no acknowledgment of a realised eschatology or indeed of a Jesus who is concerned to reform Jewish social and political life.[26]

An equally important case for eschatology in the life of Jesus has been made by J. P. Meier in *A Marginal Jew: Rethinking the Historical Jesus*, Vol. 2. Meier presents through the employment of the critical-historical method strong evidence for the existence of both a future and present eschatology in the life of Jesus.[27] Meier's presentation is a most impressive, detailed and persuasive examination of historical data that points towards the existence of eschatology in the life of Jesus. Through the skilful use of criteria of similarity, discontinuity, multiple attestation, and coherence Meier selects and analyses a significant body of eschatological sayings and actions in the life of Jesus.

In spite of this *tour de force* by Meier one must express some reservations. For example, Meier claims that 'Jesus was not interested in and did not issue pronouncements about concrete, social and political reform either for the world in general or for Israel' and that 'there is an important difference in emphasis between Jesus and some of the great Old Testament Prophets'.[28] Such statements will leave many readers from first- and third-world theologies uneasy. Further, Meier's analysis of the eschatological significance of the kingdom of God material begins with Jesus' proclamation of the kingdom as future. This could give the impression that Jesus began his mission with an emphasis on the future whereas from an historical point of view it is at least equally probable if not more likely that Jesus began his mission, having moved from the position of John the Baptist, as a prophet with an emphasis on the reign of God as present. These reservations about Meier's work, however, do not detract from the impressive historical analysis he offers of the eschatological sayings and actions relating to the kingdom of God material within the Gospels.

Where does this thumbnail sketch of the 'third quest' of the historical Jesus leave us concerning the eschatology of Jesus? In raising this question we must recognise the twofold difficulty of tracking down reliable material about the historical Jesus and at the same time of locating an eschatological dimension within that historical material. Equally problematic is the difficulty of moving from a twentieth-century outlook to the very different horizon of the first century AD. It would be naive to expect twentieth-century eschatological concerns to be addressed by the eschatological outlook of the first century. At the same time, the eschatology of Jesus is an important factor in any reconstruction of a contemporary Christian eschatology – not in any positivistic sense but in terms of outlook, principle and orientation.

In response to those who seek to eliminate eschatology from the life of Jesus the following observations must be made. The religious matrix of the life of Jesus is Judaism – a religion that is itself eschatological in orientation as we have seen. The near universal acceptance of the Jewishness of Jesus presupposes at least this eschatological mindset. Further, Jesus' close association with John the Baptist, 'the one person who had the greatest influence in Jesus' ministry'[29] suggests some form of eschatological consciousness in the life of Jesus – even though, as we shall see, Jesus modifies John's eschatology very early on. In addition Jesus' preoccupation with the kingdom of God in word and deed throughout his life is surely eschatological. Other expressions of an eschatological awareness in the life of Jesus include his sayings about the Twelve Tribes of Israel and the Banquet theme as well as his actions instituting a new table fellowship, performing healings and exorcisms, and the cleansing of the Temple in Jerusalem. Lastly there are the enigmatic Son of Man sayings in the ministry of Jesus which, though clearly influenced and shaped by the early Church, cannot be completely disassociated from Jesus.

To eliminate eschatology from the life of Jesus would be to remove him from his thoroughly Jewish roots, to sever his connection with John the Baptist, to ignore the Pauline material and to negate a substantial part of the Gospel material, all of which cannot be explained away simply as the creation of the early Church. This rather recent fashion seems motivated more often than not by an exclusively other-worldly view of eschatology which is largely a twentieth-century creation projected back into the life of Jesus. Such a view of eschatology is out of touch with the eschatology of the Hebrew Scriptures and is quite contrary to much of the eschatology in the life of Jesus as we shall presently see.

The public mission of Jesus comes close on the heels of the preaching of John the Baptist. John appeared in the style of a prophet calling people to repentance through baptism, proclaiming the imminent coming of a figure who would bring judgment and restoration to Israel (Matt. 3:11; Luke 3:17). John's eschatology is futuristic and apocalyptic. As a disciple of John, Jesus initially at least accepts his baptism and his message. At the same time, however, Jesus goes beyond John's baptism and message. A shift takes place very early on in the life of Jesus.[30] This shift is effected by John's arrest, Jesus' perception of John as the fulfilment of the expectation of the return of Elijah and as the forerunner of the Messiah. The spirit of this shift is summed up in Jesus' reply to the question from the disciples of John the Baptist: 'Are you the one who is to come, or are we to wait for another?' Jesus replies: 'Go and tell John what you hear and see: the blind receive their sight, the lame walk, lepers are cleansed, the deaf hear, the dead are raised up and the poor have good news preached to them' (Matt. 11:3–5). Clearly the emphasis has moved from the future to the present. 'What for John had been a focus on the future, has become for Jesus a focus on the present.'[31] This new emphasis on the present is continued in other sayings and actions of Jesus, especially in relation to the realisation of the reign of God in the present. For example: 'But if it is by the Spirit of God that I cast out demons, then the kingdom of God has come to you' (Matt. 12:28; Luke 11:20) – a saying regarded by many as authentic on the basis of criteria of discontinuity and coherence.[32] Here we have Jesus connecting his exorcisms with the coming reign of God in the present. A further reference to the kingdom of God as present can be found in Luke where Jesus points out in response to the Pharisees who are wondering about when the kingdom was coming, that 'the kingdom of God is among you' (Luke 17:20–21). This reply of Jesus shows an eschatological awareness of the reign of God as present, however fragmentarily, in his own ministry of healing and teaching. Other less obvious though nonetheless real instances of a this-worldly eschatology are found in the sayings where Jesus announces beatitude on the eyes and ears of those who see and hear what this generation see and hear (Matt. 11:15–17) and in the incident where Jesus dispenses his disciples from the need for fasting as long as the bridegroom is with them (Mark 2:18–20).

In contrast to the futuristic apocalyptic eschatology of John the Baptist, Jesus declares that the future reign of God is erupting now in the present in and through his ministry of healing , exorcising and table-fellowship. The reign of God is no longer only an other-worldly reality out there in the future, but rather the gracious presence of God bursting forth in present history. In a very real sense the future is being glimpsed, anticipated and realised in the present through the ministry of Jesus.

Some of the language used by Jesus in this first phase of his ministry parallels the language of the prophets of old. For example, the focus on good tidings in Isaiah 40:9; 52:7; 60:6; 61:1, is found also in the preaching of Jesus in Mark 1:14 and Luke 4:18. Likewise the emphasis in Isaiah 42:1–4 about my servant, the chosen one, marked by the Spirit, bringing forth justice on earth, is also present in the preaching of Jesus in Matthew 12:18–21. Similarly Isaiah 40:3 which talks about a voice crying out in the wilderness to prepare the way of the Lord is also echoed in Mark 1:3. These parallels and others clearly place Jesus within the tradition of prophetic eschatology and mark him out as one who within that tradition is explicitly concerned with the presence of the reign of God as a reality affecting life in this world. To this extent the initial eschatology of Jesus is an eschatology of good news in contrast to the eschatology of gloom which was present at certain moments in Judaism and also present in the preaching of John the Baptist.[33] Further, the eschatological praxis of Jesus at this stage is also an inclusive reaching out to all: sinners, tax collectors, the poor, the imprisoned. Clearly the eschatology of Jesus at this early stage in his ministry is this-worldly in focus and not other-worldly. This does not mean that the eschatology of Jesus bears no reference to the future; it does include the future as we shall see but the primary focus at this stage is the urgency of the present time (*kairos*) with a radical call to conversion whereas references to the future (*Eschaton*) are indeterminate just as they were in the eschatology of the prophets of old. Thus we find Jesus saying the time is fulfilled (Mark 1:15), the kingdom of God has come near (Mark 1:15), the kingdom of God has come to you (Luke 11:20) – even though the full manifestation of the kingdom is something for the future, a future that is now very near. It is this emphasis on the nearness, the presence and actuality of the reign of God in the ministry of Jesus that justifies the accuracy of describing Jesus as the eschatological prophet who calls people to faith, repentance and conversion, and at the same time inaugurates the coming reign of God. Eschatological fragments of salvation are gaining an historical foothold in the ministry of Jesus.

At the same time, however, there is an equally impressive body of sayings and actions of Jesus which point towards an imminent future of the reign of God.[34] One important piece of evidence signalling a future realisation of the reign of God is the second petition of the Lord's Prayer: 'Your kingdom come' (Matt. 6:10; Luke 11:2). On the basis of the principle of discontinuity the substance of the Lord's Prayer is regarded as authentic without, however, denying the presence of redactional changes within it. The first petition, 'Hallowed be thy name', is the immediate context of the second petition, 'Thy kingdom come'. To sanctify the name of God, according to Ezekiel 36:16–38, parts of the Qumran manuscripts, and the Jewish prayer of *Kaddish*, was to call forth the glory of God by defeating the Gentiles and regathering the scattered tribes of Israel.[35] This eschatological thrust of the first petition is continued in the second petition. To pray 'Thy kingdom come' is to request in an abstract way that God would come as King to restore Israel and to reign over his people.[36] These two petitions taken together have a clear eschatological orientation to them and as such indicate an expectation by Jesus of a future, yet imminent kingdom of God.

A second saying of Jesus recorded at the Last Supper talks about no longer drinking the fruit of the vine until he drinks it in the kingdom of God (Mark 14:25) – a saying regarded as authentic via the criteria of multiple attestation and discontinuity. This *logion* belongs to the Last Supper narrative and is issued in the context of Jesus' awareness of his approaching death. The saying is an expression of Jesus' trust and hope that in spite of his death or indeed because of his death the kingdom of God will come in the near future.

A third saying of Jesus that points to the future reign of God is one which talks about the many who will come from the east and west to recline at table with Abraham while others will be cast out (Matt. 8:11–12; Luke 13:28–9). This saying of Jesus according to most commentators is best interpreted from outside the textual context in which it appears in the Gospels. The 'many' is usually taken to mean the 'Gentiles' and the 'others' – 'Sons of the kingdom' (Matthew) or 'You' (Luke) – probably refers to Jesus' contemporaries in Israel who were rejecting his message. What is clear in this saying of Jesus is a belief in a future coming reign of God symbolised by the banquet theme. [37]

A fourth set of references concerning the coming reign of God can be found in the Beatitudes of the Sermon on the Mount (Matt. 5:3–12; Luke 6:20–23). What is significant about the Beatitudes is the putting together of wisdom beatitudes with eschatological beatitudes – something that begins to appear at the end of the Book of Daniel. Jesus the wisdom teacher and the eschatological prophet are united in three core beatitudes about the poor, mourners and the hungry that belong to the Q tradition and are regarded as coming from Jesus on the basis of discontinuity and coherence with other sayings of Jesus.[38] These core beatitudes solidify the case for future eschatology as an essential part of Jesus' preaching. [39]

What can we say about the eschatology of Jesus in the light of this survey of eschatological sayings in the life of the historical Jesus? Is there anything we can learn from the eschatology of Jesus? To answer these questions it must be acknowledged that Jesus' eschatology is grounded in his experience of God – an experience that exists on the one hand in continuity with the Jewish experience of Yahweh and on the other hand which surpasses that Jewish experience and interpretation. As already noted, a fundamental element in the religious experience of the Jews is the experience of God as active in history in a manner that contains an important element of promise for the future. This experience of God by Jesus is now expressed in the tensive and multi-layered symbol of the reign of God which refuses clear definition. The God of Jesus' eschatology is a God of blessings and promises on offer in the present and future consistent with his Jewish background. Jesus' statement about God acting in the future is based on his experience of God acting in the present. If this is the case, it is unhelpful and indeed inaccurate to depict Jesus as an end-of-the-world figure. In continuity with the prophets of old and on the basis of his own unique religious experience Jesus is concerned to highlight the action of God breaking into the present in his own ministry and at the same time to signal the significance of that divine action in the present for the future.

Given these observations it must be said that, insofar as anything can be said historically, Jesus did not have anything like what we today would call a worked out, systematic eschatology. Instead Jesus' eschatology is an eschatology in process of historical development bound up with his experience of God in the present right up to the time of his death. It is unrealistic, therefore, to expect a consistent eschatology in the life of Jesus. At best it can be said that there are different stages and phases ranging from what he inherited from his Jewish background, his association with John the Baptist, and his own unique experience of God. There is a shift from a future eschatology to an eschatology of the present after he takes over from John the Baptist. There is a further development or better interplay between the present and the future in the unfolding historical ministry of Jesus. An additional shift occurs when he goes up to Jerusalem at the time of Passover and cleanses the Temple towards the end of his ministry. This additional shift introduces an apocalyptic element into the eschatology of Jesus which we will examine below. In other words there is a movement from John the Baptist's futuristic eschatology to an eschatology focusing on the present and its future fulfilment to an eschatology embracing apocalyptic motifs towards the end of his life in the face of his imminent death.

Further, the eschatology of Jesus is not simply other-worldly, or purely spiritual, or apolitical. To this extent Marcus Borg, and many others like Richard A. Horsley and Sean Freyne,[40] are right to insist on the socio-political dimensions of the preaching and praxis of Jesus. It is surely clear that the action of God in the ministry of Jesus is affecting/subverting the social, political, economic and religious *status quo* by transforming the situation of those who are hungry, poor, ill and marginalised. Poverty and hunger are political issues; the preaching and praxis of Jesus is addressed to those realities in the lives of people; above all the preaching and praxis of Jesus unmasks a God who canonises such realities by announcing the reign of God as active in a way that transforms the present. This transformation of present inequalities by Jesus has implications for the future as symbolised for example by the parables of growth and the prophetic actions of Jesus in table fellowship and the miracles of healing.

Moreover, Jesus does not make a sharp distinction between the present and the future in his own ministry. There is an important sense in which the present embodies the future and the future erupts into the present. More specifically the distinction between 'this age' and 'the age to come' is by and large a Rabbinic distinction rather than a distinction of Jewish literature before AD 70 or of the teaching of Jesus. This distinction is found in apocalyptic text towards the end of the first century AD and when it is found in the words of Jesus it 'is most likely due to the redactional work of the evangelist'.[41] Consequently it is more accurate to say the eschatology of Jesus is a unified eschatology embracing the present and the future as one. Further, the sharp distinction drawn by modern theology between prophetic eschatology and apocalyptic eschatology is not to be found in the preaching and praxis of Jesus, nor in the life of the early Church. Instead, apocalyptic thinking contains within itself the seeds of a prophetic social critique of the here and now. Close links exist between the experience of Jesus and the future, between the prophetic and the apocalyptic. Likewise it is more accurate to say that the eschatology of Jesus is more inclusive than exclusive insofar as it reaches out beyond the boundaries of Israel (e.g. Matt. 8:11).

APOCALYPTIC ELEMENTS IN THE LIFE OF JESUS

The next distinctive phase in the ministry of Jesus is signalled by the Passion predictions, even though these are examples of material written up by the Church in the light of the resurrection of Jesus. There is a period in the ministry of Jesus when the imminence of his own death becomes apparent and this influences the horizon of his preaching and praxis. The prospect of death, not uncommon in the lives of the prophets, has to be integrated by Jesus into his preaching about the nearness of the reign of God. Gradually it becomes clear that his death is bound up with the coming reign of God, that his death will be somehow or other instrumental in the realisation of the reign of God, and that God will not abandon him in death. This particular phase in the ministry of Jesus represents a certain shift from a prophetic eschatology to an apocalyptic eschatology. It would be an exaggeration to claim that Jesus had a clearly worked out apocalyptic eschatology – apocalyptic thinking does not admit of such clarity. What does emerge is that the apocalyptic elements begin to make their presence felt in the teaching of Jesus, especially those elements relating to the Son of Man sayings and references to a general judgment.

In the light of this phase it becomes necessary to examine the Son of Man sayings in the Gospels in view of their apocalyptic associations and

more particularly in the light of Marcus Borg's discrediting of their relia-
bility. These sayings have been hotly debated throughout this century
with little consensus emerging.

There are some eighty Son of Man references in the Gospels and all but
two of these are self designations by Jesus. It is estimated that of these
eighty references, fifty-one make up actual sayings, with fourteen in
Mark and ten in the sayings-source.[42] Further, these sayings are usually
grouped into references about the earthly ministry of Jesus, the death of
Jesus, and the future coming of Jesus in glory and judgment. Most commentators, including Marcus Borg, have suggested that these sayings are
interpretative creations by the early Church. This particular thesis, however, has been called into question, or at least qualified, in the last few
years by some very reputable Scripture scholars.

John P. Meier raises a series of questions about the use of the Son of
Man in the Gospels that are difficult to answer for those who hold that
this tradition is a creation of the early Church. For example:

> If . . . Son of Man did not exist as a title in Judaism before the time of
> Jesus . . . what caused the church to invent this? Why does it occur
> almost exclusively on the lips of Jesus in the New Testament? Why is it
> represented in so many strata of the Gospel tradition, yet almost
> nowhere else outside of the Gospels . . . why does belief in the Son of
> Man never appear in the primitive cradle statements, liturgical formu-
> las, and summaries of Christian preaching?[43]

Further, the references to Jesus as a glutton and a drunkard (Matt.
11:19) and the relegation of him to the status more or less equivalent to
that of John the Baptist make it unlikely that all these sayings were
created by the early Church. Such difficulties have prompted Meier to
conclude 'it seems likely that the peculiar Son-of-Man locution goes back
in some way to Jesus, however much it was developed later by the
Church'.[44]

Raymond Brown in *The Death of the Messiah* is even more forceful and
explicit in attributing the Son of Man tradition to Jesus. Like Meier,
Brown wants to know why the Son of Man tradition has left no trace in
the non-Gospel tradition. Brown challenges the accepted view that there
was no developed Jewish understanding of the Son of Man outside of
Daniel 7. He argues that in the non-canonical literature of the second and
first century BC and the first century AD there may have developed a certain Jewish apocalyptic understanding of a heavenly Son of Man through
reflection on Daniel 7, and that it is not outside the bounds of possibility

that Jesus would have been in touch with this development directly or indirectly. To substantiate his case, he refers with the help of John Collins to the 'parables' section of 1 Enoch 37–71 as an example of Jewish apocalyptic influenced by reflection on Daniel 7. But even if this is not the case, Brown argues that he is not happy with the 'peculiar prejudice of modern scholarship' that if a concept is traceable to a biblical background then it cannot be of Jesus. Brown is uneasy with this approach because it seems to rule out that Jesus did not reflect on the Old Testament and that he did not use the interpretative techniques of his time. Such assumptions for Brown are 'a non realistic projection'.[45]

In particular, Brown wants to keep open the possibility, indeed the likelihood, that Jesus could have reached the conviction that if he were rejected and put to death as the prophets of old were, God would vindicate him. In other words Jesus would have used and expanded the symbolic Son of Man tradition as a way of understanding his own death as God's instrument in effecting the realisation of God's plan of salvation. After all Jesus had proclaimed the imminence of the reign of God and this is called into question by the prospect of his own death, and so within this changed context Jesus draws on the given Son of Man tradition to work out his role and place in effecting God's reign in the face of death. Surely Jesus would have reflected on Daniel 7 since it is one of the few places in the Hebrew Scriptures where there is reference to the reign of God.[46] Brown concludes his analysis by saying that the early Church did develop the Son of Man tradition 'precisely because this description was remembered to have come from Jesus in a very affirmative manner'.[47] In particular, Brown suggests that even though all of Mark 14:61–2 is phrased in the language of the 60s AD: 'there is reason to believe that in Mark 14:62 we may be close to the mindset and style of Jesus himself'.[48]

This analysis by Meier and Brown of the Son of Man tradition and its attribution to Jesus is both impressive and persuasive. It is persuasive because it takes into account the different phases in the ministry of Jesus and it recognises that there was development in Jesus' own self-understanding and interpretation of what was going on in his own experience. Most of all, the vindication and justification of the Son of Man tradition and its attribution to Jesus paves the way for moving from a prophetic eschatology to an apocalyptic eschatology in the life of Jesus. We are now in a position to address this apocalyptic eschatology which emerged as a distinct perspective in the final phase of the ministry of Jesus.

In affirming the presence of an apocalyptic eschatology in the second phase of the life of Jesus we do not wish to give the impression that Jesus had developed an apocalyptic eschatology prior to his death nor do we want to imply that the Son of Man sayings as given in the Gospels represent the historical *ipsissima verba Jesu*. Instead with Meier and Brown we suggest that there is a middle position between outright scepticism concerning the Son of Man tradition and the naive acceptance of all these sayings as coming directly from Jesus. This middle position implies that Jesus initially used the Son of Man language as a 'circumlocution for man' or 'a human being'. A good example of this would be: 'the Son of Man is Lord even of the Sabbath' (Mark 2:28). In this instance Jesus is referring not to himself but to man in general since he has just said 'the Sabbath was made for human kind' (Mark 2:27). Further, there are occasions when he seems to use Son of Man as a title for himself. In addition there are references by Jesus to the Son of Man coming in glory to judge the world and these clearly reflect the interpretation of the Christ-event. However, the question must be asked: Is it possible that Jesus' awareness of himself as eschatological prophet enabled him to move in hope when faced with death towards some understanding of himself as apocalyptic Son of Man within Judaism? Given his Jewish heritage and his personal commitment to the coming reign of God in word and in deed, some such development, however ill-defined, from being a prophet of the end time to the Son of Man, does seem justified. Positing this development helps to understand the confidence with which the early Church subsequently understood Jesus as the apocalyptic Son of Man and at the same time provides an important point of continuity between the historical Jesus and the Christ of Faith of the early Church.

The Gospel in which the Son of Man tradition is most prominent is Mark, and it is in Mark 13 that we find one of Jesus' two apocalyptic discourses. The chapter can be divided into five sections.

In the introduction (Mark 13:1–4) Jesus predicts the destruction of the Temple of Jerusalem and in doing so stands in the tradition of Old Testament prophets (e.g. Mic. 3:12; Jer. 26:18). Most scholars hold today that this prediction of Jesus does not reflect the events of AD 70 as was once thought to be the case. It should be noted that Jesus is sitting in the Mount of Olives opposite the Temple during this discourse – a location that has eschatological connotations in the Hebrew Scriptures (see Zech. 14:1–4).

Section two (Mark 13:5–13) deals with the sufferings that the disciples must endure, pointing out that there will be false prophets (5–6), wars and rumours of wars (7–8), and persecution (9–13) which are all part of the divine plan for the coming reign of God.

Section three looks to a future time of tribulation (Mark 13:14–23). The reference to 'the abomination of desolation' (v. 14) comes from Daniel 9:27 and 11:31 which talks about a heathen altar built by Epiphanes IV and put over the temple of burnt offerings in the year 168 BC.

Section four is about the triumph of the Son of Man (Mark 13:24–7) in which Daniel 7 is clearly invoked and the cosmic upheaval accompanying the advent of the end is emphasised in a way that echoes different texts from the Hebrew Scriptures (e.g. Isa. 13:10; Ezek. 32:7; Amos 8:9; Joel 2:10, 31; Isa. 34:4).

The final section, section five (Mark 13:28–37), is a call to vigilance, coupled with a stark refusal by Jesus to specify the hour or the day of the end of time.

This overview of Jesus' apocalyptic discourse in Mark 13 reflects the influence of the early Church's theological thinking on the final events in the life of Jesus. At the same time, however, we must agree with Raymond Brown that it is difficult to understand how the early Church could have developed this apocalyptic discourse in such detail unless it remembered how Jesus himself made these symbolic eschatological connections directly or indirectly in his own words and deeds. Perhaps even more telling is how this apocalyptic discourse of Mark's Gospel captures the eschatological atmosphere of early Christianity inspired by Jesus.

The second apocalyptic discourse of Jesus is found in Matthew 25:31–46 which has been variously dubbed 'a description of the final judgment', 'a summary of Christianity', or 'an apocalyptic parable'. Unlike the Markan apocalypse it has no parallel in the synoptics. The text describes how the Son of Man coming in glory at the end of time will judge as King the nations on the basis of mercy and charity shown to the poor, the thirsty, outsiders, the naked, the sick and the imprisoned. Up to the nineteenth century the least of Jesus' brothers and sisters were understood to be the suffering members of the Christian community. However, at the beginning of the twentieth century the final judgment has been given a universalist application requiring care and mercy to be shown to all the needy of the world. The precise application of this apocalyptic discourse continues to be a matter of debate among Scripture scholars.[49] Perhaps the most significant feature about this apocalyptic parable is the way it highlights the practical demands of the eschatology of Jesus for life in the present. If proof positive of the this-worldly character of the eschatology of Jesus were required then it can be found unambiguously here in this apocalyptic parable. A close relationship between the prophetic and the apocalyptic is estimated in this parable. Equally significant within this apocalypse is the quest for justice and its resolution by the Son of Man at the end of history. A third important point in this apocalyptic story is the way oppression and suffering are finally overcome at the end of time. It is a characteristic of apocalyptic literature that issues of justice and suffering are addressed and their resolution overcome by appeal to judgment by God in the fullness of time. Probably the most telling element in this apocalyptic discourse of Jesus is the eschatological challenge for a liberating praxis of all who are in need in the present. These implications of this apocalyptic parable will be taken up later on in Chapter 10.

By way of conclusion to this overview of eschatology in the life of Jesus we must now return to the centrality of the reign of God. It is the primacy of the reign of God within the ministry of Jesus initiated at the Jordan and concluded at Calvary that shaped his eschatological vision. This announcement of the reign of God by Jesus called into question the prevailing social and religious *status quo*: it opened up the possibility of an alternative world, it held out the promise of establishing a different kind of community, it sought to bring about a new set of inclusive relationships, it unmasked a view of God that enslaved people, in favour of a God who frees and liberates. This proclamation of the reign of God demanded a radical restructuring of life, a restructuring symbolised in the parables that talk about advent, reversal and action[50] and which is manifested fragmentarily in the miracles.[51] The announcement of the reign of God by Jesus implied a critique of the inherited symbols, rites, customs, institutions, laws, relationships, and religious practices that structured the world in which Jesus lived. To this extent the preaching and praxis of Jesus was ideologically explosive: disturbing the Sadducees who controlled the Temple, threatening the Pharisees who were the theological guardians of the social order, and unsettling the Romans who sought to maintain political peace.[52] But above all the message of the coming reign of God awakened a new hope among the disciples of Jesus not only for the future but also for the present (cf. Luke 24:21).

The source of this hope-filled vision and praxis in the life of Jesus would have been his Jewish inheritance and above all else his personal experience of God.[53] As noted earlier, the foundational Jewish experience of God exemplified in Moses was one that included a strong sense of the faithfulness of Yahweh to Yahweh's promises. These promises of Yahweh are now sensed and experienced by Jesus in a new and radical way, especially in his experience of Yahweh as *Abba*. This deep experience of God as *Abba* is understood, interpreted and articulated by Jesus consistently throughout his ministry in terms of the coming reign of God.

Further, this experience of God as *Abba* by Jesus is radically hope-filled and hope-centred. This commitment to the eschatological dawning of the reign of God that led to Jesus' death must now addressed in the next chapter.

7

THE ADVENT OF THE *ESCHATON* IN CHRIST

Eternal life is revealed in time, it may unfold itself in every instant as an eternal present. Eternal life is not a future life but life in the present, life in the depths of an instant of time.

(Nicholas Berdyaev, 1960)

THE LIFE, DEATH AND RESURRECTION of Jesus taken together as a single event constitutes the eschatological turning-point of history, which began with the proclamation of the coming reign of God, came into symbolic view in the exorcisms, miracles and messianic meals in the ministry of Jesus, and reached fulfilment in the death and resurrection of Jesus and the outpouring of the Spirit. The last chapter looked at the eschatology operative in the preaching and praxis of Jesus as well as the actual inauguration of that eschatology in the ministry of Jesus. In the life of Jesus, especially the preaching and praxis, and particularly the death and resurrection, the *Eschaton* is experienced by the disciples as having dawned. This chapter sets out to explore the advent of the *Eschaton* in the death and resurrection of Jesus and to describe the early Church's theological articulation of this eschatological experience. Although the death and resurrection are an eschatological unity it is necessary to analyse them as distinct moments within the dawning of the *Eschaton*.

THE DEATH OF JESUS AS APOCALYPTIC

The immediate context for understanding the death of Jesus must surely be his proclamation of the coming reign of God. We have seen how the proclamation of the reign of God was eschatological. This eschatological horizon is heightened in the second phase of the ministry of Jesus when he becomes aware of his own death as imminent. The increasing number of references to the Son of Man by Jesus, the final journey up to

Jerusalem, the incident in the Temple, the arrest and the trial, each in their own way intensify the growing apocalyptic consciousness of Jesus. Indeed the life of Jesus is driven by his commitment to the coming reign of God and it is this radical commitment to the advent of God's reign that leads to his death on the Cross.

The Passion narrative is present and prominent in all four Gospels. Martin Kähler in the last century described the Gospels as Passion narratives with extended introductions. Indeed the Passion narrative brings us to the heart of the Christian reality, especially from an eschatological point of view. The Gospel accounts of the death of Jesus are a mixture of history and interpretation, facts and faith. There is agreement among most – not all – Scripture scholars that the primary theological category for understanding the Passion narratives is eschatological.[1] More specifically, and in the light of our discussion of the two distinct phases in the ministry of Jesus, it is within the framework of apocalyptic eschatology that the drama of the death of Jesus unfolds. As already seen it was out of prophetic eschatology that apocalyptic eschatology emerged within post-exilic Judaism and we can now see something similar happening in the life of Jesus.

When we look at the Passion narrative we find many literary and theological qualities that are characteristic of apocalyptic thinking. For example, apocalyptic thought arose by way of a response to a crisis taking place in the context of persecution and suffering, employing symbolic and allegorical categories, invoking cosmic perspectives, containing an awareness of the imminence of death, turning to God to intervene, and adopting a certain pessimism about the present. Such qualities now seem to come together in varying degrees in the Passion of Jesus. It is as if the historical drama of late Judaism that provoked apocalyptic thought is now being played out at a personal level in the life of Jesus. The forces of good and evil, the sons of light and the sons of darkness found in the war scroll of Qumran, coalesce in combat in the Passion of Jesus.

This high drama in the closing stages of the life of Jesus is present in all four Gospels. By far the most developed and most apocalyptic expression of this drama is to be found in Matthew's description of the phenomena surrounding the death of Jesus:

But from the sixth hour darkness came over all the earth until the ninth hour. But about the ninth hour Jesus screamed out with a loud cry saying 'Eli, Eli, lema, Sabachtani?', that is, 'My God, my God, why have you forsaken me?' But some of those standing there, having heard, were saying that 'this fellow is crying to Elijah' . . . And behold the veil of the sanctuary was rent from top to bottom. And earth was shaken, and the rocks were rent. And the tombs were opened and many bodies of the fallen asleep holy ones were raised. And having come out from the tombs, after his raising they entered into the holy city and they were made visible to many.[2]

The *darkness over the earth*, recorded in Matthew, Mark and Luke, is an apocalyptic quality associated in Judaism with the end of time and described as 'the day of the Lord' understood as 'a day of darkness and gloom' (Zeph. 1:15; see also Joel 2:2, 2:10, 2:31, and Amos 8:9–10). Even though it is true that darkness was associated in the ancient world with the death of great figures this should not detract from the apocalyptic interpretation of what was happening at Calvary – given the eschatological preaching of Jesus and the other apocalyptic features surrounding his death.

The reference to *the coming of Elijah* in Mark and Matthew is also apocalyptic. Many expected Elijah to return at the end of time as a forerunner to the coming of God:

Lo, I will send you the prophet Elijah before the great and terrible day of the Lord comes. He will turn the hearts of parents to their children and the hearts of children to their parents so that I will not come and strike the land with a curse. (Mal. 4:5–6)

We should not forget that the figure of Elijah has already been juxtaposed to the ministry of John the Baptist and the messianic life of Jesus.

The *tearing of the Temple veil* from top to bottom connected with the death of Jesus is symbolic in at least two senses. On the one hand it connotes the ending of the economy within Israel which confined the presence of Yahweh to the Temple. One of the functions of the veil was to shut the holy place off from the profane world. From now on in the light of the life and death of Jesus access to God is available to all. Secondly, the tearing of the veil would be understood by those reading Matthew after the Romans had physically destroyed the Temple as a fulfilment of what was originally signified by the rending of the veil. In both instances there is a strong eschatological and apocalyptic sense that the death of Jesus is a turning-point within Judaism. In the words of one commentator it 'symbolises the opening of the way to God effected by the death of Jesus, or alternatively, and perhaps at the same time, the end of the Temple system'.[3] The next four lines according to Raymond Brown should be taken together as a quatrain because they exist in contrast to the preceding and succeeding verses, and because they represent a cosmic reaction to the death of Jesus. These cosmic signs of 'the earth shaking, rocks renting, tombs opening, and bodies rising' are highly symbolic and thoroughly apocalyptic in import. To debate their historical actuality would be to miss out on the eschatological significance and interpretation of the death of Jesus being offered here by Matthew.

In the Hebrew Scriptures there are many references to *the earth shaking* as a sign of divine judgment or of the last times (e.g. Judges 5:4; Isa. 5:25; 24:18; Ezek. 38:19). The linking of darkness and the shaking of the earth as expressions of divine judgment are associated by the prophet Joel with the day of the Lord: 'The earth quakes before them, the heavens tremble. The sun and the moon are darkened, and the stars withdraw their shining' (Joel 2:10).

The death of Jesus as God's chosen one evokes God's apocalyptic judgment which is now expressed in terms of the earth shaking.[4] Another way of describing God's judgment at the end of time in the Hebrew Scriptures is to talk about *the renting of the rocks.*[5]

The *opening of tombs* is something that seems to follow from the rending of rocks, especially if the rocks rent are associated symbolically with those of the Mount of Olives which would have contained many of the dead of Israel. This opening of the tombs recalls the prophecy of Ezekiel relating to the end of time: 'I am going to open your graves and bring you up from your graves, O my people; and I will bring you back to the land of Israel' (Ezek. 37:12).

The fourth element within this quatrain is *the rising of the fallen asleep holy ones* which is one of the positive signs of divine judgment resulting from the death of Jesus, whereas the previous three signs have been negative. Speculation as to who the holy ones are misses the overall impact of this quatrain which is to dramatise the effect of the death of Jesus and the atmosphere surrounding that death. What is important here is the inbreaking of God's power signifying that the end of time has begun and divine judgment inaugurated through the death of Jesus.[6]

In turning to Matthew 27:53 which says 'and having come out from the tomb, after his rising they entered into the holy city ...' we see the style of writing change, moving from the aorist passive to an active phrasing. Further there is an anomaly here because the impression is given that the holy ones are raised prior to the resurrection of Jesus. Brown suggests that a better reading of Matthew 27:53 would be 'and having come out from their tombs (on Friday), after Jesus' resurrection (on Sunday) they entered into the holy city'.[7] Tension seems to exist between the effect of the death of Jesus and his resurrection. A subtle shift from the apocalyptic phenomena associated with the death of Jesus to the eschatological phenomenon of the resurrection has taken place in Matthew.

In reviewing this section of Matthew's Gospel note should be taken of the poetic parallelism that exists within the quatrain verses driving home the dramatic effect of the death of Jesus. Likewise the comprehensive apocalyptic impact of the death of the Son of God on the whole world moving from the heavens to the earth and under the earth should be recognised. In view of the fact that Matthew's Gospel opens with cosmic signs accompanying the beginning of the life of Jesus (stars at his birth and the opening of the heavens at the beginning of his ministry), it is appropriate for Matthew that the closing of the life of the Son of God should be accompanied also by cosmic symbols.

It must surely be clear that this part of Matthew's Gospel is primarily concerned to convey the meaning of the death of Jesus through a process of apocalyptic and theological interpretation. To reduce this apocalyptic meaning to historical fact would be to confuse the categories of event and interpretation as well as to lose sight of the eschatological significance of what was happening in history and the life of Jesus at Calvary. This does not mean that apocalyptic interpretation is without historical foundation. To the contrary, the historical realities of the preaching and praxis of Jesus about the reign of God, the change in tempo concerning that preaching and praxis in the second phase of the ministry of Jesus, the going up to Jerusalem, the encounter in the Temple, the Last Supper, and the death all constitute historical aspects of Matthew's apocalyptic interpretation. This apocalyptic interpretation of these events signals that the life and death of Jesus inaugurates the end of time, that the death of Jesus has human and cosmic implications, that this death of Jesus evokes divine judgment and that this judgment is one which raises up the holy ones of Israel. On the wider theological front, Matthew's interpretation of the death of Jesus redefines the presence of God from the Temple to God's people and the relationship of God to human suffering – issues we will take up later on.

THE RESURRECTION OF JESUS AS ESCHATOLOGICAL

The resurrection of Jesus is the other side of the death of Jesus and therefore should not be separated from the Cross. At the same time we must recognise that in moving from the historical death of Jesus to the mystery of the resurrection we are moving into a realm of reality which though related to the death is nonetheless quite different and discontinuous. The resurrection of Jesus from the dead is about the entry of Jesus into a new mode of existence which we call eschatological. The resurrection of Jesus is variously described as fulfilment of Jewish hopes, the anticipation of the end of history, the dawning of the new age, and the embodiment of the reign of God. As eschatological, the language of resurrection is subject to the limitations that attach to all eschatological statements. To this extent the language of resurrection is metaphorical, symbolic and analogical. This does not mean that the resurrection is unreal or without foundation in human experience but it does mean that it transcends ordinary everyday human history. The word 'resurrection' (*anastasis*) is a metaphor taken from the experience of rising up from sleep or recovering from illness to convey a sense of the transition and transformation that characterises resurrection. Most commentators would agree with Paul that 'if Christ has not been raised from the dead, then our proclamation has been in vain and your faith has been in vain' (1 Cor. 15:14). The resurrection of Jesus is accordingly one of the foundation stones of Christian eschatology.

If we are to appreciate what it means to say that the resurrection of Jesus is eschatological, that is, the fulfilment of Jewish hopes and the foundation of Christian eschatology, then we need to look once again at Jewish eschatology as the context for these claims. As already seen in Chapter 6 there are prophetic and apocalyptic dimensions to Jewish eschatology. We have also noted that Jewish eschatology is grounded ultimately in the Jewish experience of Yahweh, that the structure of this experience is one of promise and fulfilment, and that this twofold structure of promise and fulfilment is expressed in the Jewish understanding and theology of covenant.

Within these perspectives Jewish eschatology, both prophetic and apocalyptic, is predominantly social with the main emphasis on the corporate destiny of the people of Israel. For a large part of Hebrew eschatology there was no theology of life after death: the dead were confined to Sheol, a shadowy form of empty existence untouched by the reign of Yahweh.[8] Instead the main emphasis in Jewish eschatology is on the transformation of the individual, society and nature within this life. Within the apocalyptic period during the persecution of the Maccabeen wars questions were raised about the destiny of those who were martyred for the Jewish faith. It was out of the context of martyrdom that a general belief in resurrection arose and this finds expression in Daniel of the second century BC:

Many of those who sleep on the dust of the earth shall awake, some to everlasting life, and some to shame and everlasting contempt. Those who are wise shall shine like brightness of the sky and those who lead many to righteousness like the stars for ever and ever. (Dan. 12:2–3)

While this text is usually singled out as the beginning of Jewish faith in resurrection⁹ it should be acknowledged that the content of this faith is far from clear and we know that at the time of Jesus the Sadducees did not believe in resurrection. Insofar as there was belief in the resurrection especially as this developed in the intertestamental apocalyptic literature, it was associated with the advent of the end of time and the fullness of salvation.

In the preaching of Jesus there are references to the general resurrection of the dead at the end of time (e.g. Mark 12:18–27; Matt. 13:36–43; John 5:28–9; 6:52–9) and this belief is one of the presuppositions of his teaching about the coming reign of God. Further, this belief in the general resurrection of the dead is also taken for granted by Paul in 1 Corinthians 15:13: 'If there is no resurrection of the dead; then Christ has not been raised.' It is against this background that we must look at the New Testament evidence of the resurrection of Jesus and its eschatological meaning.

In approaching the evidence for the resurrection of Jesus we must remember that the death of Jesus was a moment of crisis for his disciples. Their faith was shattered and their hopes dashed: 'But we had hoped that he was the one to redeem Israel' (Luke 24:21). A deep sense of loss, disappointment and exasperation followed the death of Jesus. This was the atmosphere prevailing after Calvary which is dramatically turned around and transformed by the experience of the resurrection of Jesus.

The New Testament evidence for the resurrection is notoriously complex, and a major part of the problem is that event and meaning are so intimately linked in the different narratives that it is extremely difficult to describe what really happened. The earliest accounts of the resurrection of Jesus are found in resurrection *kerygmata* or short credal statements:

God the Father raised him from the dead. (Gal. 1:1; Eph. 1:20; Col. 2:12; 1 Peter 1:21)
God exalted him. (Phil. 2:9; Acts 2:33; 5:31)
He was taken up in glory. (1 Tim. 3:16; John 17:1–5; Luke 24:26)
Christ died and lived again. (Rom. 14:9; 2 Cor. 13:4)
He ascended. (Eph. 4:7–10; John 20:17; Acts 1:9–11)
He (Jesus) breathed on them and said: 'Receive the Holy Spirit'. (John 20:22; Acts 2:1–4)

A particularly reliable and early example of a resurrection *kerygmata* is 1 Corinthians 15:3–6 which can be traced back to the middle 30s:

> For I handed on to you as a first importance what I in turn had received: that Christ died for our sins in accordance with the Scriptures and that he was buried and that he was raised on the third day in accordance with the Scriptures and that he appeared to Cephas, then to the twelve.

These short credal statements in turn are developed later into elaborate narratives about the appearances of Jesus and the existence of the empty tomb in the Gospels.

The appearances of Jesus, even though they may have undergone several redactions within the early Church, are an important description of the effects of the resurrection of Jesus on the disciples. Whereas the resurrection *kerygmata* captured the eschatological consciousness of infant Christianity, the appearances have mainly christological and ecclesiological functions. The empty tomb tradition operates as an important reminder that it was the whole Jesus, body and soul, that was raised up, thereby countering any reduction of the resurrection to a purely spiritual or merely mystical experience.

Another significant piece of evidence for the resurrection is of course the reality and dynamism of the first Christian communities, that is the existence of the Church itself. The birth of Christianity is difficult to explain without reference to the reality of the resurrection and the outpouring of the Spirit. We will confine ourselves however to a consideration of the early resurrection *kerygmata* because of their connection with the advent of the *Eschaton* in Jesus.[10]

Various theories have been put forward to explain the origins of these different accounts of the resurrection of Jesus. For example it is suggested that the resurrection is merely an interpretation of the life and death of Jesus. Rudolph Bultmann holds that Jesus rose into the *kerygma* of the early Church and Willie Marxsen suggests that the resurrection stories are simply ways of saying that the cause of Jesus must continue in the world today. The difficulty with these approaches is that they fail to explain, given the scandal of the Cross, what triggered off these interpretations and responses to the life of Jesus. In particular these approaches do not account adequately for the dramatic recovery and renewal of faith in the followers of Jesus or the significant change of vision and praxis in the lives of the frightened disciples after the death of Jesus.

In contrast to this approach we propose that after Calvary the disciples had new experiences of Jesus, that these experiences gave rise to a new interpretation of Jesus and that this new understanding is expressed in the resurrection *kerygmata* and developed later on in the Gospel narratives. Lying behind the New Testament accounts of resurrection are the presence of new and real experiences that occurred to the disciples after the death of Jesus. The kind of experiences we are talking about here are only available indirectly in the post-crucifixion interpretations of Jesus. As we have just seen these interpretations are quite varied, embracing theological statements about the destiny of Jesus in terms of resurrection, exaltation, glorification, ascension, living again and the outpouring of the Spirit. These statements are quite deliberative, capturing one or other aspect of the same experience. The experience in question is principally an eschatological experience, an experience summing up the full flowering of the eschatology implicit in the ministry and death of Jesus. As one commentator points out: 'The particular choice of discourse used of the fate of the crucified Jesus is related to the eschatological convictions of the earliest disciples.'[11]

These different expressions of one and the same eschatological experience are seeking to communicate that the crucified Jesus is alive, transformed into a New Creation, and present now in a new way to his disciples; these expressions are in effect an attempt to convey that the *Eschaton*, the end of time, has arrived in the crucified one. This new presence and this new reality of the risen Jesus embodies symbolically the advent of the *Eschaton*. The variety of language, namely resurrection, exaltation, glorification, ascension, living again and Pentecost highlights 'the surplus of meaning' belonging to this foundational eschatological experience. These different symbolic expressions capture one or other aspect of the advent of the *Eschaton*.

'Resurrection' among other things points towards the arrival of the end of time. 'Exaltation' symbolises Christ sitting at the right hand of God the Father and now exercising a new reign over humanity and the world. 'Ascension' is about making way for the universal life-giving Spirit of the risen Jesus which initially had been particularised in Palestine. 'Glorification' is a way of saying that the crucified Jesus shares fully in the perfection and fullness of the glory of God. 'Living again' gets across the triumph over death. 'Pentecost' is about the outpouring of the Spirit of Jesus over the whole of humanity and creation – one of the significant signs that the end of the ages has arrived as foretold in the prophet Joel. It is important that these different expressions of the advent of the *Eschaton* be kept together as a check and control on how we understand the *Eschaton*. When these expressions become separated from each other distortions begin to creep in and this happened quite early on in Christianity.

Towards the end of the first century the language of resurrection had moved to the centre of the Christian stage. When resurrection is separated from the other equally important eschatological elements of exaltation and glorification then resurrection runs the risk of being literalised and distorted. After the first century the language of resurrection of the body begins to be replaced by the Hellenistic language of the immortality of the soul and then eschatology tends to become reduced to teleology or mystical union with Christ, as happened in different periods within the Christian tradition.[12] In this regard it is important to remind ourselves that the resurrection of Jesus is not about the return of Jesus to a pre-existent heaven, but rather the resurrection as eschatological is about the establishment of a New Creation in the crucified Jesus which becomes the blueprint or prototype of the future of humanity and creation.

One further expression of the eschatological character of the resurrection of Jesus can be found in the credal statement used by Paul: 'He was raised on the third day in accordance with the Scriptures' (1 Cor. 15:4). The phrase 'on the third day' occurs in the Gospels in reference to the Passion predictions, the sayings about the sign of Jonah and the raising of the Temple. The source of this technical Jewish expression is the Hebrew Scriptures where it is used to designate the day of deliverance and the dawning of salvation (see Hosea 6:1–3). For example it is 'on the third day' that Abraham is delivered from offering his son in sacrifice (Gen. 22:4), that Joshua and the Israelites entered the promised land (Joshua 3:2) and that Yahweh appears on Mount Sinai (Ex. 19:10–11). The third day, therefore, is a way of symbolising the eschatological arrival of salvation. To state that Jesus rose 'on the third day' is to make a profound eschatological statement about the meaning of the resurrection. The import, therefore, of this technical expression is primarily theological and not historical. This eschatological meaning attaching to the resurrection of Jesus is further confirmed by the expression 'in accordance with the Scriptures'. In this short credal statement the resurrection of Jesus comes across clearly as the fulfilment of Jewish hopes and expectations.

To sum up, we can say that after the death of Jesus the disciples had a new experience of Jesus distinct and different from the experience they had of the pre-crucified Jesus. This new experience is an experience of the eschatological reality of the risen Christ caught in the wide variety of eschatological symbols. The risen Christ gathers and assembles and missions the disciples. It is this new eschatological presence of Christ that animates and empowers the disciples to go forth proclaiming and witnessing to the good news of resurrection. This news of resurrection shapes the faith, mission and ministry of the early Christians.

In the light of this analysis we can now say at least what the eschatological reality of Jesus is not. It is not a physical resuscitation or a return to historical existence; it is not simply something that happened to the disciples but rather something that occurred objectively to Jesus and therefore had a transforming effect on the disciples; it is not simply a response or an interpretation of the life of Jesus but a new reality subsequent to the death of Jesus affecting the disciples; it is not a purely spiritual reality but rather something embracing the whole person of Jesus as transformed. In a word the resurrection of Jesus is God's eschatological action on the life and death of Jesus within history. To understand this divine action more fully we must now turn to the christological eschatology of Paul and John.

THE CHRISTOCENTRIC ESCHATOLOGY OF THE EARLY CHURCH: PAUL AND JOHN

A recent debate about the centre of Paul's theology helps us to situate the prominent presence of a christocentric eschatology within the Pauline corpus.[13] Out of this debate comes agreement that the centre of Paul's theology is not simply 'justification by faith' or 'being in Christ', even though these are important themes. Probably most would agree that Christ is the centre of Paul's theology, and that the Pauline corpus is an elaborate interpretation of the meaning of the death and resurrection of Christ,[14] or as Joseph A. Fitzmyer says, the whole of Paul's theology is orientated to the development of a 'christocentric soteriology'.[15] J. Christiaan Beker argues that the coherent centre of Paul's Gospel 'is a Christian apocalyptic structure of thought'.[16] For Beker there are three elements within this Christian apocalyptic structure: the primordial experience that Paul had, interpreted by the Christ-event, within an apocalyptic framework.

The value of Beker's description of the centre of Paul's theology is that it picks up the emphasis we have already put on experience in trying to understand Jewish eschatology and the eschatology of Jesus – an emphasis that highlights the experience of Moses, of Jesus, of the disciples after the death of Jesus and now of Paul in the genesis of eschatology. Further, the key to interpreting the experience for Paul is the Christ-event and the horizon is Jewish apocalyptic eschatology. In the light of this debate about the centre of Paul's theology we suggest that eschatology was at least a vital ingredient – a distinguishing dimension? – in early Christian experience and that consequently eschatology is a pervasive element within Paul's interpretation of Christian experience. Indeed it is hardly an exaggeration to hold that there is a prominent – if not central – christocentric eschatology throughout Paul's theology. Eschatology and christology interact creatively and continuously in the Pauline corpus to such an extent that one cannot be understood without the other.

Since Christ is 'the fullness of time' (Gal. 4:4; Eph. 1:10) Paul can say 'if anyone is in Christ, he is a New Creation. The old has passed away and the new has come' (2 Cor. 5:17). Further, because Christ is 'the revelation of the mystery which was kept a secret for long ages but is now disclosed' (Rom. 16:25; 16:26; see also Col. 1:26; Eph. 1:9–10; Eph. 3:4–5; 1 Cor. 2:7) he has 'abolished death, brought life and immortality to light' (2 Tim. 1:10). In virtue of the fact that we are now living in 'the end of ages' (1 Cor. 10:11) and in the 'latter times' (1 Tim. 4:1) we are encouraged 'to put away the old man and (to) put on the new man' (Eph. 4:22; Col. 3:9). Above all it is the risen Christ who is 'the first born among many' (Rom. 8:29; Col. 1:18) and 'the first fruits of those who have fallen asleep' (1 Cor. 15:20). A new ontological unity and solidarity has been established between Christ and humanity in and through the resurrection of Jesus. To highlight this, Paul draws a parallel between Adam and Christ: 'For since death came through a human being, the resurrection of the dead has also come through a human being; for as all die in Adam, so all will be made alive in Christ' (1 Cor. 15:21–2).

For Paul the death and resurrection affects not just the destiny of the individual but also the destiny of humanity and also of creation. This focus on the cosmic significance of the Christ-event is brought out in the contrast Paul makes between creation and the New Creation, between the old and the new. In Romans Paul talks about the whole of creation groaning in travail to be 'set free from its bondage and (so) obtain the glorious liberty of the children of God' (Rom. 8:18ff.). The ultimate foundation for the future of the individual, society and creation is the promise of resurrection which for Paul has been realised in Jesus who is now the firstfruit of God's harvest.

Within this christocentric perspective it is possible to outline four phases or moments or aspects in Paul's eschatology. The first phase is focused almost exclusively on the imminence of the Parousia, that is the expectation that the second coming was about to occur, and this is summed up in the Aramaic prayer, *Maranatha*, 'Come Lord Jesus' (1 Cor. 16:22). The prominence of this concern with the Parousia is found in the first letter to the Thessalonians, especially 1 Thessalonians 4:13–17.

The focus in Thessalonians is the immediate expectation of the Parousia, and the context (1 Thess. 4:13) is that in spite of the nearness of the Parousia some of the faithful have already died and consequently there is a concern that they may be at a disadvantage when the Parousia does arrive. To address this concern Paul returns to first principles, stating that 'since we believe that Jesus died and rose, even so through Jesus, God will bring with him those who have died' (v. 14). He then goes on to assure the Thessalonians 'that we who are alive . . . will by no means precede those who have died'. He then describes in apocalyptic terms the sequence of events at the Parousia as the descent of the Lord from heaven, the command of the Lord, an archangel's cry, the sound of a trumpet, the resurrection of the dead and the taking up of those who are alive with the risen dead in the clouds to meet the Lord in the air (vv. 16–17). The interpretation of these verses is varied from understanding the dead literally being brought back to life in this world (that is reconstituting their earthly bodies) and translated into heaven with the living like Enoch and Elijah to an affirmation of full bodily resurrection for the dead and the living – the latter being the more favoured interpretation today.[17] Clearly Paul expects to be alive for the Parousia and his primary interest here is the imminence of the coming of Christ.

This interest in the Parousia shifts to the resurrection and Parousia in 1 Corinthians 15 with the resurrection assuming importance in its own right. Paul now affirms the resurrection of Christ in the past (vv. 3–11) and connects this with the resurrection of the faithful in the future at the end of time (vv. 12–19). He notes that since 'all die in Adam, so all will be made alive in Christ' (v. 22) at his coming and then goes on to describe the element of transformation that belongs to resurrection (vv. 35–8; 50–6) stating 'we will all be changed' (v. 52). Within this chapter 15 of 1 Corinthians Paul develops a rich theology of resurrection to which we will return later on.

A third moment in Paul's eschatology is the presence of scattered references to resurrection immediately after death. The focus now seems to be on the possibility of being united with Christ immediately after death. 2 Corinthians 5:1–10 seems to suggest that resurrection will take place after death. The similarity in language that exists between 2 Corinthians 5:1–10 and Romans 8:18–27 and 1 Corinthians 15:50–5 in terms of being 'naked' and being 'clothed' as well as having the Spirit as a guarantee implies that Paul envisages resurrection immediately after death. Further, Paul's declared preference for being 'away from the (physical) body and at home with the Lord' (2 Cor. 5:8) also suggests resurrection after death.[18] In a similar manner Philippians 1:21–3 contrasts the difference between living 'in the flesh' in this life and being united 'with Christ' in the hereafter in a way that suggests resurrection takes place after death. Likewise Philippians 3:21, in talking about the transformation of the earthly body 'to be conformed to the body of his glory' (v. 21) implies resurrection after death.

A fourth phase in the eschatology of Paul moves resurrection into present existence. Paul talks about being 'in Christ' in this life and walking in newness of life through baptism (Rom. 6:3–6) and the gift of the Spirit that has been poured out into our hearts as a guarantee of the future (2 Cor. 5:5; 2 Cor. 1:22). A process of dying and rising with Christ, of putting off the old and putting on the new, of 'being transformed . . . from one degree of glory to another' (2 Cor. 3:18) in this life is present in the later Pauline literature.

These different phases in Paul's eschatology have prompted many to posit a high degree of development in his christocentric eschatology. However, a more modest degree of development seems nearer the truth when we remember that Paul would have been theologising out of his knowledge of late Judaic literature on eschatology (canonical and non-canonical), the teaching of Jesus about the resurrection (e.g. Mark 12:18–27) and the actual Christ-event itself.[19] These four phases in Paul's eschatology can be drawn into a single synthesis by holding that in the Pauline corpus there is an underlying tension between 'the already' and 'the not yet', between being 'in Christ' and becoming 'in Christ', between realised eschatology and futurist eschatology. For Paul the risen Christ is the beginning of the end, the first fruits of those who have fallen asleep, the initiation of the New Creation. The Spirit of the risen Christ has been poured out as a pledge of something greater to come in the future (Rom. 8:23; 2 Cor. 1:22; 2 Cor. 5:5). A new age has come into being through the resurrection of Jesus from the dead. At the same time however there is caution, indeed reservation about the present age and we are encouraged to keep up the struggle for the sake of what is yet to come. This tension between the present and the future which surrounds Paul's eschatology is not well maintained subsequently in the Christian tradition, with the result that more often than not the importance of the future takes over and distracts from the significance of the present as we shall see later.

As will be apparent it is impossible to present a single account of Paul's eschatology. Instead the strength of his christocentric eschatology is that it resists any easy categorisation, moving as it does from dialectic (the already and the not yet) to paradox (dying and rising in Christ) to a mysticism of being and becoming in Christ. What is clear is that the

Christ-event has introduced the new into our world. The resurrection and the outpouring of the Spirit of Christ affects the direction that humanity and history and creation are now moving. Sin and death have been overcome by the Cross and replaced by grace and new life in Christ Jesus.

When we turn to the Gospel of John we find a not too dissimilar christocentric eschatology. If it is true to say that Mark's Gospel is concerned with the future, then it is equally true to suggest John's Gospel is about the present. The fourth Gospel is outstanding for its emphasis on realised eschatology and for this reason it is sometimes called the Gospel of eternal life. Yet it must be acknowledged that there is also a futurist eschatology running throughout John's Gospel. This juxtaposing of realised and futurist eschatologies in the one Gospel is seen by many as a problem of inconsistency calling for explanation or resolution. Thus Rudolph Bultmann held that the futurist eschatology was an addition by an ecclesiastical redactor.[20] In contrast others have held that the present eschatology of John derives from the editor of the Gospel.[21] A more realistic approach recognises the deeply theological character of the Gospel of John and sees an underlying unity or coincidence of realised and future eschatology deriving from John's particular christology.

For the fourth evangelist, Jesus is the unique revelation of God – the Messiah and Son of God sent by the Father as Saviour of the world. Consequently the time of judgment is 'now' and disciples are called to make a decision in the present. Flowing from that decision is the eschatological offer of eternal life and the gift of the Holy Spirit. The promise and fulfilment come together in Jesus Christ who is one with the Father. The *Eschaton* is present in Jesus who is now the actual source of realised eschatology. The blessings belonging to the future are experienced in the present by the Johannine community in different ways. The Spirit / Paraclete, as eschatological gift, is poured out in the present not only on Jesus (John 1:33; 3:34) but also on his disciples (John 20:22). Eternal life, a blessing of the future, is now a present possession for those who believe in Jesus (John 3:36; 5:24, 40; 6:40, 47, 54, 68; 10:10). Judgment, usually associated with the end of time, is now taking place in the present (John 3:36).

These strong expressions of realised eschatology, however, create a problem for the Johannine community as indeed they do for us today. That problem is the reality of death. How is it possible to reconcile this realised eschatology with the presence of death in the world? This question is addressed by the fourth evangelist in the story of the raising of Lazarus (John 11:17–27).[22] For the Johannine community the present primary question is not so much the delay of the Parousia as it was with

110

Paul but rather, given that Jesus has brought the gift of eternal life, why do we have to die? It is the drama of this question that is played out in the story of the raising of Lazarus. The issues of life and death are to the fore and so Jesus says 'this illness (of Lazarus) does not lead to (ultimate) death' and yet Lazarus dies. Martha complains 'if you had been here my brother would not have died' (v. 21). Jesus reassures her 'your brother will rise again' (v. 23) but Martha protests 'I know that he will rise again in the resurrection on the last day' (v. 24). In response Jesus gently corrects this reference by Martha to a purely futurist eschatology by pointing out 'I am the resurrection and the life. Those who believe in me, even though they die, will live, and everyone who believes in me will never die' (John 11:25–6).

In this important dialogue Jesus transposes and transforms the reference to future eschatology into the present. What is determinative is not the future but belief now in Jesus. What is at issue is eternal life which does not yield to physical death so that even though the believer dies nevertheless he will live for ever. This eternal life is a present possession coming from belief in Jesus. Resurrection therefore is not some dim and distant future reality out there on 'the last day'; instead the resurrection as a future reality is already present in the life of the believer who follows Jesus.

The message of Jesus within this story is that he is the source of eternal life to those who believe in him and that this eschatological gift of eternal life conquers death without, however, abolishing death. In this way Jesus brings the present and the future, realised and final eschatology together into a single unity and coincidence. The primary emphasis is on realised eschatology and it is this focus on the present that shapes the future. In other words the role and function of future eschatology in the Johannine community is to ratify and validate the present gift of eternal life that comes from abiding faith in Jesus (John 12:48).[23] What makes this story about Lazarus all the more significant is that in John's Gospel, with all its theological subtlety and nuance, it marks the turning-point in the life of Jesus when 'the chief priests and Pharisees had given orders that anyone who knew where Jesus was should let them know, so that they might arrest him' (John 11:57). The theological truth of this important exchange with Martha and Mary about their brother Lazarus is subsequently given historical and theological justification by the personal passover of Jesus at Calvary. Death and exaltation, the present and the future are one in the christocentric eschatology of John's Gospel – a unity that needs to be recovered in any retrieval of eschatology for today.

8

THE CRUCIFIED AND RISEN CHRIST AS THE HOPE OF THE WORLD

As all die in Adam, so all will be made alive in Christ. But each in his own order: Christ the first fruits, then at his coming those who belong to Christ.
(1 Cor. 15:22–3)

IT IS SOMETHING OF AN UNDERSTATEMENT to suggest that a theological vacuum exists in relation to eschatology today. Past formulations command little contemporary credence. Yet the questions that gave rise to these formulations of the past continue to haunt humanity. Issues about the meaning of life and death, about the range of hope, and about the destiny of the world simply will not go away. These questions burden everybody at some stage of life; all too often discussion of these disturbing issues is postponed and when the issues reappear they almost overwhelm us in a manner reminiscent of *The Death of Ivan Illich*. In this chapter we will try to correlate these perennial concerns with the advent of the *Eschaton* of the crucified and risen Christ. In particular we will seek to grasp the underlying dynamic of the Paschal Mystery of Jesus for contemporary life and then go on to correlate the resurrection of Jesus with human experiences and conclude by answering the important question: What can we hope for today?

AN ESCHATOLOGY OF THE PASCHAL MYSTERY

It has been fashionable in the last twenty-five years to emphasise the centrality of resurrection in eschatology. That trend was challenged by Jürgen Moltmann in *The Crucified God: The Cross of Christ as the Foundation and Criticism of Christian Theology*.[1] Moltmann reminds us that 'The Cross is the form of the coming, redeeming kingdom'[2] and that therefore our eschatology must become an *eschatologia crucis*. However, an eschatology of the Cross only succeeds to the extent that it includes an *eschatologia resurrectionis*. The crucified Christ is the centre of eschatology because the crucified One is risen. Catholic theology, especially since Vatican II, talks about the importance of the Paschal Mystery and by this term intends the dynamic unity that exists between the life, death, resurrection and the outpouring of the Spirit. To this extent what is needed today is an eschatology of the Paschal Mystery.[3]

The death and resurrection of Jesus from the dead was experienced in the early Church as the decisive eschatological action of God in history. As seen in the last chapter the language used to describe the experience of the death and destiny of Jesus is predominantly eschatological: exaltation, resurrection, glorification, ascension, and Pentecost.

The preaching and praxis of Jesus concerning the reign of God comes to a point of fulfilment and realisation in his death and resurrection. On a wider front the hopes of Judaism are crystallised and transformed in the Passion of Jesus. And in a still wider horizon the puzzling pattern of life and death in the rhythm of nature is given new meaning in the Paschal Mystery of Jesus. It is these three different points of contact with the death and resurrection of Jesus that prompted the early Church to interpret the historical reality of the crucified and risen Christ as representing the advent of the *Eschaton*. What happened in the life of Jesus was experienced and perceived to have absolute significance for understanding the meaning of life, of death, and the future of history and creation. In effect what happened in the life of Jesus is understood to have significance for the future of the self, society and the world. Consequently Christian eschatology is about the application of christology to the future of the individual, the community and creation.

This eschatological action of God in the life, death and resurrection of Jesus establishes a new order in the world. The reality of the crucified and risen Christ is described as 'the beginning, the first born from the dead' (Col. 1:18; Rev. 1:5), 'the first fruits of those who have died' (1 Cor. 15:20), 'the first born within a large family' (Rom. 8:29). These images suggest that the Paschal Mystery of Jesus is the turning-point, the centre and goal of history. From now on history and humanity are moving in a different direction, namely the New Creation already established in the death and resurrection of Jesus. This new direction for humanity is at least visible in the new community of women and men who confess the crucified-risen One as the Christ who is the Lord of history and creation. The eschatological action of God in raising Jesus from the dead reverses what up to now has been the apparent success of injustice and death. In the death and resurrection of Jesus, God confronts the forces of darkness, and engages the powers and principalities of this world. The resurrection of Jesus is therefore a re-ordering and a restructuring of life in such a way that we can now believe that out of death comes life, darkness yields to light, and self-surrender leads to transformation.

The creative paradox proclaimed by Jesus in terms of losing one's life to save one's life through conversion receives verification in the historical death and resurrection of Jesus. From now on the Paschal Mystery of the death and resurrection becomes normative and paradigmatic for the disciples of Jesus in understanding the future. It is normative in terms of summing up the meaning and structure of salvation, and paradigmatic in terms of the process required for becoming part of the *Eschaton* already established in Christ. Contact with the crucified and risen Christ, becoming a disciple, involves a personal process of dying and rising, of passing over into Christ, a movement of decentring the self in order to recentre the self in Christ.

This process takes place at different levels of Christian existence: ethical, sacramental and eschatological. The ethical aspect is shaped by love; the sacramental is determined by faith; the eschatological is influenced by hope. Of course these aspects should not be separated; taken together they represent the Christian response to the Paschal Mystery of the death and resurrection of Jesus. What is important is that the eschatological is not isolated but seen as an intrinsic part of Christian existence. Hope in the present and the future is not some kind of optional extra to Christian faith; instead hope is a constitutive dimension not only of human existence but also of Christian living. The character of that hope for the Christian is, as already pointed out in Chapter 4, influenced decisively by the death and resurrection of Jesus. We noted there that the shape of Christian hope is cruciform, and that there is no credible future that bypasses the reality of the Cross in this life or at the moment of death. At the same time, however, due emphasis must be given to the resurrection dimension of Christian hope in the future lest we be overwhelmed by the pain and suffering of the Cross.

Part of the context for understanding the resurrection of Jesus is the Jewish hope of a general resurrection of the dead at the end of time. We find Paul alluding to this when he writes that 'if the dead are not raised, then Christ has not been raised' (1 Cor. 15:16). There has been a tendency to move from the individual resurrection of Jesus to an affirmation about the general resurrection of the dead. Instead the prior context for appropriating the resurrection of Jesus is the Jewish hope of a general resurrection of the dead at the end of time. The individual resurrection of Jesus is an anticipation of the general resurrection of the dead.

Also important in this context is the Jewish hope of a general resurrection as something which is inclusive not only of all the people of Israel but also of the whole of humanity. Further, this Jewish hope in a general resurrection of the dead, especially through the development of an apocalyptic eschatology, also has a cosmic dimension to it. These two elements of Jewish hope, namely the inclusive and cosmic elements, are exemplified in the individual resurrection of Jesus.

The personal resurrection of Jesus is a prototype of the universal resurrection of humanity. This representative aspect of the resurrection of Jesus is emphasised by Paul when he draws a parallel between Adam and the crucified-risen Christ as the new Adam: 'For as all die in Adam, so all will be made alive in Christ' (1 Cor. 15:22). The Adam-Christ parallel is developed in Romans 5:12 in terms of sin and justification and is repeated extensively in 1 Corinthians 15 in terms of death and resurrection. The gift of resurrection is for all and is as universal as death itself. This analogy between Adam and Christ highlights that the promise of resurrection is for the whole of humanity. Just as Adam was the symbolic head of historical humanity so now the crucified and risen Christ is the head of redeemed humanity destined for resurrection.

In addition to the universality of the resurrection there is also the cosmic dimension of resurrection. Just as the fall of Adam had cosmic implications so the resurrection of humanity in Christ also has cosmic implications. This is especially evident in Romans 8 where Paul talks about the whole of creation groaning in travail, awaiting the same kind of redemption as humanity so that the risen Christ can be described in Colossians not only as the firstborn of the dead but also as 'the first born of all creation' (Col. 1:15). For this reason the second letter to the Corinthians states that 'if any one is in Christ', that is in the crucified and risen Christ, that person 'is a New Creation: the old has passed away; see everything has become new' (2 Cor. 5:17). There is an important sense in which faith in the resurrection is an extension of faith in God the creator.

Closely related to this focus on the inclusive and cosmic implications of the resurrection of Jesus is the strong emphasis on his bodily resurrection. It is the whole person of Jesus, body and soul, spirit and matter, person and flesh that is raised up and transformed. The bodily resurrection is affirmed quite explicitly in the appearances and the empty tomb tradition. This means that the resurrection is more than the immortality of the soul, more than spiritual survival, more than memory. Equally the bodily resurrection is more than a physical resuscitation, more than a re-animation of the dead body of Jesus, more than a return to earthly existence. Instead the bodily resurrection of Jesus embraces identity within transformation, sameness within difference, continuity within discontinuity. There are important elements of transformation, re-creation and newness attaching to the bodily resurrection of Jesus that exceed anything we can know or experience on this side of death. At best we can only express these elements symbolically and very inadequately in terms of the seed, the flower and the gardener, the acorn and the oak tree, the plant and the forest, the caterpillar and the butterfly. It is important to acknowledge the limitations that belong to all symbols of resurrection by applying the *via negationis et eminentiae*. What is central here is the eschatological element of human fulfilment, wholeness and completion that is symbolised in the bodily resurrection of Jesus. In other words the resurrection of Jesus is not simply about Jesus' return to heaven from where he came; instead the resurrection of Jesus is about the eschatological inauguration and establishment of a new ontological order destined for eternal communion with the Spirit of God in glory: exaltation, glorification, ascension and Pentecost.

A number of important consequences flow from this understanding of the bodily resurrection of Jesus. The focus on the bodily resurrection helps us to appreciate how we can hold that the resurrection of Jesus has cosmic implications. If the whole Jesus, body and soul, spirit and matter is the subject of transformation in resurrection then it follows that part of the material creation has already been glorified in the resurrection of Jesus. Further, since the resurrection of Jesus is about the eschatological wholeness of humanity, then we have a new basis for going beyond Niet-zsche's nihilistic myth of eternal recurrence. The bodily resurrection of Jesus symbolises a point of arrival for humanity and the completion of creation – and not therefore simply more of the same. The bodily resurrection of Jesus is about the fulfilment and transformation of human identity. We have seen how the human self is both radically relational and permanently embodied. That relationality and embodiedness reaches fulfilment in the bodily resurrection of Jesus as the blueprint of humanity. Close links exist between anthropology and the eschatological reality of the resurrection as we outlined in Chapter 3.

A third point about the bodily resurrection of Jesus is that it confirms our faith in God the Creator. The God who creates is the God who trans-forms in resurrection. A fundamental consistency and coherence exists therefore between a theology of creation and an eschatology of resurrec-tion or the New Creation.

In making these statements about resurrection we must be careful not to claim too much or appear to be too clear about the object of Christian hope. To do this would be to reduce the content of Christian hope to purely human proportions, or even worse, to a mere human projection. We need to remind ourselves that the language of resurrection is symbolic and that the logic of Christian hope therefore is not the logic of inference but of imagination. Further, the rhetoric of resurrection must not be allowed to cover over the historical existence of so much pain, suffering and death in the world. These negative realities continually challenge every theology of resurrection and highlight the need to keep the Cross and resurrection together in creative tension. The pain of the world demands a praxis of liberation and we must now seek a foundation for that praxis in solidarity and hope.

RESURRECTION AND HUMAN EXPERIENCE

The resurrection of Jesus is the foundation stone of Christian eschatology, but if the reality of resurrection is to succeed as the fulcrum of eschatology then it must be seen to be related to human experience – not just the experience of the disciples two thousand years ago but also the experience of the contemporary disciples of Christ. Where and how does resurrection touch contemporary experience? How can we fuse the Christian tradition of resurrection with our peculiarly twentieth-century experiences? Is there any point of contact today between the first-century experience of resurrection and twentieth-century experiences? Can the resurrection empower the Christian community today in the way it energised the despondent and frightened first disciples after the death of Jesus?

In raising these questions we do not want to give the impression that the resurrection of Christ is something that can be experienced in this life like any other empirical reality. Nor do we wish to deny the uniqueness of the resurrection experience that the first disciples had. Rahner is right when he reminds us in this regard that 'the whole of the resurrection experience is more than the sum of its individual parts'.[4] We have already seen that the original resurrection experience was expressed in a great variety of languages and that therefore no one particular expression captures the fullness of the power and presence of the Spirit of the risen Christ animating the first Christian community. However, it needs to be emphasised that it is the same Spirit of the risen Christ that continues to animate the Christian community today in a great variety of different experiences: the struggle for equality and justice, the quest for human and ecological wholeness, the search for peace, reconciliation and unity. Every generation needs to seek out its own particular points of contact with the risen Christ.[5] We will confine ourselves here to two particularly pressing experiences that pose searching questions for any eschatology of resurrection – the experience of hope and the unity or disunity of human history.

As seen in Chapter 4, hope is a universal phenomenon and an essential element in the make-up of the human condition. Without hope the human declines and disintegrates. We also noted in Chapter 5 that something of an interplay takes place, sometimes tacitly and at other times explicitly, between human, historical hopes and primordial, fundamental hope. We saw that fundamental hope sustains human hopes, especially when they break down and collapse. But this begs the question as to what sustains primordial hope? What keeps primordial hope going? Is there any foundation in history for fundamental hope?

The theologian who has given most thought and careful consideration to this question is Karl Rahner. Rahner shows that primordial hope or what he calls transcendent hope 'is the horizon of understanding within which, and within which alone something like a resurrection of Jesus can be expected and experienced at all'.[6] It is the resurrection of Jesus that sustains primordial hope even though many people may never actually move from primordial hope to the resurrection of Jesus. Conversely Rahner also argues that the openness of transcendental hope only becomes clear under the impact of its categorical fulfilment in the resurrection of Jesus.[7] Rahner readily admits that there is a mutual conditioning and reciprocity between transcendental hope and its categorical expression in salvation history: 'the circle between transcendental and categorical experience is operative everywhere'[8] especially in regard to transcendental hope and the resurrection of Jesus. Transcendental hope searches history for confirmation and fulfilment, and finds this concretely in the resurrection of Jesus from the dead.[9] The universal experience of transcendental hope is the necessary supposition for appropriating the particular experience of the resurrection of Jesus. This universal experience of transcendental hope arises out of the individual's innate quest for fulfilment in the future. Every human being looks to the future for fulfilment, especially in exercising personal acts of freedom and responsibility. These acts are called into question by the reality of death and can only be resolved by accepting death as that final act in which a person comes to some form of definitive self-determination. This transcendental hope 'seeks historical mediation and confirmation in which it can become explicit'[10] and finds this expressed in the resurrection of Jesus. For Rahner it is only against this background of transcendental hope that people are able to experience and understand the resurrection of Jesus.

At the same time, however, the resurrection of Jesus not only grounds fundamental, primordial hope but also legitimates this fundamental hope even though many may never seek either foundation or legitimation for their fundamental hope. Primordial hope provokes questions that are ultimately religious in nature. These questions relate to broad issues about the meaningfulness, purpose and goal of life as well as particular issues about the future fulfilment of the self, especially the future of the self as embodied because that is the only kind of experience that the self knows. But we have seen that the most fundamental experiences of the embodied self are relational and therefore such experiences raise questions not only about the future of the embodied self but also about the self as bound up with others in community and as connected to the earth. To this extent transcendental hope raises questions about the future of the individual as a part belonging to the whole. It is the unique capacity of the resurrection of Jesus to embrace the individual, community and creation that makes the resurrection of Jesus the foundation of transcendental hope.

The second contemporary human experience that the resurrection of Jesus sheds light on, concerns the unity of history. Is there any underlying unity to the history of humanity? Is history merely a flow of discrete, atomised and contingent moments in time that have no relationship or influence or responsiblity to each other? In particular, is our human participation in history a series of accidental events and incidental eruptions without coherence? Is the action of individuals on the so-called stage of history a mere puff of smoke that eventually evaporates? Can humans exempt themselves from all responsibility for the greater good belonging to the past, present and the future? In brief is there any unity to history, or solidarity to life?

These questions have been addressed imaginatively by the critical theorists of the Frankfurt School of Philosophy in this century, especially in a famous debate between Max Horkheimer and Walter Benjamin. This debate raises the question whether history is closed or unclosed and in focusing on this issue has been described as 'one of the most theologically significant controversies of our century'.[11]

In 1937 Walter Benjamin wrote an article about historical materialism in which he pointed out: 'The work of the past is not closed for the historical materialist.'[12] Horkheimer reacted by saying that 'the supposition of an unclosed past is idealistic . . . past injustice has occurred and is closed. Those who are slain in it were truly slain.'[13] Horkheimer was repeating what he had often said on other occasions: 'What has happened to those human beings who have perished does not have any part in the future. They will never be called forth to be blessed in eternity.'[14] And then as if to clinch the issue against Benjamin he says: 'In the end your statements are theological.'[15] Benjamin replies: 'The corrective for this sort of thinking lies in the reflection that history is . . . a form of empathetic memory. What science has settled, empathetic memory can modify.'[16]

Benjamin wants to work out a theory of history that does not ignore our unity in history with past generations, especially those who have been oppressed. He realises, however, that most attempts to write history seem to require empathy with the victor and this makes us incapable of grasping 'history as the history of the suffering of the world'.[17] What is really needed therefore in the writing of history is an 'empathetic memory' that keeps alive the knowledge of how badly people have been victimised in the past. In this way Benjamin believes he can keep past history open and unclosed. Refusing to go down this road because of its affinity with theology, Horkheimer admits that 'a metaphysical sadness pervades the writings of the great materialists' and that these materialists are acutely aware of the 'unlimited loneliness of man' because the past is indeed passed.[18] Horkheimer, with characteristic pessimism, speaks out against the idea of perfect justice: 'It can never be . . . realised in history. For even if a better society takes the place of the present disorder it will not redress the penury of the past nor the injustice done to non-human nature.'[19]

A similar expression of this problem about history can be found in an important article by the political scientist Christian Lenhart in 1975.[20] He invites the reader to consider three successive generations: G1 as the generation of enslaved predecessors, G2 as enslaved contemporaries who emancipate themselves, and G3 as the generation of emancipated successors. What should be the attitude of the generation of emancipated successors, G3? Can they enjoy life without reference to their predecessors in G1 and G2? Are G2 and G1 to be forgotten and reduced to the status of deadwood in the evolution of humanity? Is oblivion the precondition of bliss? Would the generation of emancipated successors, G3, be really liberated if they ignored, forgot and erased the memory of the struggles of G2 and G1? The generation of emancipated successors, G3, seems to have everything and owes nothing – but if it is to live nobly it must learn that it owes everything and possesses nothing.[21] In response to this apparent paradox, Lenhart proposes what he calls 'anamnestic solidarity', i.e. a solidarity in remembrance. If the struggle for the revolutionary cause is to continue, then it must be informed by some kind of larger historical solidarity with the dead comparable to ancestral worship. In putting the issue this way Lenhart realises that he 'comes dangerously close to a violation of the Marxist prohibition of graven images'.[22] This link with worship will be taken up in the final chapter which will deal with the relationship between the Eucharist and eschatology.

One can hardly fail to be moved by the passion and depth of feeling expressed in the dialogue between Benjamin and Horkheimer, and replayed by Lenhart. The issues raised may sound theoretical but they have a very practical and existential bearing on the way we live life. Every human being has been faced with searching questions about the meaning of the innocent suffering of the dead and the apparent triumph of injustices. The history of the twentieth century is peppered with question marks about the value of unselfish commitment to the causes of humanity, especially in terms of peace-making, the work of justice and more recently the care of the earth. Is it all in vain? Is commitment to the flourishing of humanity merely a puff of smoke? Is the pursuit of peace and the praxis of liberation purely illusory? Is the selfless service of larger realities like the common good and the cause of truth a waste of time? These are not just theological questions, they are deeply eschatological issues affecting how one reads two world wars, the Jewish holocaust, and the ongoing holocaust in the Third World, the persistent presence of so much innocent suffering, the seeming success of so much injustice and the exploitation of the earth. The suggestion that we read history in terms of an 'empathetic memory' and universal solidarity are indeed important and creative responses. Herbert Marcuse's perception of the emancipatory power of memory is worth quoting here:

> Remembrance of the past can allow dangerous perceptions to dawn upon us . . . remembrance is a way of detaching oneself from the given situation, a kind of 'intervention', which for an instant interrupts the omnipotence of the given situation.[23]

Similarly solidarity continues to be the lynch-pin of Habermas' theory of communicative action[24] and the importance of action for justice in our world today. However, these important responses contain their own inner tensions, as well as begging further questions which are clearly theological and ultimately eschatological. What is the goal of empathetic memory and is there any lasting finality to its exercise? Is there any ground or continuity to human solidarity with the disadvantaged, the good of the community and the care of the earth?

It may be objected that at first sight our discussion about the underlying unity of history has wandered away from the primary intention of grounding resurrection and human experience. But on second reflection it must surely be evident at this stage that our discussion of the questions raised by the critical theorists of the Frankfurt School of Philosophy has opened up horizons within which the resurrection of Jesus takes on a new urgency and significance. It is instructive to recall that the hope for resurrection in late Judaism before the common era arose out of questions similar to those discussed by the critical theorists. The context of second-century Judaism before the common era which produced belief in the resurrection was the persecution of innocent people, their fidelity to Yahweh in the face of death and the extraordinary witness borne by Jewish martyrs at the hands of Antiochos Epiphanus IV. More particularly the death of Jesus arising out of his solidarity with humanity for the sake of the coming reign of God and his apparent abandonment by the God in whose name he had claimed liberation are all called into question by his death on the Cross. Are not the macro-anomalies raised by empathetic memory and universal solidarity also present in microform in the death of the innocent Jesus on the hill of Calvary? Is not the value of the costly love of God and neighbour exemplified in the life of Jesus challenged in a most fundamental way by his shameful death on the Cross? Is the life of Jesus lived out of empathy and solidarity with others and God to become, as appears with so many other lives, the mere 'refuse of history'?

In response to these questions it must be stated that the resurrection of Jesus reverses the outward appearances and re-orders the direction of history. The resurrection of Jesus is an expression of God's solidarity with everything that Jesus stood for, especially his promotion of the causes of justice, freedom and love in his preaching and praxis of the coming reign of God. The resurrection of Jesus is also a vindication by God of the innocent suffering unto death of Jesus on behalf of others. In the context of the above discussion the resurrection of Jesus is the triumph of Jesus' empathetic memory with Judaism and his universal solidarity with humanity out of love. The resurrection of Jesus means that his memory and solidarity with others out of love is not in vain, is not empty, is not useless; instead the solidarity in remembrance is fruitful, productive and enduring.

Helmut Peukert states tersely that 'faith in the resurrection of Jesus is at once solidarity with all others. And as anamnestic solidarity, it is universal solidarity in the horizon of all humanity and of one unified history.'[25] Peukert is anxious to bring out the link between the resurrection of Jesus and the solidarity of humanity. In this way he argues for the unity of history as grounded in the resurrection of Jesus.

It is Wolfhart Pannenberg more than most who develops a theology of history in the light of the resurrection of Jesus. For Pannenberg the resurrection of Jesus is an anticipation of the end (*prolepsis*) and as such is, therefore, a disclosure in principle of the future to come. Through the resurrection of Jesus, the reign of God has come into existence, a new world has dawned, and history has been given a radical orientation towards the future. The resurrection of Jesus is the pre-appearance of the end, the arrival in outline of the future, giving us a preview as it were of life to come, a prototype of the future.[26]

In brief, the resurrection of Jesus fulfils human hope, grounds universal, primordial hope and is the object of Christian hope. At the same time the resurrection of Jesus provides a centre of unity for past, present and future history as well as keeping history open; the resurrection of Jesus also transforms the role and importance of memory and solidarity within history. In this way the resurrection of Jesus addresses and empowers contemporary human experience in a manner resembling, in part at least, the way it addressed and empowered the experience of the first disciples after Calvary.

WHAT CAN WE HOPE FOR?

In the light of this relationship between the resurrection of Jesus and contemporary experience we are now in a position to return to the question asked in Chapter 4, namely: What can we hope for? This particular question takes us to the storm centre of modern eschatology. The way we answer this question will shape most of the horizons of contemporary eschatology. Michael Scanlon helpfully lays out two quite different answers to this question: for some the answer to the question is 'Eternal life after death for purified souls' and for others 'Yes, ultimately eternal life, but penultimately a more just, more peaceful world order.'[27] The Irish theologian, Gerry O'Hanlon, SJ, raises the same kind of question in an article entitled 'May Christians hope for a better world?'[28] O'Hanlon, anxious to avoid any evolutionary view of hope, answers 'that our primary hope is directed towards God; that this will be realised definitively only in heaven; and that in a secondary sense we may hope for this-worldly anticipations of this primary hope'.[29] The same issue was raised in an important Symposium in Dublin entitled 'Impotent or Powerful: the Catholic Church in Ireland' in 1994. The titles of two key papers capture the tensions of two distinct theologies of hope: 'The Transformation of the World' and 'We Have Here No Lasting City'.[30]

Christians are divided on how they answer this important question about hope, and most of the division derives from different perceptions of eschatology which affect a host of issues within practical theology such as the relationship between prayer and politics, liberation and salvation, the religious and social mission of the Church, and faith and justice. Ultimately these different views of eschatology evolve around the stubborn tension that exists between a this-worldly eschatology and an other-worldly eschatology, between what is often called the elements of 'the already' and 'the not yet' of the Christ-event.

Before attempting to answer the question about what can we hope for, something must be said about the new, changed context in which this question is asked today. A clue to this changed context may be found in the fact that Emmanuel Kant, often described as the father of the Enlightenment, also asked the question 'What can we hope for?' Kant was asking the question in the context of the Enlightenment and that Enlightenment, sometimes called the first Enlightenment, continues to be at least part of the context in which we ask the question today. The Enlightenment brought with it a new sense of historical consciousness and human responsibility for the shape of the world in which we live. The Enlightenment continues to challenge theology today, especially eschatology. At the same time we cannot ignore that the Enlightenment brought promises of progress through the advances of science and technology which have turned out to be both destructive and deceptive. There is a growing awareness today of the downside to modernity which must also be recognised as part of the new context in which we ask the question: What can we hope for? Humanity is burdened more than ever before in the face of the ongoing nuclear threat and the possibility of ecological collapse with a soul-searching responsibility for the survival of the world. If the first Enlightenment was about knowing and understanding the world then the second Enlightenment which we are presently experiencing is about praxis, the possibility of assuming responsibility for the world in terms of action for justice, liberation and transformation.

It is increasingly clear that it has been inattention to the ethical consequences of so much modern scientific and technical progress that is responsible for many of the negative effects of modernity. The need to move beyond a modern mechanical perception of the world towards some form of post-modern, inclusive, processive paradigm is receiving growing acceptance among scientists and theologians alike.[31] The issue facing humanity as it approaches the end of the second millennium is how to move from theory into praxis, from an instrumental rationality to a liberating wisdom, from an ethic of domination to a new ethic of social and ecological solidarity.

There is a growing awareness that these more recent perceptions of the world in which we live carry with them a different way of seeing God: no longer 'on the margins and in the gaps but in the middle of life and of the world, and finding Him as the mystics say in all things'.[32] The image of God that is used in the context of the question 'What can we hope for?' is all-important and therefore warrants some further clarification here.

If we are to move beyond the monism of a this-worldly eschatology and the supranatural dualism of an other-worldly eschatology then new images of God are necessary; these have been developed quite extensively in theology under the impact of feminism and ecology but have failed to have much influence on eschatology.[33] The image of God available in a theology of Pantheism is helpful here. It suggests that God is present in the world and the world is present in God without however identifying God with the world in the way Pantheism does. The biblical foundation for this image of God can be found in the doctrines of creation, covenant and incarnation – each of which highlights a relational God. God is related to the world and the world is related to God, and this relationship is personalised irrevocably in the incarnation of God in Jesus. Within this perspective Jesus of Nazareth represents the fullness of God's loving self-communication to the world and humanity's self-transcending outreach towards God. A new communion is established between God and humanity in Jesus so that we can now talk about the co-presence of God to humanity which is the basis of a human–divine co-responsibility for the future of the world. This relational understanding of God receives its fullest expression in the Christian understanding of God as Trinity.[34] Within this perspective emphasis is placed on the full equality, mutuality and communion of three persons in the one God.[35]

An additional new image of God can be found in the nature–grace relationship which is also very important for developing an eschatology that goes beyond the dualism of classical theology. Under the influence of Henri de Lubac and Karl Rahner a unity within distinction is seen to exist between nature and grace. Every human being comes into the world graced by God; that is, every human being is called by God to communion.[36] This divine call has a real effect on the very constitution of every human being and implies that the human person is born turned towards God. This fundamental disposition, what Rahner calls the 'existential supernatural', demands a free response of acceptance from the individual. This response in turn is the beginning of the active life of grace: a personal relationship with God in this life. Every human being is surrounded by the love of God and therefore graced by God from the beginning of life. This more nuanced, and certainly more dynamic, view of the nature–grace relationship developed in this century retrieves neglected aspects of Aquinas' theology of the natural desire to see God.[37] An echo of this intrinsic relationship between nature and grace can be found in Newman's famous dictum: Grace in this life is glory in exile and glory is grace at home.

The foundation for these images of God as radically relational is given in the revelation of God in the person of Jesus. It is still a matter of great concern and alarm at how little theology has allowed the revelation that took place in the life of Jesus to transform the concept of God from classical antiquity with its emphasis on the transcendence, immutability, impassability and omnipotence. The failure of christology to modify this pre-Christian perception of God has had and continues to have an inhibiting effect on the development of a contemporary eschatology. The God revealed in Jesus continues to be the God concealed but the revelation that did take place must be allowed to transform the God of the philosophers. It is surely ironic that the philosopher Alfred N. Whitehead could complain that the 'brief Galilean vision of humility flickered throughout the ages uncertainly . . . but the deep idolatry of fashioning God in the image of Egyptian, Persian and Roman rulers, was retained. The church gave unto God attributes that belonged exclusively to Caesar.'[38] Karl Barth has argued that it is not enough simply to add christology to the Aristotelian notion of God. Instead the revelation of God in Jesus must be allowed to break up and reform the Aristotelian understanding of God.[39] Some fifty years later Walter Kasper observes: 'The Christian . . . understanding of God in the light of Jesus' Cross and resurrection leads to a crisis, even a revolution, in the way of seeing God.'[40]

Similarly David Calvert points out that 'christology . . . leads to a revision of our concept of God'.[41] But what, it will be asked, is this transformation, this revolution, this revision of God that the mystery of Jesus effects? A bare outline can only be sketched here. When Jesus talks about God he talks about the reign of God as present reality and future promise. This coming reign of God, depicted in parables and actions, is about establishing in the present right relationships between rich and poor, outsiders and insiders, through a new liberating praxis of love. It is important to remember, in the words of Jon Sobrino 'that Jesus came following a tradition of hope for the oppressed' and that 'the first impression he made was above all in continuity with a hope-filled tradition' of Judaism.[42] This hope-filled tradition is developed by Jesus in his preaching and praxis about the reign of God. God is experienced as active in the present in a new way through the liberating praxis of Jesus: healings, exorcisms, the offer of unconditional forgiveness, and a new table-fellowship.

A second revision of the concept of God is provoked by the Cross which reveals a God personally immersed in the pain and suffering of humanity in history. This revelation of God in Jesus stands out in sharp contrast to the immutable and omnipotent God of Greek philosophy. The God of the Cross is an involved and compassionate God – a God who suffers in and with humanity even unto death. This God, revealed in the suffering and death of Jesus, is a God of self-emptying love and self-limiting power. The God of Jesus Christ is a God who has freely chosen to limit the expression of God's power in history out of love for the gift of human freedom bestowed upon humanity in creation. A corollary to the divine self-limitation revealed in the Cross of Jesus is the freedom and therefore responsibility of humanity for the world. This freedom and responsibility is highlighted by the call of Jesus to all to participate in bringing about the reign of God in the present and the future. A joint responsibility between God and humanity, a new partnership between the divine and the human, is forged in the light of the Christ-event.

A third transformation in our understanding of God is revealed in the resurrection of Jesus which, as already noted, reveals the absolute solidarity of God with the cause of humanity, especially at that point in which humanity is most vulnerable and most at risk, namely death itself. This expression of divine solidarity with humanity in death is not simply one of effecting survival for humanity but the gratuitous offer of a radically new life symbolised by the gift of resurrection. The promise of resurrection to humanity in virtue of the resurrection of Jesus is pure gift resulting from God's solidarity with the world.

These three transformations of our image of God are given formal expression in the doctrine of the incarnation. The radical unity between God and the world, between divine and the human, between grace and freedom is summed up in the mystery of the eternal Word made flesh in Jesus. The incarnation is about the unity that obtains between God's gracious self-communication to the world and humanity's dynamic self-transcendence towards the divine. In the person of Jesus, God and humanity have become one, a divine–human threshold has been crossed, a new relationship between grace and nature has been established. Consequently the gulf between heaven and earth, between the eternal and the historical, between the divine and the human, between the sacred and the secular, between the natural and the supernatural have been overcome in Christ as the Word incarnate. From now on we glimpse heaven on earth, the eternal in the historical, God in the world, the divine in the human, the supernatural within the natural. This funda-mental unity within distinction between God and humanity has been defined by the Council of Chalcedon as that which exists 'without confu-sion and without change, without division and without separation'.

It may seem we have strayed from the question under review – 'What can we hope for?' However, an adequate Christian response to this question requires that we move beyond the monism of a this-worldly eschatology and the dualism of an other-worldly eschatology. The foun-dation of this move is the doctrine of the incarnation as outlined. Equally important in this move is the image of God operative in one's theology of hope and this is shaped by the revelation of God in Jesus. Also significant in any answer to this question is the role accorded to human responsibil-ity, and this is linked up with the historical ministry of Jesus announcing the advent of the reign of God in the present through word and deed. The source of human responsibility for the world is not simply some sense of transcendence, but rather engagement with the historical immanence of God's transcendence – however fragmentary and elusive this may be – made manifest in the mystery of Jesus.

If the world is God's creation and if creation is the sacrament of God's active co-presence to humanity, then surely the object of hope must embrace this world as well as the next world. More specifically, if the mis-sion and ministry of Jesus is focused on the actual presence of God's reign in this world as well as something that is to come, then Christian hope must be directed to this life and the next. A central part of the mission of Jesus was about bringing good news to the poor, release to cap-tives, sight to the blind, and liberty to the oppressed in a manner that engendered hope in this life. These worldly objectives must surely belong to Christian hope today. The realisation of these hopes is provisional, frag-mentary and anticipatory of the full dawning of the reign of God; yet it was these fragmentary anticipations of the reign of God that activated and sustained hope for the disciples of Jesus in the promised realisation of the reign of God. Without some experience of good news, freedom and a new vision of life, references to the next world become dangerously close to escapism. In this sense, a hope which abandons this world is not in con-tinuity with the this-worldly hope of the preaching and praxis of Jesus and therefore cannot be called a truly Christian hope. To abandon hope for this world is to vacate the co-presence of God in this life from the movements of creation and history. To talk about primary and secondary hope runs the risk of playing down the seriousness of hope for this life. The prophetic preaching and praxis of Jesus for the reign of God within this world cannot be reduced to secondary importance.

Consequently, in answer to the question 'What can we hope for?', a complementary emphasis must be given to a this-worldly hope as well as an other-worldly hope. The logic of recognising the world as God's creation and of affirming God's personal incarnation in Jesus and God's ongoing sacramental presence in the Christian community carries with it hope for this world and the next life. A unity within a distinction between this-worldly and other-worldly hope must permeate Christian eschatology. In effect, Christian hope embraces this life and the next life. We are faced, therefore, in this debate as in so many theological questions, with what Karl Barth has called the 'blessed *and*' of catholic theology. Christian hope embraces this life *and* the next life, the immanence of God in the world *and* the transcendence of God, divine presence in history *and* in eternity. Christian hope for the next life must assume an incarnational presence in this life if it is to be more than a wishful projection.

While it would not be accurate to say that the Second Vatican Council formally addressed this question about hope, nonetheless it is true that the *Pastoral Constitution on the Church in the Modern World* (1964) did lay down principles which go beyond the dualism of classical and neo-scholastic eschatology. On several occasions that Constitution says that 'Hope in a life to come does not take away from the importance of the duties of this life on earth but rather adds to it by giving new motives for fulfilling those duties.'[43] Further, the same document goes on to say that there is an internal relationship and unity between hope for this life and the world to come. While it distinguishes clearly between earthly progress and growth of Christ's kingdom, it also states that the cultivation of this world is able 'to make ready the material of the celestial realm' and 'is able to give some kind of foreshadowing of the new age'.[44] In addition, this pastoral constitution also takes account explicitly of what we have called the new and changed context of modernity in which hope finds itself by pointing out that this new context has given rise to 'the birth of a new humanism, one in which man is defined first of all by his responsibility towards his brothers and history'.[45] This new humanism and the sense of responsibility it generates is grounded in hope for this world and therefore coincides with important aspects of Christian hope.

It was these perspectives, especially of the *Pastoral Constitution on the Church in the Modern World*, that paved the way for the development of political, liberation, feminist and ecological theologies in more recent times – each of which has a strong though by no means exclusive emphasis on this-worldly hopes. These developments in turn have been accompanied by the articulation of the social teaching of the Church

which assumes both this-worldly and other-worldly eschatologies. Two
examples will suffice to illustrate the point in question. The 1971 Synod
prophetically declares that: 'Action on behalf of justice and participation
in the transformation of the world fully appear to us as a constitutive
dimension of the preaching of the Gospel.'[46] This emphasis on the
this-worldly dimension of the Gospel is also taken up by Paul VI in his
Apostolic Exhortation on *Evangelisation in the Modern World* which
asserts: 'The Church . . . has the duty to proclaim the liberation of millions
of human beings, many of whom are our own children – the duty of
assisting the birth of this liberation, of giving witness to it, of ensuring
that it is complete.'[47]

Action for justice and assisting the birth of liberation of people are
premised on hope for this life. These conciliar and post-conciliar
developments have had the effect of inserting the praxis of liberation in
history within the horizon of Christian hope. In more recent times, since
the mid-1980s, the work of justice has come to embrace the care of the
earth. Thus Christian hope includes as intrinsic to itself hope for justice,
peace and the integrity of creation both in this life as well as the next life.
A new appreciation is emerging of the radical unity of hope that exists
between the mystical and political, contemplation and action, liberation
and salvation.

The concluding word on this discussion about what can we hope for
must be given to contemporary poets. The Irish poet and Nobel Prize
recipient, Seamus Heaney, captures much of the above debate in his now
famous and widely quoted lines:

> History says, *Don't hope*
> *on this side of the grave.*
> But then once in a lifetime
> the longed-for tidal wave
> of justice can rise up
> and hope and history rhyme.[48]

The longed-for tidal wave has appeared in the prophets of Israel and in
the life of Jesus; it continues to appear in our own times in liberation, ecological and feminist movements. Contemporary examples include the
Jewish–Palestine peace accord, the end of apartheid in South Africa, and
the fragile peace process in the north of Ireland. The praxis of Christian
hope is indeed about hope and history rhyming in this life.

Equally evocative are the words of the American poet Denise Levertov
dedicated to the memory of Karen Silkwood and Eliot Gralla:

We have only begun
to love the earth.
We have only begun
to imagine the fulness of life.
How could we tire of hope?
– so much is in bud.
How can desire fail?
– we have only begun
to imagine justice and mercy,
only begun to envision . . .
we have only begun to know
the power that is in us if we could join
our solitudes in the communion of struggle.
So much is unfolding that must
complete its gesture,
so much is in bud.[49]

9

RETRIEVING THE *ESCHATA*

A truth that is merely handed on, without being thought anew from its very foundations, has lost its vital power.

(Hans Urs von Balthasar)

H AVING STRESSED THE PRIMACY of the *Eschaton* over the *eschata* in Chapter 2 and having examined the advent of the *Eschaton* in Christ in the last two chapters, we are now in a position to look at some of the individual *eschata*: death, heaven and hell, and purgatory. We have already seen that one factor contributing to the current crisis in eschatology has been the divorce of the *eschata* from the advent of the *Eschaton* in Christ. Indeed from the Middle Ages onwards the individual *eschata* had very little direct connection with the paschal reality of the death and resurrection of Christ. Any reconstruction of the *eschata*, therefore, must seek to recover at least the christomorphic character of the *Eschaton*. A further difficulty in classical eschatology is its pre-Copernican intellectual framework, or what others have referred to as its strange 'supernatural geography'.[1] This difficulty has been compounded by literalisation of this supernatural geography by the popular mind. This particular difficulty demands that any re-examination of the *eschata* must at least take account of the emerging post-modern, relational and cosmocentric anthropologies. If the literalisation of eschatological symbols is to be avoided, then a more rigorous application of the hermeneutical principles discussed in Chapter 2 must be invoked. An additional problem with classical eschatology has been its excessively juridical approach to God's gift of salvation in Christ. This legal emphasis can be seen in the language of satisfaction, expiation and the payment of debt due to sin. This kind of eschatological discourse operates with images of God that do not reflect adequately the revelation of God as love in the life of Jesus.

Attempts to retrieve the *eschata*, therefore, must take account of these difficulties and seek to be in touch with human experience, a reconstructed anthropology and the mystery of Christ.

INDIVIDUAL DEATH

Among the *eschata* perhaps the hardest one to talk about is death. It is ironic that so much can be said about heaven and hell and so little about death. The refusal to take death seriously is one of the outstanding characteristics of contemporary culture. As noted in Chapter 4 we live in a death-denying culture and this has life-denying consequences. Not only contemporary culture but contemporary theology is also relatively silent about death – with some notable exceptions.[2] And yet it is death that poses serious questions about the meaning of life and the presence of God in the world. It is only when one has fully accepted the disturbing reality of one's own death and perhaps even more importantly the death of others that one can authentically know God in hope. Indeed the cultural conspiracy to cover over death is in part connected with the decline of hope in God. By this we do not mean to imply that God is some kind of refuge or great escape from the troubling issue of death since there is abundant evidence that believers and unbelievers alike find death difficult to accept.

The question of death challenges all our images of God, especially the images of the all-powerful, unrelational and monarchical God. Although these classical images of God cannot be totally dismissed they only assume their real significance after some appreciation of the Christian God as radically relational and incarnational. More specifically the question of death challenges our understanding of the human self. The self is threatened in so many different ways today: by the ever-increasing bureaucratisation of society, the decline of community values and the rise of competitive capitalism. The human self is endangered by an inward-looking self-centred individualism. The crisis in anthropology discussed in Chapter 3 influences the way we perceive death. The contemporary culture of individualism makes it increasingly difficult to hope beyond death because hope is something that takes place in communion with others and is grounded in a deep awareness of the incompleteness of the human self – two particular responses that lie outside the contemporary cult of individualism.

In trying to work out a theology of death we need to draw on the relational character of the human self already developed in Chapter 3. The human self is derivative in origin and likewise equally derivative in destiny. The first step in approaching the question of death is the need to decentre the self from its own isolation in order to recentre the self in its radical relatedness with others, the cosmos and the Triune God. Thus the first step, as seen in Chapter 5, in the genesis of hope is the realisation of our belongingness to each other and the life of the cosmos and the mystery of God. Only when this relationality of the human self has been discovered can we think of facing death with some kind of hope.

It is from within this relational context that we must ask what is it from life that survives death? Does anything remain after the destruction of death? For many it is sufficient to affirm some form of social immortality in terms of family, artistic creativity, or some other contribution to the human enterprise. This popular response has been given considerable sophistication through the work of Charles Hartshorne who under the influence of Alfred Whitehead argues in favour of objective immortality in God without positing any subjective immortality. For others there is the dualism which affirms the immortality of the soul after death. A third position gaining popularity is one that sees the human self as evolutionary and that death is simply a step within the evolutionary spiral.

In contrast to these views I want to suggest an eschatology of communion, that is an eschatology which affirms communion with God initiated in this life through first and second grace which cannot be broken by death but is rather transformed in death. Death is not about transition but transformation, not about mere continuity but recreation. The radical relationship existing between God and the individual *ab initio* and sustained historically by grace throughout life is taken up and transformed in death. What survives in death is the radical relationality of the human self which is transformed by the Trinitarian God who is the fullness of relationality in communion. The myriad relationships that make up human identity, especially those that require decentring and recentring, as well as the dialectic of living and dying survive death and are transformed by God in their own unique distinctiveness into a New Creation and communion in Christ. In saying this we must realistically recognise the definitive finality of life as we know it in death and at the same time affirm an openness to the radically new. The moment in which the human is most helpless, namely death, is precisely the moment in which God is most creative. As Werner Jeanrond points out: 'Where we become totally powerless in death, God becomes powerful. Where we cannot do anything any longer God is there for us.'[3]

In support of an eschatology of communion I wish to draw on three distinct though related arguments, namely the fundamental and final option theories, the underlying unity of creation, redemption and the consummation of all things in Christ, and the challenge to face death within the memory of the Cross of Christ. The 'final option theory' about death has been put forward by Ladislaus Boros in an influential book entitled *The Mystery of Death* .[4] According to Boros 'Death is man's first completely personal act, and is, therefore, by reason of its very being, the place above all others for the awakening of consciousness, for freedom, for encounter with God, for the final decision about eternal destiny.'[5] Although Boros does not ignore the individual acts that have taken place before death he does seem to exaggerate or give excessive weight to the final moment of death. In spite of the fact that Boros was a student of Rahner and seeks to invoke his teacher Rahner, nonetheless Rahner himself has expressed some dissatisfaction with Boros' final option theory:

> . . . to ascribe to the moment of medical disease a theological signifi-
> cance that cannot belong to any moment in the rest of life, to assert that
> in the moment of clinical death and only at that point there occurs
> man's real and comprehensive act of freedom in the total disposal of
> his existence for or against God . . . is an assertion which is not proba-
> ble in the light of empirical psychology and biology (and) can be
> supported only with the aid of ideas savouring up mythology, and
> which theologically is neither probable nor necessary.[6]

Rahner prefers to focus on the importance of what has gone on in life before death and suggests that this has influence on the personal act of dying. Above all Rahner, mirroring the influence of Heidegger, empha-sises that dying is something that is going on throughout life in a variety of different ways in acts of love, forgiveness, standing up for the truth, acting with compassion, doing justice, and caring for others. Death, therefore, is not an act simply coming at the end of life; it is something that permeates the whole of life and enables living. In this sense a close relationship exists between the way we live, what is often called our fundamental option, and the way we die, namely our final option. Given this unity between living and dying throughout life and especially at death Rahner sees the final act of dying as something in which we fully participate and describes this final act as a maturing self-realisation which embodies the results of what the individual has made of himself or herself during this life, namely the achievement of self-possession.[7]

Consistent with what has already been said about death in Chapter 4, especially the dialectic between living and dying as well as dying and living and what has also been said about the beginning of resurrection in this life in Chapter 8, our fundamental thesis about death is that the divine–human communion with God initiated in this life through first and second grace is not broken but transformed in death.

The Fathers of the early Church expressed this important theological truth by holding that in death there is destruction so that there may be reconstruction, that is, the disintegration of death results in reintegration through the creative power of the Spirit of God. The Fathers of the early Church likened the human condition to that of a work of art containing a flaw, as in a piece of sculpture, which needs to be broken down so that it may be fully restored. Death within this context is perceived as a process of human disintegration and divine reintegration.

The God who created the human out of love is the same God who recreates the human in death into a New Creation. The first creation is a *creatio ex nihilo*. The second creation is a multilayered process of recreation influenced by the grace of historical existence, shaped by the second grace of the gift of redemption in Christ, and completed by the third grace of the love of God's creativity expressed paradoxically in death itself.

The first creation is the foundation of our hope for life beyond death. If we have been loved into existence by God the Creator, and this is the heart of the Christian doctrine of creation, then we can dare to hope beyond death. The doctrine of creation is the first ground of hope beyond death and it was this foundation that the Jews kept on returning to in their troubled history of success and failure. The New Creation established embryonically 'in Christ' is the confirmation of that initial creation-based hope turning it into Christian hope. What happened in the life, death and resurrection of Jesus prefigures the future of the human race and the world. The drama of christology is a microcosm of the drama facing humanity and the world to come. The story of the Christ-event is the story of creation. This concentration of creation within the Christ-event continues to take place in the present in and through the creative activity of the Spirit of God in the world – a Spirit that draws humanity and history to a point of fulfilment and completion in Christ. The focal point of this drama is the reality of personal death that takes place in the shadow of the Cross of Christ.

This focus on the unity of the fundamental and final options and on the link between creation, redemption and consummation of all things in Christ does not remove the awesome reality of individual death. How can the Christian face death with hope in his or her heart? How can the Christian confront the darkness of personal death?

Honesty requires an acknowledgment that there is no easy way around the threatening reality of death. At the same time, however, the

Christian is surely someone who approaches the crisis of personal death within the memory of the death of Christ on the Cross. The memory of the Cross of Christ enables the individual to face death with hope knowing in the first instance that Christ died out of solidarity with the human race and that now in death we die in solidarity with the death of Christ. It is the Cross that is the great sign of hope for the individual in death. An essential element within the memory of the Cross of Christ is the personal act of self-surrender made by Christ in the face of death: 'Into your hands O Lord I commend my spirit.' Care must be taken not to romanticise this moment which we know from the Gospel narrative was prefaced by a disturbing sense of abandonment by God (Matt. 27:46). Death, individual death, every death is an apparent abandonment by God the Creator – the Creator who graced us with life appears to abandon us in death just as he appeared to have abandoned Christ in death. And yet the central claim of Christianity is that God did not abandon Christ in death, that God transformed the dead Christ into a living New Creation, that this New Creation is described in a plurality of terms such as glorification, exaltation, resurrection, ascension and Pentecost, that this initially God-forsaken but ultimately glorious destiny of Christ is the prototype of the destiny of every individual in death. In this important sense the Christian faces death with his or her eyes fixed on the death of Christ, dying as it were within the liberating memory of the Cross.

HEAVEN AND HELL

Heaven and hell have a habit of appearing in surveys and in discussions about religion as if they were equal sides of the one coin and therefore of the same theological importance. It must be stated from the very beginning that heaven and hell do not enjoy the same philosophical or theological status within Christian eschatology. Karl Rahner has consistently pointed out that 'The eschatology of salvation (heaven) and of loss (hell)' are not on the same plane[8] and that the human capacity to say 'Yes' or 'No' to God belong to two different orders. For Rahner there is only one predestination within Christian eschatology and that is the victorious grace of Christ offered to the world.[9] This does not mean that we eliminate the possibility of damnation; eternal loss always remains a disturbing possibility in virtue of the human freedom to reject God but it must be remembered that this human freedom is already surrounded and upheld by the grace of God given in creation and redemption. In other words where sin exists, grace abounds all the more in the light of the Christ-event.

In a somewhat similar vein Hans Urs von Balthasar suggests that in the Old Testament there was a symmetrical relationship between reward and punishment. The individual was faced with equal possibilities, says von Balthasar, in the Old Testament. However, after the Christ-event there has been a radical 'change of the ages' and from now on there is a 'fundamental asymmetry' between heaven and hell in virtue of the saving death and resurrection of Christ.[10]

This basic difference between heaven and hell is clearly evidenced by the historical fact that neither Scripture nor the Church has ever judged anyone to be in hell whereas both sources have confidently declared many people to be in heaven. In spite of this, hell has had a prominent place in preaching over the centuries and indeed many would argue an exaggerated importance. A good example of this can be found in Joyce's *Dubliners* which contains a typical and by all accounts an accurate portrayal of the prominence hell played in preaching in the early 1900s. This preoccupation with hell illustrates how far Christian eschatology had strayed from its christological core and how influential a juridical understanding of God had become. What is needed in contemporary eschatology is not a denial of the possibility of hell but a modification of the prominent place it has had within the Christian tradition, especially throughout the second millennium. Primacy must be restored to the good news of salvation in Christ which is offered to all and the practical implications that this has for the way we order life in the present.

While the Christian doctrine of heaven has roots in the Jewish Scriptures it nonetheless acquires its own particular shape in and through the mystery of Christ. A number of particular images rooted in the life and destiny of Jesus are used in the New Testament to convey the meaning of heaven. For example, heaven is described as the coming reign of God announced by Jesus. This new reign of God is about establishing right relationships in this life which include God and are fulfilled in the next life (Matt. 25:31–46). Heaven is also described as eternal life which is described in terms of knowing God and Jesus Christ whom God sent (John 17:3). Other images of heaven in the New Testament include that of the wedding feast (Matt. 25:10) and the experience of having a vision of God (Matt. 5:8). Each of these images, the reign of God, eternal life, the wedding feast and the vision of God is mediated by the relationship we have with Christ, especially the crucified and risen Christ who is the way, the truth and the life. Heaven, in effect, is about being in personal communion with the paschal Christ who introduces the human person to the eternal life of the Trinitarian God. Personal union with Christ has socially and ultimately cosmic implications. Thus we find that the later writings of the New Testament talk about heaven in terms ultimately of a 'new heaven and a new earth' as well as a 'New Creation'. And yet in spite of these rich and varied images we are reminded that it has not yet been revealed what the future will be like beyond simply stating that when God appears we shall be like him (1 John 3:2).

From the Middle Ages onwards heaven is described almost exclusively in terms of the beatific vision. This particular account of heaven owes much to the constitution of Pope Benedict XII, *Benedictus Deus*, promulgated in 1336 which stated that the souls of the just 'see the divine essence with an intuitive vision and even face to face without the mediation of any creature by way of object of vision; rather the divine essence immediately manifests itself to them plainly, clearly and openly, and in this vision they enjoy the divine essence'.[11] This definition of Benedict influenced all subsequent eschatology down to the present day.

The vision of God, especially the Trinitarian God, is of course the centrepiece of heaven but the whole point to the mystery of Christ, especially in terms of the incarnation, death and resurrection, is to mediate the life of God to humanity. Christ is the mediator, the new and eternal mediator between God and humanity and the world. Karl Rahner more than any other theologian in this century has sought to recover the mediating role of Christ in eschatology. For Rahner it is the humanity of Christ, especially the glorified humanity, which mediates the immediacy of God to the individual, humanity and the world:[12] 'the humanity of Jesus is the medium through which our immediate relationship with God is achieved'.[13] Neglect of this mediating role of the glorified humanity of Christ in eschatology has had a distorting effect on our understanding of the individual *eschata*. For one thing it has resulted in an excessive individualism which by-passes Christ, reducing eschatology to a private relationship between the individual and God. As a result there has been up to the middle of this century considerable neglect of the social and cosmic implications of eschatology. The work of social justice and the care of creation are of fundamental importance to any eschatology. In the words of Vatican II we will find these different activities 'freed of stain, burnished and transfigured . . . when Christ hands over to the Father a kingdom eternal and universal: "a kingdom of truth and of love, of holiness and grace, of justice, of love and peace"'.[14]

Heaven, therefore, is about sharing in the fullness and communion of God's Triune life in a manner that incorporates the historical unity between the self, society and the world. This unity between God and the world has been established in the crucified and risen Christ who is the eternal Word of God made flesh. Not only humanity but the cosmos has been adopted and accepted by God in and through the death and bodily resurrection of Christ. It is the paschal Christ as the eternal Word of God made flesh who mediates, opens up and inserts humanity and the world into the eternal life of the Trinity. In particular it is by being in communion with Christ in this life through baptism and especially the Eucharist that we gain access to the relational life of the Triune God in eternity. We become adopted sons and daughters of God the Father in Christ through the life-giving energy of the Spirit poured out into the world. In this sense heaven is something that begins in this life and not just after death; it is about historical and eternal communion with God in Christ through the Spirit – a communion opened up and mediated by the crucified and glorified humanity of Christ. The by-passing of Christ and his mediating role in history and eternity has given rise to an eschatological mysticism that neglects the social and cosmic challenges of a truly Christian eschatology.

Heaven, therefore, according to Christian eschatology is about participating in the eternal life of God in and through the glorified humanity of Christ; it is about communion with one another and the world in God through the mediation of Christ as the second person of the Blessed Trinity. In highlighting the mediating role of Christ it becomes necessary to say that entry into heaven at death is more than 'absorption into God' or 'dying into God'[15] or being retained objectively in the memory of God.[16] These particular descriptions play down the importance of human subjectivity and the significance of the mediating role of Christ in understanding heaven.

Within this christocentric understanding it is important to retain the link between human experience and heaven. This link is to be found in the hope for human fulfilment, the yearning for wholeness and the passion for communion. These experiences and others are activated by human acceptance and forgiveness, by healing and reconciliation, and above all the offer of love or indeed the hunger for love in virtue of its absence.

In contrast to the theological reality of heaven, the concept of hell is primarily a statement about the seriousness of human freedom and its potential for absolute self-isolation. If heaven can be described in the extroverted terms of the joy that issues from relationality and communion, then hell is about the darkness that results from freely chosen negative introversion and self-isolation. Heaven is a theological affirmation about God's intention for the world whereas hell is a statement about the possible frustration by human freedom of that divine plan for every human being. It must be stated clearly, therefore, that hell is not God's creation, that hell is not the outcome of some additional divine sentence for punishment or retribution, that hell is not 'a place' to which God sends sinners. Instead hell is a freely chosen human creation, entailing the punishment and suffering that results from a persistent lifestyle of self-isolation in deliberate opposition to God's permanent call to communion.

The source of much thinking in Christian circles about hell goes back to the Jewish Scriptures and at times some of that thinking seems to have persisted without taking account of its transformation brought about by the good news of Jesus Christ. It needs to be said that different expressions of hell can be found in ancient Greek and Roman cultures as well as the Hebrew and Christian Scriptures.[17] These expressions of hell arise from a convergence of ideas about divine punishment, retribution, justice and judgment.

Within Judaism the dead were confined to a shadowy and nameless existence in a place called *Sheol* which existed under the earth in contrast to the heavens above. Gradually, the belief developed that God would reward the just and punish the wicked at the end of time. This gave rise to a division of *Sheol* into two levels – one for the just in paradise, and the other for the wicked in *Gehenna*. The judgment involved seems to be one of divine retribution, a judgment sometimes described in terms of two equally possible ways of salvation or damnation.

The principal case for hell in the teaching of Jesus is to be found in the parable of the sheep and goats (Matt. 25:31–46), the parable of the talents (Matt. 25:14–30), and the reference to the unforgivable sin against the Holy Spirit which carries eternal guilt (Mark 3:29; Matt. 12:32). Also significant is the teaching of Jesus about the debtors who are thrown into prison and who will not get out until they have paid the last penny (Matt. 5:25–6) – a view which seems to qualify the eternity of hell. This teaching of Jesus clearly affirms the possibility of hell without however claiming that anyone is in fact in hell. Whether Jesus is putting forward a new doctrine of hell or simply referring to the existing belief about hell as a way of exhorting people to faith and repentance is a matter of debate which is not easily resolved. What does seem clear in the teaching of Jesus is that hell is a real possibility for those who choose permanently to ignore God's offer of grace in history.

In addition to this teaching of Jesus on hell, there is in the New Testament the tantalisingly brief reference to the descent of Jesus into hell after his death. This New Testament symbol which is an article of faith in the Apostles' Creed and prominent in eastern Christianity has in recent times become the subject of considerable theological attention, especially in the writings of Hans Urs von Balthasar and Karl Rahner. Suffice it here to note that the new *Catechism of the Catholic Church* quotes an ancient homily for Holy Saturday night explaining most eloquently the theological richness of this neglected Christian symbol:

> He (Christ) has gone to search for Adam, our first father, as for a lost sheep. Greatly desiring to visit those who live in darkness and in the shadow of death, he has gone to free from sorrow Adam in his bonds and Eve, captive with him – He who is both their God and the son of Eve . . . 'I am your God, who for your sake have become your son . . . I order you, O sleeper to awake. I did not create you to be a prisoner in hell. Rise from the dead, for I am the life of the dead.'[18]

This highly symbolic expression of Christ's solidarity with sinners and the offer of universal salvation it implies must surely be allowed to influence the shape of Christian eschatology in the future, especially in regard to the doctrine of hell. In the past the descent of Christ into hell received considerable attention in the apocryphal Gospels and the icons of the Byzantine church as well as becoming the subject of a mystery play entitled 'The Harrowing of Hell' in thirteenth-century England.

It is the rich symbolism associated with the descent of Christ into hell alongside a contemporary recovery of the soteriological significance of the death and resurrection of Christ that justifies the asymmetrical relationship that exists between heaven and hell within Christian eschatology.

Allowing for this fundamental difference between heaven and hell, theology has differed in its accounts of hell. The traditional view about hell emphasises the reality of eternal punishment stressing the pain that results from freely choosing to cut oneself off from the love of God. In more recent times some theologians talk about a kind of self-annihilation resulting from anthropological isolation[19] and others hold out for hell as 'being with no one at all' which they describe as 'the indefinite (and so, non-definite) persistence or endurance of a free "No" to God' that does not achieve 'finality or eternity' because the proper finality of human freedom as a gift from God is God.[20]

The extinction model of hell has come to the fore in recent times through the 1996 report of the Doctrine Commission of the Church of England entitled *The Mystery of Salvation*, which says that hell 'is not eternal torment' but rather 'total non being' and 'annihilation'.[21] The difficulty with the annihilationist model is that it goes against the grain of the Christian understanding of God: God as the Creator of heaven and earth, Christ as the Redeemer of the world, and the Spirit as the Giver of life. This understanding of God is powerfully expressed by Jesus when he talks about 'The God of Abraham, the God of Isaac, and the God of Jacob' as the 'God not of the dead but of the living' (Mark 12:26–7; Matt. 22:32). There is something incongruous about affirming God as a God of the living alongside a hypothesis about hell as the annihilation of people. For this reason preference must be expressed for a view of hell as the possibility of a form of self-isolation and absolute aloneness resulting from a deliberate turning away from all communion with others and God. This possibility of turning away from communion with others and God must always be balanced by reference to the primacy of God's omnipresent offer of salvation to all in this life – a point we will take up in the next chapter.

PURGATORY

The next *eschata*, Purgatory, is a very good example of the theological principle *lex orandi, lex credendi,* namely that liturgical praxis influences the shape of what we believe. The practice of remembering the dead in prayer is found in the Jewish and Christian Scriptures, and is given liturgical expression in the early centuries of Christianity in the celebration of the Eucharist. It was not until the thirteenth century, however, that the doctrine of Purgatory was given formal ecclesial expression by way of response to this ancient Christian practice. Here we will review briefly the practice of praying for the dead, the teaching of the Church on Purgatory, and then seek to retrieve its meaning for contemporary eschatology.[22]

It would be contrived to suggest or even imply that a Christian doctrine of Purgatory is given in the Bible. In truth there is no direct, explicit evidence in Scripture for the existence of Purgatory. What we do find in the Jewish–Christian Scriptures, however, are some few references to the practice of praying for the dead: 2 Macc. 12:42–5 recounts how Judas Maccabeus 'took up a collection . . . and sent it to Jerusalem to provide for a sin offering' to make atonement on behalf of Jewish soldiers who had died in battle carrying idols of Jamnia which were forbidden by law. The implication here is that the prayer and sacrifice for the dead will help to deliver these soldiers from their sin. In looking at this text we must be careful not to read back too much into this particular incident. What is striking about the event is the evident expression of solidarity which seems to exist between the living and the dead.

The other text frequently referred to concerning Purgatory is 1 Corinthians 3:12–15:

Now if anyone builds on the foundation with gold, silver, precious stones, wood, hay, straw – the work of each builder will become visible, for the Day will disclose it because it will be revealed with fire, and the fire will test what sort of work each has done. If what has been built and the foundations survives, the builder will receive a reward. If the work is burned up, the builder will suffer loss; the builder will be saved but only as through fire.

The context here is a quarrel going on in the Corinthian church about the work of Paul and Apollos in building up the community. The reference to fire in the text is primarily the fire associated with the final judgment and is not really concerned with the purification of sins by fire immediately after death. To this extent the text is not, strictly speaking, about what has subsequently become known as Purgatory. Nevertheless this text was taken up by many of the early Fathers and used to work out a theory of purification by fire after death before entering Paradise. The symbol most frequently invoked is that of 'The Flaming Sword' which acts like a temporary sanctifying fire on the soul preparing it for Paradise. For example, Clement of Alexandria says in the *Stromata* that sinners who die reconciled with God but without time to do penance are 'sanctified' by 'a fire which is not a consuming fire like the fire of a forge, but an intelligent fire which penetrates the soul traversed by it'.[23] Similar ideas can also be found in Origen, Cyril of Jerusalem, Basil, and Gregory Nazianazen who also invoke 1 Corinthians 3:12–15. Gregory of Nyssa captures much of this patristic perspective when he says that 'no one can share in divinity who has not by means of a purifying fire purified his soul of stains with which it is marked'.[24]

It should be remembered that the background to this patristic theology is the existing liturgical practice of praying for the dead. This practice is present in Eucharistic celebrations as early as the second century. For example the Roman Canon and the Eucharistic prayer of Basil explicitly remember and pray for the dead. The Christian community remembers the faithful departed and makes intercession on their behalf. The underlying supposition is that the dead may still have need of forgiveness for their sins before entering eternal life.

By the fourth century the liturgy of Christian burial also included the practice of offering the Eucharist for the dead. In addition to this Eucharistic practice there was also the early Penitential practice which posited that those who sinned after baptism could only be restored to communion after doing penance for their sins. If they died before completing their penance, it was estimated that their penance could be continued and completed after death through a process of purgation. This early Christian practice of praying for the dead in the celebration of the Eucharist seems to imply a process or action of purification after death before entry into Paradise.

The practice of praying for the dead and the thinking associated with it received special representation in medieval art. When the practice does receive doctrinal definition in the Middle Ages, particular care is taken to avoid the use of the word 'fire' or the possibility of giving the impression that Purgatory is a 'place'. The first official teaching on Purgatory derives from a profession of faith required of the Emperor Michael Paleologus in 1267 which was adopted by the Second Council of Lyons in 1274. That Council says that the souls of the faithful who have died 'truly penitent and in charity' are 'purified after death by purifying pains' and that 'the prayers of the living serve to relieve their pains'.[25] This same teaching is repeated almost verbatim at the Council of Florence in 1439 in its decree for the Greeks. Given the difference between the Greeks who saw Purgatory as a process of maturation and the Latins who focused more on the need for satisfaction/expiation the Council is careful to exclude reference to 'fire' and to avoid any description of Purgatory as 'a place'.

The Council of Trent towards the end of its deliberations, reacting against the reformers reaffirms 'the doctrine of Purgatory passed on by the Fathers and earlier Councils'. It issues a timely appeal for caution in preaching concerning details about Purgatory. Trent also emphasises primarily the value of prayers and the offering of the sacrifice of the altar for the souls of the departed.

The Second Vatican Council in its dogmatic Constitution on the Church, *Lumen Gentium*, makes passing reference to Purgatory:

This most sacred Synod accepts with great devotion the venerable faith of our ancestors regarding this vital fellowship with our brethren who are in heavenly glory or who still are being purified after death. It proposes again the decree of the Second Council of Nicea, the Council of Florence and the Council of Trent. At the same time, as part of its pastoral solicitude the Synod urges all concerned to work hard to prevent or correct any abuse, excesses, or defects which may have crept in here and there, and to restore all things to a more ample praise of Christ and of God.[26]

This doctrine of Purgatory is reaffirmed by the Congregation for the Doctrine of the Faith in 1979: 'The church believes there may be

purification of the elect previous to the vision of God, which is nevertheless different from the pains of the damned.'

Purgatory also receives attention in the 1991 document of the
International Theological Commission on eschatology[27] and in the new
Catechism of the Catholic Church.[28]

It is surely significant to note in the teaching of the Church the consistent reserve and appeal for caution in the way Purgatory is presented. It
should also be pointed out that descriptions of Purgatory as a place are
avoided, that references to 'fire' and the duration of Purgatory are exclud-
ed, and that statements about the nature of punishment are omitted.

In the light of this overview of the traditional teaching about
Purgatory we are now faced with a challenge of making sense of this
doctrine to the contemporary world. For many the doctrine of Purgatory
has lost credibility. The language of 'punishment due to sin' and making
satisfaction for sin, and of souls suffering for a period of time, sounds to
many quite anachronistic. Further, for some the fact that the doctrine is
not clearly taught by the Scriptures seems to give it some kind of secondary and therefore almost optional existence. Above all, the image of
God portrayed by this language seems to contradict the revelation of the
love of God in the life, death and resurrection of Jesus. In a word, the
question must be asked: Is the doctrine of Purgatory worth retrieving or
can it not be quietly forgotten about?

There can be no doubt that in the past there have been gross exaggera-
tions in popular preaching and teaching about Purgatory and that at
times more was said about the pain of Purgatory than about the love and
mercy of God. If there is to be any credible retrieval of Purgatory therefore, then it must be in terms that are connected to human experience,
anthropology and christology.

Turning to human experience, every human being senses the extraordinary distance and difference that exists between the Creator and the
creature. All too often it is clear how inadequately and poorly the
creature reflects the image of the Creator. Further, within that experience
we become aware of the tension within the human personality that exists
between the fundamental faith-option for God and the day-to-day living
out of that decision. More specifically the conversion of the individual to
God after sin often contains inner tensions and contradictions between
intention and behaviour, a strain between aims and outcomes; there are
few who would deny the presence at least of inconsistencies between
what we say and what we do in regard to our relationship with God.

This tension between what Paul called 'the good I would' and 'the evil
I do' can be developed more extensively in the context of an anthropology

of human and divine relationality. Human life and the individual person are made up of a complex network of relationships operating at different levels: physical, psychological and spiritual. At the centre of these relationships is a radical belongingness to the mystery of God and a rootedness in the stock of Adam. The human person is graced *ab initio*, invited to communion with God in Christ. This 'supernatural existential', this graced orientation of the human person, can be affirmed or denied in freedom. Indeed realism requires we acknowledge that as creatures we are caught between original blessing and original sin, between the unbounded love of God and the selfishness of the human personality, between the divine call to communion and the human propensity to self-centredness. Within this ambiguity we are faced with the offer of God's second grace in Christ, opening up the way of salvation through baptism, Eucharist and the life of discipleship. In spite of our membership in the body of Christ and the gift of a new communion in Christ, there continues to exist an inner struggle between conversion to Christ and the lure of the world in the Johannine sense. The reality of evil and selfishness persist, the possibility of sin and estrangement remain.

It is against this background that we must seek to retrieve the doctrine of Purgatory. What does it mean to talk about temporal punishment due to sin or indeed a need for purification after death? As to temporal punishment due to sin it must be stated clearly that this is not something imposed *ab externo* by a vindictive God. The temporal punishment due to sin, insofar as one can talk like this, derives not from God but from sin itself; it is a consequence flowing from the reality of sin. In turning back to God after sin, there will remain within the human personality some of the after-effects of sin: the inner contradiction embedded in the different layers of human personality between being turned once again to God, and self-centred connections and traces of selfishness that remain after conversion. The fundamental decision for God is something that takes time to unfold, permeate and transform the whole personality. Traditional theology talks about the need to engage in penance, prayer and good works after conversion in order to turn around the many different orientations and complex levels of the human personality. If one should die before fully turning around these different aspects of the human personality, then the tradition says that one is in need of Purgatory.

Another way of saying this is to talk about the fundamental relationality of the human person in this life and in death. Included in this relationality is our relationship with God which affects all other relationships. To reshape our relationship with God through conversion requires the reshaping of our relationship with others. To decentre the inward-looking self demands that we recentre an outward-looking self focused on the mystery of God. This reshaping and recentring is a process that takes time in this life; it does not happen all at once – even though the conversion to God is decisive. Whatever is left within that process at the time of death, whatever remains to be done or undone, whatever perdures of self-centredness within the human personality, is the primary concern of church teaching on Purgatory. Purgatory, therefore, is about finalising a process, or better, completing the divine–human relationship already decisively initiated by God in this life through grace and only gradually accepted from a human point of view in this life.

The question about 'when' Purgatory takes place is one that allows different answers. According to some, Purgatory can take place in this life, through penance, prayer and good works. For others, and this seems to be the emerging view, Purgatory happens in death: 'We may take it to mean that everything happens in death itself, that the "purification" in Purgatory is an aspect of death itself and can be made intelligible in the light of different characteristics of death itself.'[29] For Rahner and others[30] the process of re-integration and transformation required in the fundamental option for God takes place in death itself. A third view, less popular today, suggests that Purgatory takes place some 'time' after death.

Consistent with the second view is the presence of a shift among theologians from seeing Purgatory as a place to a moment of personal and transforming encounter with the love of God.[31] Many, including Ratzinger, caution against quantifying the 'transforming moment of this encounter with God as either "long" or "short"'.[32]

So far we have spoken about the after-effects of sin on the human personality as the basis of Purgatory. More important in any understanding of Purgatory is an awareness *coram Deo* (before God) of how much we need to change and to be changed in this life and in death in virtue of the infinite love and mercy of God, especially as this has been made manifest in Jesus as the crucified and risen one. The unconditional love of God offered to humanity in Christ calls forth in this life and in death a personal response that involves a purging conversion and transformation. That response is ultimately one of being configured to the crucified and risen Christ both in this life and in death. Anyone who is in touch with the ambiguous dispositions of the human self and who has at the same time some sense of the gracious forgiving love of God will hardly find it difficult to accept that eternal life with God will require a radical transformation and adjustment in the life of the individual; it is this transformation and adjustment that is at issue in the doctrine of Purgatory.

10

DISPUTED QUESTIONS IN ESCHATOLOGY

Salvation from death preoccupies much of the western world, but the state beyond death remains a troubled question mark.
(The Doctrine Commission of the Church of England, 1995)

IT WILL BE CLEAR from the last chapter that a host of questions remain unanswered: What happens between death and the end of the world? When does resurrection take place? Where does the second coming of Christ fit into a contemporary eschatology? Will many people be saved? What are we to make of claims about the possibility of a second chance in life through a process of rebirth? These questions do not admit of clear-cut, ready-made answers. Of all the areas of theology, eschatology more than most calls for humility and diffidence. We know very little about the next life, especially when it comes to particular details. The experience of hope, especially Christian hope, opens up a variety of perspectives on the future. However, care must be taken not to allow hope to be overtaken by exaggerated claims about the future. Hope must be allowed to remain hope; that is, a knowledge embracing a 'bright-darkness', a *chiaroscuro*, relating to the future. At the same time this must not prevent us from trying to address contemporary questions while acknowledging that we are often moving into the realm of disputed, controversial and sometimes speculative issues. We will confine ourselves in this chapter to the following complex, disputed questions: the so-called intermediate state and its relationship to resurrection, the possibility of universal salvation, and the question of reincarnation.

THE INTERMEDIATE STATE, INDIVIDUAL RESURRECTION AND THE *PAROUSIA*

According to classical eschatology the answer to the question 'What happens at death?' is that in death there is a separation of the body and soul, followed by the body going back into the earth to await the general resurrection of the dead and the soul as immortal entering into eternity to enjoy the beatific vision. This classical eschatology was reaffirmed by the Congregation for the Doctrine of Faith in Rome in 1979:

> The church affirms that a spiritual element survives and subsists after death, an element endowed with consciousness and will, so that the 'human self' subsists, though deprived for the present of the complement of its body. To designate this element the church uses the word 'soul', the accepted term in the usage of scripture and tradition.[1]

This statement has been developed at length in an important document issued by the International Theological Commission in 1992 entitled 'Some Current Questions in Eschatology'. If the statement by the Congregation for the Doctrine of the Faith in 1979 was striking for its brevity, then the document of the International Theological Commission is striking for its length.[2]

The document of the Theological Commission amplifies the position stated by the Congregation for the Doctrine of the Faith in 1979. It does this by developing what it calls an 'anthropology of duality', an 'eschatology of souls' and a 'twofold phase' eschatology. By an 'anthropology of duality' it means 'a duality of elements (the 'body-soul' schema) which can be separated so that one of them ('the spiritual and the immortal soul') subsists and endures separately'[3] in what is known as the intermediate state. This anthropology of duality is the foundation of the 'eschatology of souls', which asserts that the separated soul exists in an intermediate state and that finally it is reunited with its body at the end of time with the second coming of Christ.[4] This presentation of classical eschatology is reaffirmed in the 1992 *Catechism of the Catholic Church*.[5]

Statements promulgated by the Church are rarely issued in a vacuum and this is certainly the case regarding the documents of the CDF in 1979, the International Theological Commission in 1992 and the new Catechism of 1992. Part of the background and context here is a theological controversy that has been taking place in Germany since the 1970s. Certain theologians in Germany had become uneasy with the classical position about what happens in death and they put forward what has been called an eschatology of 'resurrection in death'. These theologians, unhappy with the dualism of classical anthropology and eschatology, proposed a view of the total death of the person in death followed by the immediate resurrection of the person in death, thereby doing away with the need for the second coming of Christ. In effect, resurrection and *Parousia* take place for each person in the moment of death.[6] This particular thesis has been rigorously refuted by Professor Joseph Ratzinger, the theologian,[7] and Cardinal Joseph Ratzinger, the Prefect of the Congregation for the Doctrine of Faith. This particular German debate has influenced statements by the magisterium of the Church since the 1970s.

Walter Kasper has described the controversy as an 'overdrawn polemic' characterised by 'mutual misunderstanding' and 'impassioned language'.[8] Peter Phan describes Ratzinger's response to the thesis of resurrection in death 'as excessively sweeping and labouring under non-sequiturs'.[9]

The issues involved in this controversy may be summarised first of all in terms of the immortality of the soul versus the resurrection of the body – a debate which of course is older than this particular controversy of the 1970s between Ratzinger and certain theologians in Germany.[10] The problem here is ultimately one of anthropology. The second issue is about the relationship that exists between individual eschatology and collective eschatology, that is the relation between the destiny of the individual in death and the significance of the second coming of Christ.

To the outsider these questions may seem rather academic, but in reality they are more than merely matters of academic interest; they are of considerable existential significance in their implications. The way these questions are answered affects the credibility of eschatology in general and its relationship to the rest of theology. Further, these issues have a direct bearing on the pastoral practice of the Christian community. In addition, every human being is concerned about his or her own death as well as the destiny of loved ones. Finally, a credible response to these questions has a direct pastoral bearing on the attitudes of the living to the dead and will influence a community's respect for the memory of its living dead and the way this is celebrated in Word and Sacrament.

Many commentators today are unhappy with the dualistic anthropology of body and soul that supports the conceptuality of classical eschatology. The idea of a disembodied soul surviving death, that is to say the classical theory of the immortality of the soul, no longer receives the ready acceptance it once enjoyed philosophically. The renewal of anthropology outlined in Chapter 3 with its emphasis on the primacy of relationality and embodied existence demands that we go beyond the pre-scientific perception of the person as a body and soul

united that become separated in death. The individual person is an irre-
ducible unity of embodied relationships: divine, human, historical,
social and cosmic. Many commentators today would agree with the
observation of Wolfhart Pannenberg that 'the development of modern
psychology and neurology make it increasingly difficult to speak of a
soul or a self-conscious mind that could exist and operate independently
of bodily functions'.[11] There is an ever-increasing appreciation of the
metaphysical unity between spirit and matter that must be applied also
to the person as an indivisible soul and body.

Dissatisfaction with the immortality of the soul is about an unease with
what after all is basically a pre-Christian concept. This unease is not
altogether foreign to the Christian tradition. For example, we find Tertullian talking about the separated soul as 'half a person' and using this as an
argument in favour of resurrection: 'How unfitting it would be for God to
raise half a person to salvation.'[12] Likewise Aquinas is quite clear that 'my
soul is not I'. By this he means that a disembodied soul is not a person.[13]
Further, the International Theological Commission readily admits that
'the separated soul . . . is an ontologically incomplete reality'.[14]

Somewhat paradoxically the International Theological Commission
uses this anthropological dualism to defend the concept of the immortality of the soul and justify the validity of the intermediate state; it does this
to highlight the need for the second coming of Christ against those who
argue for resurrection in death. However, it could just as well have used
this defect with the concept of the immortality of the soul to argue
against the validity and viability of immortality of the soul as intrinsic to
the intermediate state. Surely there is something at least incongruous if
not contradictory about claiming that all who have died since the beginning of time and in particular since the salvation of the world in Christ
merely exist as 'half-persons', 'not-I's' and 'incomplete ontological realities' enjoying the beatific vision? One wonders how a half-person could
enjoy the beatific vision? What has become of the God of the living so
strongly affirmed in the preaching of Jesus? More particularly it must be
asked what has happened to the good news of salvation brought about
by the saving death and resurrection of Jesus. What of the paschal
theology of 'new life' in Christ effected by the sacrament of baptism and
celebrated in the Eucharist? Is the New Creation in Christ to be suspend-
ed until the second coming of Christ? What about the realised
eschatologies of Paul and especially of John in the New Testament?
Above all, what has happened to the mediating role of the crucified and
risen Christ in God's plan of salvation for the world and humanity?

It would seem that the concern to safeguard the classical theory of the

immortality of the soul and in particular the intermediate state has created more anthropological anomalies and christological lacunae than these
particular theories as theories deserve. Do we not have here a good
example of how far classical eschatology has strayed from its moorings
in the mystery of Christ?

Is there any way around these theological difficulties generated by a
particular debate in Germany which offers a meaningful account of individual salvation after death and at the same time safeguards the social
significance of the second coming of Christ? The International
Theological Commission properly insists on preserving the *Parousia* as
essential to the Gospel which does seem to be neglected by those who
put forward resurrection in death. Is it possible to go beyond the apparent impasse in this domestic German debate which is anthropologically
credible and faithful to the advent of the *Eschaton* in Christ? Is it not
possible to retain the fundamental truth lying behind the immortality of
the soul, namely that the individual subsists in a new form after death,
by affirming the triumphant grace of Christ within a framework which
takes account of contemporary developments in anthropology and at the
same time recognises the full eschatological significance of the revelatory
event of the death and resurrection of Christ?

One way of resolving these questions is to suggest as Rahner does that:

> it is by no means certain that the doctrine of the intermediate state is
> anything more than an intellectual framework . . . So whatever it has to
> tell us (apart from statements about the commencement through death
> of the final form of man's history of freedom, and about the inclusion
> of the body in this final form) does not necessarily have to be part of
> Christian eschatology. We might put matter differently and say: no one
> is in danger of defending a heresy if he maintains the view that the
> single and total perfecting of man in 'body' and 'soul' takes place
> immediately after death; that the resurrection of the flesh and the gen-
> eral judgment takes place 'parallel' to the temporary history of the
> world; and that both coincide with the sum of particular judgments of
> individual men and women. As long as he can produce good reasons
> for his view he can go on maintaining his opinion provided that he
> does not mean that the time scheme of world history itself can also be
> eliminated from his theological statement.[15]

Rahner's proposal is attractive; but is it fully satisfactory? He is surely
right in suggesting that 'the final form of man's history of freedom can
take effect in death'. But is he altogether correct in going on to say that 'the

total perfecting of man in "body" and "soul" takes place immediately after death'? If the total perfection of man takes place after death, is there any room left for the social significance of the second coming of Christ for the individual? Rahner says such a view can be maintained provided it 'does not mean that the time scheme of world history itself can also be eliminated from' this theological position. There is a tension here in Rahner between saying that the total perfection of the individual can take place in death while at the same time seeking to keep open the theological scheme of world history. Can the perfection of the individual take place without reference to the perfection of the totality of the world symbolised by the second coming of Christ? Is there not a risk in Rahner's position as stated that the second coming of Christ loses its intrinsic connection with and relationship to the destiny of the individual? Is it not true to hold that the *total* perfection of the individual involves the perfection of humanity and the cosmos because of the underlying unity between the creation and the radical relationality of all individuals to each other within that creation? If Rahner's position can be understood to retain this intrinsic connection between the destiny of the individual in death and the destiny of the world at the end of time, then it can be said that he has provided a way forward beyond this domestic dispute in Germany.

Another way forward is to retain the doctrine or schema of the intermediate state without its association with the immortality of the soul. This could be done by suggesting that individual resurrection – as distinct from general resurrection – takes place after death and that this individual resurrection is finally completed and perfected at the end of time in the general resurrection symbolised in the doctrine of the second coming of Christ. This proposal has a number of advantages. It retains some continuity with classical eschatology insofar as it affirms an intermediate condition between the death of the individual and the second coming of Christ. Further it places the risen Christ at the centre of individual and collective eschatology and in doing so recovers the essential mediating role of Christ in the beatific vision as we shall presently see. In addition it also safeguards the eschatological importance of the second coming of Christ. Fourthly it brings the doctrine of the resurrection back to the centre of the eschatological stage: in this life, at death and the second coming of Christ.

The theological grounds for this proposal include a re-reading of the New Testament material, especially the Pauline corpus concerning salvation 'in Christ'. Secondly, the recovery of the Paschal Mystery at the Second Vatican Council seems to support the thesis of resurrection in life, at death and the second coming of Christ.

When we turn to the New Testament we find that the Pauline literature has much to say about the place of resurrection in Christian living
and dying. The Letters of Paul and the literature influenced by Paul span
a period of some fifteen years. The early Paul, believing that he would be
alive for the second coming of Christ, emphasised the link between
resurrection and the second coming. For Paul, the resurrection is directly
connected with the second coming of Christ:

> But we would not have you ignorant brethren, concerning those who
> are asleep . . . For this we declare to you by the word of the Lord, that
> we who are alive, who are left until the coming of the Lord, shall not
> precede those who have fallen asleep. For the Lord will descend from
> heaven . . . and the dead in Christ will rise first; then we who are alive,
> who are left, shall be caught up together with them in the clouds to
> meet the Lord in the air. (1 Thess. 4:13–17; see also 1 Cor. 15:23–4)

With the passing of time Paul realises that he may not be alive for the
second coming and so the emphasis shifts from the resurrection–*Parousia*
couplet to an emphasis on the intrinsic link between death and
resurrection. The later Paul, therefore, developed a theology for the interim period between the historical resurrection of Christ and the second
coming. The focus now is on a mystical and sacramental dying and rising
with Christ in this life as a preparation for the next life. According to
Paul, resurrection for the individual begins in the present life and comes
to some kind of climax in death. Through baptism the Christian is
initiated into the resurrection of Christ:

> Do you not know that all of us who have been baptised into Christ
> Jesus were baptised into his death? We are buried therefore with him
> by baptism into death, so that as Christ was raised from the dead by
> the glory of the Father, we too might walk in newness of life . . . so you
> must consider yourselves dead to sin and alive to God in Christ Jesus.
> (Rom. 6:3–4, 11; see also Col. 1:12)

The experience of 'being alive to God in Christ Jesus' for Paul is a constant struggle: 'Our outer nature is wasting away, our inner nature is
being renewed every day' (2 Cor. 4:16) because we 'are being changed
into his likeness from one degree of glory to another' (2 Cor. 3:18). This
struggle is a process of dying and rising with Christ: 'For while we live
we are always being given up to death for Jesus' sake, so that the life of
Jesus may be manifested in our mortal flesh' (2 Cor. 4:11).

155

For Paul this new and developing life 'in Christ' reaches a point of finality in death when individual resurrection takes place. In death our relationship with Christ comes to term and a new condition of individual resurrection is realised. The clearest expression of this is found in the Second Letter of Paul to the Corinthians:

> For we know that if the earthly tent we live in is destroyed, we have a building from God, a house not made with hands, eternal in the heavens. Here indeed we groan, and long to put on our heavenly dwelling, so that by putting it on we may not be found naked. For while we are still in this tent, we sigh with anxiety; not that we would be unclothed, but that we would be further clothed, so that what is mortal may be swallowed up by life. (2 Cor. 5:1–4)

Most commentators suggest that in this text the earthly tent symbolises the physical body and the heavenly dwelling represents the new risen body given by God to the individual in death. A similar use of imagery can be found in the First Letter to the Corinthians:

> But someone will ask how are the dead raised? With what kind of body do they come? You foolish man. What you sow does not come to life unless it dies. And what you sow is not the body which is to be, but a bare kernel, perhaps of wheat or some other grain. God gives it a body as he has chosen, and to each kind of seed its own body. (1 Cor. 15:35–8)

Here Paul is appealing to the analogy of the seed, also used by Jesus, to explain what happens in death. The seed falls into the ground and dies, and what comes up is a transformed stalk of wheat. For Paul something similar happens to the Christian in death: 'What is sown is perishable. What is raised is imperishable . . . It is sown in weakness, It is raised in power. It is sown a physical body, it is raised a spiritual body' (1 Cor. 15:42–4).

The image of the seed is a particularly evocative symbol of the resurrection that takes place in death. On the one hand it gets across the element of continuity and on the other hand it also conveys the equally important element of transformation. Christian death and resurrection involve personal continuity within a process of transformation: sameness and difference, identity and newness.

A further example in Paul that seems to suggest that individual resurrection takes place at death for the Christian is the Letter to the Philippians, chapter 3. In part one of chapter 3, i.e. verses 2–11, Paul talks about the importance of knowing Christ in this life so that we may share his resurrection in the next: 'that I may know him and the power of his resurrection, and may share his suffering, becoming like him in his death, that if possible I may attain the resurrection from the dead' (vv. 10–11).

In part two of the same chapter, verses 12–21, Paul talks about the importance of keeping our eyes on the goal of resurrection in Christ in contrast to those who live as if there is no future except an earthly one: 'But our commonwealth is in heaven, and from it we await a saviour, the Lord Jesus Christ, who will change our lowly body to be like his glorious body' (Phil. 3:20–21).

A further theme in the writings of Paul suggesting that individual resurrection takes place in death is that of the gift of the Spirit in baptism; it is this same Spirit that is the guarantee and the pledge of individual resurrection in the future: 'If the Spirit of him who raised Jesus from the dead dwells in you, he who raised Christ Jesus from the dead will give life to your mortal body also through his Spirit who dwells in you' (Rom. 8:11; see also Rom. 8:14–17; 2 Cor. 5:5).

These different texts in Paul suggest that the Christian in history who has been dying and rising 'in Christ' will also be raised up in death with Christ into the new life of resurrection. What happens in death seems to go well beyond what might be called the immortality of the soul. There is more than continuity implied; there is also change (1 Cor. 15:51–7; 2 Cor. 3:18), newness (2 Cor. 5:17), and transformation (1 Cor. 15:42–3). A real difference exists between the immortality of the soul which is about continuity and survival, and the resurrection of the body which is about the fulfilment and transformation of the individual. F. X. Durwell concludes his classical study on the resurrection with the following words: 'Pauline theology does not provide a single argument to show why the individual believer's resurrection should be delayed beyond death . . . Thus physical death completes sacramental death and all other deaths in a Christian life, all of which open out into the resurrection.' Likewise Pierre Benoit's analysis of these texts leads him to conclude that those who 'die in Christ' are raised up in resurrection by being united to the risen Christ.[16]

Furthermore, a close reading of the document of the International Theological Commission reveals a certain tension between its focus on an eschatology of 'communion in Christ' as central[17] and its insistence on the immortality of the soul after death against certain unnamed theologians.[18] The International Theological Commission comes very close to the proposal under consideration here when it says 'there is, immediately after death, a communion of the blessed with the risen Christ'.[19]

In other words a strong case can be made that the human person after death becomes embodied in and through the body of the risen Christ in virtue of the person's special relationship with the body of Christ historically in and through baptism, Christian living and above all the Eucharist.[20]

But what, it will be asked, has become of the second coming of Christ in the theology of St Paul? Has he given up altogether on the importance of the *Parousia*? The short answer is 'No'. There is an equally impressive body of texts in Paul which points towards the ultimate coming together of all things 'in Christ' at the end of time. Paul has a vision of the future in which everything one day will be reunited in Christ. There is, according to Paul, 'a plan for the fullness of time, to unite all things in him (Christ), things in heaven and things on earth' (Eph. 1:10). When this happens, then Christ will hand everything over to his heavenly Father: 'then comes the end, when he (Christ) delivers the kingdom to God the Father after destroying every rule and every authority and power' (1 Cor. 15: 24–9), and 'when all things are subjected to him, then the Son himself will be subjected to him who puts all things under him that God may be everything to everyone' (1 Cor. 15:28).

How then are we to reconcile two apparently different traditions in Paul? Must we collapse the biblical tradition about individual resurrection at the time of death into the tradition about the general resurrection at the end of time as classical eschatology seems to do, or must we conflate the tradition about the general resurrection of the dead at the end of time into 'resurrection at death' as some modern German theologians have done?[21] Is it perhaps possible to retain what is of value in these two traditions by introducing some additional important distinctions?

For example, might we not distinguish here between the resurrection of the individual initiated in this life that takes place in death, and the general resurrection of the dead that occurs at the end of time? In other words is it not possible to suggest that in death, individual resurrection takes place and that this individual resurrection will be completed and perfected at the second coming of Christ by the general resurrection of the dead? The second coming of Christ therefore will entail the gathering together of the whole people of God, the living on earth with those who have been raised up individually to new life in Christ, along with history and the fruits of history, and creation itself into 'a new heaven and a new earth' (Rev. 21:1). In this vision, it should be clear that individual resurrection is incomplete to some degree without the general resurrection at the second coming, just as the part in isolation from the whole is incomplete. This incompleteness of individual resurrection is overcome through what might be called a process of socialisation and cosmic trans-formation that characterises the end of time. The Christian who under-goes individual resurrection in death continues to retain a relationship with the pilgrim people of God on earth and indeed with creation itself. It is this underlying relationship which is completed and transformed in the general resurrection of the dead at the end of time in the *Parousia.*

In effect we are proposing that resurrection is something that begins in this life through our paschal relationship with the risen Christ, that this relationship with Christ comes to a point of fruition in death through individual resurrection, and that this personal resurrection is taken up into the general resurrection at the end of time with the second coming of Christ.

The horizon of New Testament eschatology embraces a strong sense of the second coming of Christ as an event which gathers the whole of humanity, history and creation into the one body of Christ (1 Thess. 4:16–17; 1 Cor. 15:23; Tit. 2:13; John 6:39–40, 54). It is perhaps more correct to talk here not about a return of Christ but rather a coming together of all things in Christ in the fullness of time. The *Parousia* is in effect about the completion of the work of Christ on earth and in heaven. One of the most persuasive descriptions and theological justifications of the *Parousia* is provided by Origen:

> Of course, you will be happy when you pass from this world as a Saint; but only then will your happiness be complete when you are no longer missing any of your members. Indeed, you will wait, just as you are being awaited now. Now, if to you who are a member it will seem incomplete happiness as long as any member is missing, how much more must our Lord and Saviour, who is the head and creator of this body, fail to find complete happiness while he is still deprived of cer-tain of his members? . . . So he refuses to accept the fullness of his glory without you, that is, without his people who are 'his body' and 'his members'.[22]

This doctrine of the second coming highlights the social and cosmic aspects of the fullness of salvation in Christ. The *Parousia* stands out today as an important corrective and critique of the modern cult of indi-vidualism, reminding us that the individual as outlined in Chapter 3 is always an individual in relation to others, is always one who coexists within the larger communion of humanity, the cosmos and God. The theological significance and importance of the second coming of Christ for the future of creation is an important theme that will be taken up in

Chapter 11. Neglect of the second coming of Christ in theology has been responsible for the rise of individual eschatological mysticism which by-passes the importance of community and the cosmos as participants in the life of the Triuine God.[23] Above all, the Christian symbol of the second coming of Christ is a powerful reminder that salvation is never a purely private affair between me and God; instead Christian salvation is a communal reality – life in communion – grounded in the life of the Triune God mediated by Christ.

In conclusion to this section it must be pointed out that the suggestion that resurrection takes place in death and at the second coming of Christ is supported by a clear emphasis in the Second Vatican Council on the importance of the Paschal Mystery. Running through the documents of Vatican II is the persistent theme of the Paschal Mystery.[24] The work of redemption by Christ is achieved principally by the Paschal Mystery.[25] The norm guiding the revision of the liturgy is the Paschal Mystery.[26] The Church proclaims and celebrates the Paschal Mystery in her liturgical life.[27] Christians are invited to imitate the Paschal Mystery in their ordinary everyday lives.[28] Ministers of the Gospel are challenged to live the Paschal Mystery so that they initiate others into it.[29] The Council broadly describes the Paschal Mystery in terms of the Passion, death, resurrection and ascension of our Lord Jesus Christ.[30] The Liturgy Constitution of Vatican II mentions specifically the sacraments of baptism and Eucharist as celebrations of the Paschal Mystery of Christ[31] and suggests that the funeral service should reflect 'the Paschal character of Christian death'.[32] The Second Vatican Council, in at least two of its documents, points out that some individuals have already been raised up into glory. The *Constitution of the Sacred Liturgy* talks about the martyrs and the saints who have been 'raised up to perfection by the manifold grace of God' and who are therefore 'already in possession of eternal salvation'. It then goes on to say: 'By celebrating the passage of these saints from earth to heaven the church proclaims the Paschal Mystery as achieved in the saints who have suffered and been glorified in Christ.'[33]

Likewise, the *Dogmatic Constitution on the Church* affirms that certain individuals have already been raised up into glory without detracting from the second coming of Christ:

When the Lord comes in His majesty . . . death will be destroyed and all things will be subject to Him . . . meanwhile some of his disciples are exiled on earth. Some have finished this life and are being purified. Others are in glory, beholding 'clearly God himself, triune and one, as he is.'[34]

The language and vision of these texts of Vatican II seem to justify the affirmation of individual resurrection after death as well as the distinction between individual resurrection and general resurrection of the dead at the end of time.

What are the arguments in favour of this distinction between individual resurrection and general resurrection, and the particular vision it embodies? Does this vision have any advantage over the other points of view that we have referred to above?

The first point to note in favour of this vision is that it is more consistent with the language of Christian living and liturgy. If through baptism and the Eucharist we are united to Christ crucified and risen and therefore live 'in Christ', why should this relationship with Christ be severed in death by the immortality of the soul? Would it not be more consistent to suggest that our paschal relationship of dying and rising with Christ in this life comes to a point of realisation and fruition in the mystery of our death through individual resurrection?

Secondly the proposal that resurrection begins in this life, reaches a climax in death, and is completed at the second coming gives a more unified vision to the Christian mystery. A relationship of both continuity and discontinuity seems to exist between historical life in Christ, individual resurrection at death, and the general resurrection of the dead at the end of time. The life of the Christian develops in degrees between knowing Christ in this life, to personal resurrection in Christ at death, to being part of the New Creation of Christ at the end of time. The unity of belongingness with the crucified and risen Christ that marks Christian existence is something that obtains between the past, the present and the future. Further, this unified vision of life 'in Christ' is more coherent with the emerging new story of the universe as unified, relational and organic. Indeed, it becomes possible within this new vision to talk about the cosmic dimensions of the Paschal Mystery in a way that is not immediately apparent with classical doctrine of the immortality of the soul.[35]

Thirdly, the distinction between individual resurrection in death and the general resurrection at the end of time reflects more accurately the true nature of salvation as both individual and social. On the one hand the gift of salvation is about healing and making whole that which is wounded and fragmented. This sense of healing and wholeness is not immediately apparent in the doctrine of the immortality of the soul at death, whereas the possibility of individual resurrection does suggest at least the initiation of healing and wholeness, without prejudice to the reality of Purgatory which may precede individual resurrection. Further, it is difficult to see how the immortality of the soul correlates adequately with the full object of Christian hope. The logic of Christian hope is not the logic of inference which amounts to a desire for more of the same without limitations. This desire simply for continuity corresponds to what is promised by the immortality of the soul. In contrast, the logic of Christian hope is the logic of imagination which approximates more closely to what is promised in personal resurrection. On the other hand, by positing the general resurrection of the dead as something complementary in the future alongside individual resurrection, we are safeguarding the all-important social and cosmic character of salvation.

THE POSSIBILITY OF UNIVERSAL SALVATION: *APOKATASTASIS*?

The Christian doctrine of salvation is the centrepiece of eschatology. The quest for salvation, both individual and social, is universal and irrepressible. Indeed the search for wholeness is one of the many engines driving theology, and eschatology in particular. Broadly speaking there are two opposing views on salvation within the Christian tradition. On the one hand there is the optimistic view of Origen, known as *apokatastasis*, which claims that the whole of creation including sinners will be restored to a condition of wholeness at the end of time when God will be all in all. Origen's view was condemned at the Council of Constantinople in 543. In spite of the rejection of Origen's views many others in the subsequent patristic period presented modified versions of Origen's doctrine of universal salvation: St Gregory of Nazianzus, St Gregory of Nyssa, Didymus the Blind, Evagrius Ponticus, Diodore Tarsus and Theodore of Mopuestia.[36] These subsequent views within the patristic period have never been questioned by the Church.

On the other hand there is the pessimistic view put forward by Augustine which talks about a *mass damnata:* large numbers of people being lost for all eternity. This view of Augustine has had considerable influence in later theology in the Western world giving rise to an excessive preoccupation with mortal sin and eternal damnation.

There are few theologians today who would wish to defend either of these extreme positions concerning salvation. At the same time it must be acknowledged that renewed interest in this century in the theology of universal salvation has given rise to a reconsideration of *apokatastasis*. Very few theologians today, if any, teach the reality of universal salvation *simpliciter*.

The arguments against *apokatastasis* may be summarised as follows. Any doctrine of universal salvation calls into question the absolute importance of human freedom within the history of the world. Further, *apokatastasis* seriously ignores the realities of evil and sin in the course of human history. In addition a doctrine of universal salvation devalues the struggle to do good and create a more just society. Lastly *apokatastasis* clashes directly with the Christian doctrine of the eternity of hell. Put more positively, any theology of salvation must give due weight to the importance of human freedom, the reality of sin, the existence of social responsibility and the possibility of hell. Given these limitations surrounding the doctrine of *apokatastasis* we must ask what are the emerging emphases within a contemporary theology of the possibility of universal salvation?

In the first place there is a growing awareness and rediscovery of the universality of God's will to save all human beings. Evidence of this can be found in both the Hebrew Scriptures (e.g. Gen. 9:8–17; 18:18; Isa. 24:13–16) and the New Testament (especially 1 Tim. 2:4–6). The Christ-event, especially the death and resurrection of Christ, is understood to have universal significance for the whole of humanity and this is brought out in a very striking way in the Adam–Christ typology of Romans 5.

The meaning of the theory of 'outside the Church no salvation' has been reinterpreted by recent developments in ecclesiology especially at the Second Vatican Council.[37] The *Dogmatic Constitution on the Church* at Vatican II affirms that all who 'sincerely seek God and, moved by grace, strive by their deeds to do His will as it is known to them through the dictates of conscience' ... 'can attain to everlasting salvation'.[38]

Equally significant has been the development in this century of a universalist theology of grace via the work of Maurice Blondel, Henri de Lubac and Karl Rahner which found expression at Vatican II in various documents. This theology claims that God has called all human beings to communion and that all are given the opportunity directly or indirectly to be associated with the saving Paschal Mystery of Christ.[39]

It is against this background that the doctrine of *apokatastasis* has been reconsidered in this century by such contrasting theologians as Karl Rahner and Hans Urs von Balthasar. While it is true that Rahner has written very little about *apokatastasis* as such – indeed he regretted towards the end of his life that he had not given more attention to this question – nonetheless he formulated principles that have a direct bearing on the doctrine of universal salvation, especially in his theology of grace and human freedom. Many students of Rahner's theology, such as John R. Sachs and Carmel McEnroy,[40] have developed these principles into a modified form of *apokatastasis*.

Von Balthasar has written quite explicitly on the subject of *apokatastasis*, especially in a short monograph entitled *Dare We Hope 'that all men be saved'?* with *A short discourse on Hell* and *Apokatastasis: Universal Reconciliation*.[41] Both Rahner and von Balthasar are clear that they are not advocating a straightforward doctrine of *apokatastasis*. Both emphasise the tension that exists between divine grace and human freedom, between the particularity of the Christ-event and the universality of human history, between a theology of God's mercy and divine justice. Both also suggest that this tension should be mediated by a theology of hope grounded in the mystery of Christ. In addition both explicitly affirm that hell is a real possibility facing every human being in virtue of human freedom while emphasising that this fragile freedom of the individual is always surrounded and sustained by the love of God.

Von Balthasar stresses the unity and solidarity of Christ with all sinners especially in his death and resurrection. Such solidarity with sinners is most powerfully communicated in what von Balthasar calls 'the drama of Holy Saturday' symbolised by the doctrine of Christ's descent into hell. The descent into hell expresses Christ's radical solidarity with all who are separated from God. In the mystery of Holy Saturday God, as it were, erects the Cross of Christ in hell among all the dead. This divine act of oneness with all that is not of God has the power, says von Balthasar, to change the heart of even the most hardened sinner.[42]

The heart of Rahner's theology of hope for universal salvation is found in his understanding of human freedom. For Rahner human freedom from beginning to end is that event in history of God's free self-communication finding expression in the human person.[43] The individual is created and sustained by God in freedom. Freedom is from God for God and is therefore inextricably bound up with the love of God. Freedom is the human capacity for God and it must be acknowledged that without the gracious love of God the freedom of the individual would not exist. Freedom consequently is exercised not in a vacuum, not in isolation, not in autonomy but only and always as a gift from God that radically orientates every human being towards God. As already seen in the last chapter the human capacity to say 'No' or 'Yes' to God is not an equal or neutral capacity. Instead the exercise of human freedom is weighted *ab initio* in the direction of choosing God as a result of first grace given in the act of creation. This weighting of freedom in the direction of God is crystallised through the action of God in the death and resurrection of Jesus as the Christ.

Given this understanding of freedom the question arises: Is it possible for freedom to deny definitively the ground of its own existence and still be freedom? Freedom can only fully realise itself in God as its source, ground and goal. In saying this Rahner does not wish to exclude the possibility of the individual choosing in freedom to exclude himself or herself from God. Whether human freedom can irrevocably reject God as the ground of its own being and still claim to be an act of freedom is something that must at least be called into question. This in turn raises the question what such a persistent act of self-exclusion from God would entail. The logic of Rahner's position would seem to imply something like a condition of self-isolation leading to absolute aloneness or some form of frustrated freedom which retains its orientation to God without any further possibility of realising its goal in God. It is this possibility of permanent self-isolation or frustrated freedom that the Christian tradition names as hell. While such a condition remains a possibility it is increasingly difficult to see how the individual who is created in grace out of love for communion with God can definitively and irrevocably turn aside from this source, ground and goal of its own being. It is for this reason that Rahner argues that every human being can at least dare to hope for salvation and as such is obliged to hope for the salvation of all, knowing that individual salvation must include reference to the salvation of others.

Closely connected to the issue of human freedom is the even more intractable question of evil as *the* argument against any form of *apokatastasis*. The reality of evil in the world is the strongest argument against a doctrine of universal salvation. Classical and contemporary theodocies dealing with the question of evil have been found wanting on several grounds: they convey a very cold and clinical image of God, they lack any existential edge and bite, they run the risk of legitimating the existence of evil in the world.[44] There is no adequate theological response to the disturbing question of evil just as there is no satisfactory answer to the questions of Job in the Hebrew Scriptures or of Jesus on the Cross in his experience of abandonment. The nearest we can come to any response to the question of evil is resistance through solidarity and action against all forms of evil. This kind of reaction is, as we have tried to argue in Chapter 4, the beginnings of hope. Hope arises out of the experience of the negative. The reality of evil in the world therefore evokes hope and so we are thrown back once again on hope against hope in the face of evil. Such hope against evil is the first step in the movement towards hope for universal salvation.

A similar response of hope must also accompany any consideration of all human efforts to do good and to perform justice in the world. The underlying supposition behind and within the praxis of creating a better world is the hope that such human efforts are not in vain and that somehow they will endure to the end. Once again we arrive ultimately at an underlying hope for the salvation of all.

If hope for salvation is the only adequate response to the complex questions of human freedom, the realities of evil and sin, and the ethical quest, then it must be emphasised that this response of hope carries with it practical implications, including the beginnings of conversion. The hope in question implies at least a praxis of liberation in the present, a praxis that recognises individual and social responsibility for the shape of the world we live in. It is only in and through this historical praxis of liberation in the present that we can begin to talk credibly and meaningfully about the possibility of eternal salvation. The thrust of previous chapters has been that hope for the future must be grounded in experiences in the present. Without some sense and experience of wholeness in the present through the praxis of liberation, albeit fleeting, our discourse about salvation in the future runs the risk of being a mere opium or an empty rhetoric.

What was significant and decisive about the life of Jesus was the offer of salvation in the present as well as in the future. Through the preaching and praxis of Jesus, salvation gained a fragmentary though nonetheless real foothold in history.[45] This fragile foothold is vindicated through the death and resurrection of Christ and the outpouring of the Spirit. What this means in effect is that those who hope for salvation, who dare to hope for the salvation of all, must manifest the foundation of this hope in and through a praxis of liberation in the present.

In spite of this emphasis on the importance of the praxis of liberation in the present, it must nonetheless be acknowledged that salvation is always and ultimately a divine gift and grace. Salvation is a gift from God requiring a human response and co-operation. The hardest theological lesson for the modern person to learn is that he or she cannot effect his or her own salvation or indeed the salvation of others. There are fundamental eschatological truths at issue in this observation.

Salvation comes from God and is of God. Human response and co-operation, openness and conversion are important and necessary ingredients but they are miniscule in comparison to God's final gift of salvation. When we die and face God it is not ultimately our paltry 'Yes' or actions or achievements that determine our destiny; it is rather the love of God that created us in the first instance and redeemed us in Christ that ultimately saves. Anyone who doubts this fundamental truth needs to remember how fatally flawed the human condition is. Life, in spite of the fleeting moments of truth, beauty and joy, is ambiguous; the human condition is wounded by sin, human actions are tarnished by mixed motives in the pursuit of good and ultimately marked by tragedy. It has always been an essential part of the Christian tradition 'that the transcendent goal of human destiny and the depth of human sin doom all efforts to fulfil any capacity for self constitution to futility in the absence of God's grace'.[46] It is the grace of God in this life and at death that heals, transforms and recreates the brokenness of the human condition. In the end it must be acknowledged that salvation is not about finalising our fundamental option, nor is it about freezing in eternity what we may have accomplished, nor is it about some kind of stocktaking before God, nor is it the administration of human–divine or divine–human retribution. These images, all too deeply embedded in human consciousness, miss the mark and meaning of God's forgiving grace revealed in Jesus. Salvation is not about the eternal prolongation of anything that any human being has attained in this life; instead salvation is about God graciously redeeming and transforming the broken and tragic elements within the human condition.

This gracious character of salvation is most evident in the reality of death itself. As already seen, death is a process of human disintegration and divine regeneration, an event of historical reduction and gracious recreation, a painful coinciding of human destruction and divine reconstruction. It is God who brings the freely chosen human but basically ambiguous and fluctuating 'Yes' to finality and fulfilment in death. It is the grace of God given to every human being that is the seed of eternal life, the Spirit of God poured out in the act of creating every human being, that is the pledge of future glory, and the foundation of the New Creation offered in the crucified and risen Christ that grounds the hope of individual and universal salvation. In the end it must be clearly recognised that the hoped-for restoration of all things 'in Christ' is an act of God and not an act of humans. The offer of divine forgiveness is not something that any human being can earn; the gift of divine healing is not in any sense an act of self-realisation or self-fulfilment. This divine offer of grace requires some form of human co-operation. This co-operation on behalf of humanity has been offered in solidarity by Jesus as the representative of all humanity. It is this act of Jesus, especially in the Cross and resurrection of Jesus as the new Adam that draws all to God in history and at the end of time.

REINCARNATION

The doctrine of reincarnation coming from the East has begun to take hold of the Western imagination. A new fascination within the Western world exists concerning the possibility and even promise of reincarnation. In some respects reincarnation has become a new object of 'hope' for many, not only in Western Europe and North America but also in Latin America and parts of Africa.[47]

It is now estimated according to Gallup Polls in the United States (1981) and in Europe (1983) that at least one in four believe in some form of reincarnation. This statistic increases to one in three among practising Protestants and Catholics according to a more recent survey in Europe in 1989.[48] Reincarnation therefore cannot be simply dismissed as some kind of esoteric Eastern aberration. Instead it must be taken seriously and included in any contemporary search for eschatological direction among Christians today.

All that can be done here is to open up some lines of enquiry concerning this emerging fascination with reincarnation. To do this we will try to describe rather generically what is meant by reincarnation and indicate some reasons for the rise of interest in it. This will be followed by an account of the appeal that reincarnation has and we will conclude with some theological questions that should arise within any dialogue between Christian faith and reincarnation.

One of the difficulties in discussing reincarnation is the wide range of meaning attached to its usage in the East and West. Generically speaking reincarnation is about a cycle of life, death and rebirth. Within most expressions of Buddhism this process of rebirth takes place in different forms of life, involving a search for liberation, and leading ultimately to a metacosmic horizon which is metatheistic. This process of rebirth in Buddhism is not so much a transmigration of what the Western world calls the soul from body to body but rather a movement of consciousness which is better understood as a process of rebecoming. The cycle of rebecoming is itself a cosmic experience, leading finally to a metacosmic state of nirvana.[49]

Within the Western world the meaning attached to reincarnation is more difficult to tie down. One variation is to be found in Frederick Nietzsche's myth of eternal recurrence: 'Everything goes, everything returns; the wheel of existence rolls on for ever. Everything dies, everything blossoms anew; the year of existence runs on for ever ... The path of eternity is crooked.'[50]

Another variation of reincarnation is present in some strains of New Age spiritualities. These spiritualities focus on the cosmic unity and relationship of all forms of life into which we die and are reborn. A third expression of reincarnation can be found in popular forms of psychological therapy. Within this context it is suggested that personal problems in this life have been caused by or inherited from a former existence. Appeal to a life before the present existence and our reference to a life after this life become a way of dealing with the unhappy lot of this historical existence.

There can be little doubt that the ever-increasing popularity of reincarnation in the West is due in large measure to the collapse of classical eschatology. Factors such as the literalisation of eschatological symbols, the inadequate anthropology accompanying classical eschatology, especially from a contemporary point of view, the lack of reference to the cosmic dimensions of eschatology, and the dire warnings attached to the presentation of the four last things, have created a serious eschatological vacuum that is being filled at present by the new interest in reincarnation.

In particular, the inability of the traditional doctrines of the immortality of the soul and the resurrection of the body to hold the Christian imagination have produced a far too narrow focus on the so-called intermediate state and this has paved the way for some form of reincarnation. An exaggerated emphasis on the separated soul awaiting the fullness of redemption has created a breeding ground for some form of reincarnation. While it is true that the image of disembodied souls floating around in eternity hardly does justice to the classical doctrine of immortality, nonetheless this is an image that comes across all too often in popular writings. Likewise the crude physicalism attaching to many theologies of the resurrection of the body has conspired merely to marginalise the central symbol of Christian eschatology. The resulting theology of the intermediate state, already critiqued above, can no longer hold the interest of Christian faith for many.

A further factor facilitating this fascination with reincarnation in the West has been the separation of time from eternity. This removal of the temporal from the eternal arises out of the so-called enlightened proclamation of the death of God. If, in certain forms of modernity, God is no more, then time becomes absolutised and ultimately divinised. In the prophetic words of Johann Baptist Metz, time becomes 'the last remaining monarch after all the metaphysical thrones have been overthrown' and now appears as 'the only post-metaphysical fascination'.[51] A new framework is imposed for looking at life. Reality is described by giving it a date in time; human identity is truncated into time.[52] Once time is absolutised there is a real need for 'more' and reincarnation seems to fulfil this particular need.

There is much that is humanly attractive about reincarnation, especially when one becomes disenchanted with the general framework of traditional eschatology and the literalisation of its particular symbols. One should not underestimate the popular psychological plausibility of reincarnation. For one thing, reincarnation offers an attractive alternative to the irrepressible human search for immortality. Further, there is so much that seems rather arbitrary and accidental about historical birth and death that the possibility of something like 'a second chance' becomes very attractive and this appears to be offered by the cycle of birth, death and rebirth through reincarnation. Anything that offers an explanation for the apparently fated inequalities and misfortunes of life has its own intrinsic appeal. Likewise life is for so many unfinished and incomplete: so much is left undone and so many dreams remain unfulfilled.[53] In addition there is a strong sense of biological, human and social evolution, now taken so much for granted within the modern world, that certain forms of reincarnation seem able to accommodate within a vision of ongoing evolution. A link is perceived to exist for many between modern theories of evolution and reincarnation.[54]

Closely connected with this view of evolution is the frenzied individualism and consumerism of the modern world which appears to be more compatible with reincarnation than any form of finalised eschatology. The myth of more is advanced by the promise of endless rebirth. A final point about reincarnation is its opening up, however obscurely, of links between human destiny and cosmic unity. The growing interest today in post-modern cosmologies raises questions as we have seen in Chapter 3 about the relationship that exists between the human and the cosmic. Within this context reincarnation seems better able to address this development than the highly individualised, non-cosmic eschatologies of traditional Christian faith.

It is against this background of reasons for and attractive features of reincarnation that we must engage in eschatological dialogue with the doctrine of reincarnation. Our primary focus here must be with Western expressions of reincarnation.

One of the foundational questions in any dialogue with reincarnation must be the nature of time itself. Two fundamentally different conceptions of time seem to be vying for attention within this debate. On the one hand there is the largely Eastern view of time as cyclical. On the other hand the Judaeo-Christian understanding of time is linear. Within the latter, time has a purpose and goal; time is limited and relational; time is grounded and surrounded by eternity itself.

Within the Hebrew and Christian Scriptures this linear understanding of time is dramatised in at least two different but complementary ways. On the one hand the prophetic eschatology of Judaism and Christianity emphasises the existence of privileged and disruptive time technically described as *kairos*, a qualitative time, which exists in contrast to *chronos*, a quantitative time represented by continuous clock-time. On the other hand there is also within this tradition the existence of strong links between origins and endings expressed through the dramatic imagery of apocalyptic eschatology which describes the coming of the *Eschaton*, the end of time.

In Judaism and Christianity it was the prophet who read the signs of the times, discerning the time of divine visitation, a unique moment coming from God calling for conversion, offering the gift of salvation in the present, demanding a decision and action. This particular time is a *kairos*: a divine grace, opportunity and invitation. Apocalyptic eschatology on the other hand signals a dramatic break with present time, disclosing the limited character of historical time, acting as a protest against continuous time, and symbolising the possibility of an alternative time known as the *Eschaton*. This end-time in Judaism is often referred to as 'the day of the Lord' and in the ministry of Jesus as 'the coming reign of God'. A close connection is perceived to exist in the Bible between *kairos* and *Eschaton*. When *kairos* exists, the *Eschaton* is near and coming – not in terms that are measurable like hours or days or years which Jesus refused to declare but in qualitative terms concerning the relationship that obtains between the human and the divine in the present and the future.

It was Augustine more than any other Western theologian who unified these different biblical perspectives on time in the following way:

> It is now, however, perfectly clear that neither the future nor the past are in existence, and that it is incorrect to say that there are three times – past, present, and future. Though one might perhaps say: 'these are three times – a present of things future'. For these three do exist in the mind, and I do not see them anywhere else: the present time of things past is memory; the present time of things present is attentive reflection (experience); the present time of things future is expectation. If we are allowed to use words in this way, then I see that there are three times and I admit that there are.[55]

For Augustine there is ultimately only one time – namely eternity that embraces historical time through creation and the Christ-event. Historical time only makes sense in the context of eternity.

A similar understanding of time is found in the theology of Paul Tillich in this century. The human lives in the presence of the 'the Eternal Now' which includes both past and future:

The past and the future meet in the present . . . In this way the *eschaton* becomes a matter of present experience without losing its futuristic dimension: we stand now in the face of the eternal . . . This gives to the eschatological symbol (of the end) its urgency and seriousness . . . [56]

Down through the centuries authors as diverse as Meister Eckhart and George Tyrrell have spoken about the co-inciding of the eternal and the temporal, suggesting that the experience of the temporal gives access to the eternal in the present.

A second area that needs to be addressed in any dialogue about reincarnation is the question of God: Where is God and what particular image of God is operative in the doctrine of reincarnation? These questions about the mystery of God are closely connected to our remarks about the relationship between eternity and temporality. The doctrine of God as the One who creates and sustains everything in existence appears to be absent in most discussions about reincarnation. More specifically the question about the relation that exists between God and individual in the present is surely paramount to any discussion about the future. It is only in virtue of our relationship with the God who is already there that we can have hope in the future. Because we are surrounded – upheld – by the grace of God in the present and because this enables us to co-experience the omnipresence of God in history, and because this experience of God shapes human identity, it is possible to have hope in the future – hope for a personally transforming full communion with God. It is this image of the co-presence of God to the individual in the world outlined in Chapter 2 that is the basis of the intrinsic link between the eternal and temporal.

A third area requiring further clarification in any dialogue with reincarnation is that of anthropology. As noted in Chapter 3 the individual as individual is derivative from relationships with others and the absolute Other. Human identity is relational at the human, cosmic and divine levels. Removal of the individual from this relational context diminishes and dwarfs human identity. In contrast to this relational anthropology the doctrine of reincarnation suffers from a certain solitariness of the soul or human consciousness, yielding to what David Tracy calls the 'all consuming and compulsive modern ego(s)'[57] and Matthew Lamb describes as the 'individualised, monodised modern world'.[58] There appears to be too much individualism and insufficient relationality in most expressions of reincarnation.

A number of problematic consequences arise from this deficient anthropology. For example the individual within any doctrine of reincarnation becomes exempt from social and political responsibility for the world, a responsibility that follows from the anthropology of the relational autonomy developed in Chapter 3. Further, the anthropology attached to most theories of reincarnation is at variance with the importance of matter and the body in the Christian understanding of human existence – an understanding grounded in the theology of creation, covenant, incarnation and resurrection.

A final difficulty with reincarnation is the apparent disregard for the elements of failure and tragedy within life itself. Reincarnation leaves behind the destructive debris of human history: the failure and tragedy of individual acts, the realities of social injustice and ecological neglect. In contrast, Christian eschatology claims to gather up the whole of human, historical and cosmic life into a New Creation. The God of Christianity is a God immersed in the bloodied mess of history as is evidenced in the Exodus story and the Cross of Christ – raising up new life out of death, manifesting glory in darkness, revealing redemption in suffering. It is the human experience of suffering, darkness and death that generates Christian hope for the future of the world, not only for the future of the individual but also for social history and the cosmos because as we have seen in Chapter 3 there is a fundamental unity connecting these different dimensions of life itself.

Perhaps the real significance of the current fascination with reincarnation is that it forces Christian eschatology to rethink its response to the irrepressible presence of hope and the increasing interest not only in human destiny but also cosmic destiny – a question we must now address in the next chapter.

11

WHITHER THE WORLD?

The effort to understand the Universe is one of the very few things that lifts human life a little above the level of farce, and gives it some of the grace of tragedy.

(Steve Weinberg, 1979)

ONCE UPON A TIME – and this may be the right literary genre in which to begin this chapter – theology used to talk in great detail about the end of the world. This confidence, however, has been diminished by the advent of modern science and especially in the light of the Galileo crisis. Whatever discourse has remained about the end of the world in modern times has become so spiritualised and other-worldly that it is of no consequence to material creation; that is, it does not take the future of the world seriously. Of course there are some notable exceptions to these generalisations such as the work of Teilhard de Chardin and Karl Rahner.

In this chapter I want to suggest that the future of creation has once again moved to the centre of the stage and become an important theological question. Practical issues like the nuclear threat and the ecological crisis have raised searching questions about the future of creation. Likewise, new experiences of the world made possible by modern technology giving us a perception of the earth as a small blue planet within a vast universe are raising new questions about destiny of creation. Furthermore, the crisis of modernity as expressed in the collapse of the myth of progress and the growing awareness of the destructive downside of so-called development is also throwing up new questions about the future of the world. Equally, the emergence of a deconstructive post-modernity inescapably poses questions about the very meaning of creation. The nihilism of most versions of post-modernism and particularly its bleak claim concerning the collapse of all *les grands recits*, at least among some

French philosophers, raises searching questions about the point and future of creation. Finally, there is the ever-increasing apocalyptic mood about the future of the world as we face the end of a century which coincides with the commencement of the new millennium. Such a mood existed in the 990s of the last millennium and no doubt will increase as we near the year 2000.

In search of some response to these questions about the future of creation I propose to do three things in this chapter. In the first instance I will look at the world from the quite different perspectives of science and the Bible to see what these might have to say about our understanding of the world and its future. Then I will examine our perception of creation in the light of the Christ-event. Finally, I will explore the possibility of developing a creation-based eschatology.

CREATION ACCORDING TO SCIENCE AND THE HEBREW SCRIPTURES

Science has changed its views on creation several times in the modern period and this in itself should serve as a warning to theology against any easy co-option of the findings of science. It is sobering to realise that most Christian theology in the pre-modern period was done on the assumption that the world was fixed and static, that the sun and moon and five known planets revolved around the earth in seven celestial spheres, that human beings were the centre of the universe, that Europe was the centre of the world and that the earth was without limits.[1] Within the modern era the world has been understood by and large as an impersonal machine available to serve the needs of 'man'. In the emerging post-modern period theology finds itself in the midst of a paradigm shift in science which has enormous consequences for theology in general and for eschatology in particular. Theology cannot afford to ignore the findings of science, especially in view of the considerable cultural influence it has on our understanding of the world we inhabit. A new climate of constructive dialogue between science and religion is one of the outstanding signs of the times in the latter half of this century.

Contemporary science has moved from a steady-state theory of the universe, namely that the world exists throughout an infinite span of time, to a near universal acceptance of one or other versions of the so-called Big Bang hypothesis, namely that the world evolved out of a unique 'mathematical singularity' of some 15,000 million years ago. Within the context of Big Bang theories, the cosmos is perceived by some to be an open universe and by others to be a closed universe. In the open

universe theory the cosmos will continue to expand indefinitely. According to the closed universe theory, the world will eventually contract and
end in a big crunch. Within this latter theory there is the possibility of an
infinite number of oscillations back and forth between expansion and
contraction.[2] However, on the basis of the second law of thermodynam-
ics many scientists argue that the universe will eventually die through a
process of 'heat death'. This will happen when the sun, which is now estimated to be four and a half thousand million years old and about
halfway through its lifespan, will increase its temperature and
eventually swallow up the solar system. As Carl Sagan puts it: 'the sun,
ruddy and bloated' will 'envelop and devour the planets Mercury and
Venus – and probably the earth as well'.[3]

A third possibility put forward by scientists is the suggestion of what
they call a flattening out of the curve of expansion at some time in the
future. In this theory the forces of expansion will come into balance with
the forces of gravitation giving rise to an indefinite phase of stability.[4]

In view of these different possibilities it is apparent that there is no
consensus within the scientific community about the future of creation.
What is reasonably clear, however, among scientists is the presence of
broad agreement about the origins of the universe in terms of the Big
Bang theory while there is no agreement about the future of the universe.
Although there are differences in detail about the Big Bang there is general agreement about the broad picture. As one physicist, Brian Swimme,
puts it:

> For the first time in human existence we have a cosmic story that is not
> tied to one cultural tradition, or to political ideology, but instead
> gathers every human group into its meaning . . . Islamic people, Hopi
> people, Christian people, Marxist people and Hindu people, can all
> agree in a basic sense on the breadth of the sun, the development of the
> earth, the species of life and human cultures.[5]

It is surely ironic at a time when certain strains of post-modern French
philosophy are announcing the end of all the great narratives, that the
world of science is announcing the emergence of a new cosmic story that
highlights the unity, coherence and solidarity of humans, the earth and
the cosmos.

This widespread agreement about the origins of the universe among
scientists does raise questions about the future of creation. The advances
of science in this century in terms of discovering the sheer vastness of the
universe, the beauty of the earth in spite of so much ecological degrada-

tion, and the appearance of some traces of promise within nature, raise questions about the future of creation. Fascination with questions about origins – and these certainly exist within the scientific community today – implies at least some fascination with questions about endings. Such questions about the future are unavoidable for believer and unbeliever alike. While science cannot give an answer about the future of creation it does legitimate the actuality and urgency of this question. A recent issue of *National Geographic* formulates the question in the following way:

So many stars. And yet we have learned also that the universe is mostly emptiness. Cold, sometimes flickering with explosive energy, this universe taunts us with mysteries. When did it begin? How will it end? What laws of nature governed its creation and evolution? Are there other universes? If so, are they like ours? Time and again since humans first acquired a sense of wonder we have asked such questions.[6]

When we turn to the Hebrew Scriptures to see what light they might shed on creation we discover first of all that the highly influential view subordinating creation to salvation history put forward by Gerard von Rad no longer enjoys widespread acceptance.[7] Instead it is argued that the theme of creation was an integral part of Jewish faith and not something simply subordinated to salvation history. Further, it emerges that there are several theologies of creation in Judaism and not just those expressed in the early chapters of the Book of Genesis. These other theologies of creation, found especially among the prophets and the Wisdom tradition, present a strong sense of God's continuous involvement in creation in contrast to the semi-deistic views of God often associated with the Book of Genesis which inaccurately imply that God created the world in the beginning and then simply left creation to its own resources.

The sources of creation theology in the Hebrew Scriptures are varied and complex: the Psalms of Lament, Deutero-Isaiah, the Wisdom literature of Proverbs and Job, and the two distinct Genesis accounts. According to Richard Clifford the Psalms of Lament can be summed up in the following way: 'Will you, O Lord, allow your act that brought us into existence to be nullified by the present danger?'[8] When everything seems to be falling apart, the psalmist appeals to God's original gift of creation as the basic source of faith and hope in the future. The God who creates is the God who redeems. For example, Psalm 74 returns to Yahweh's original act of creation at the very foundations of the world: 'You divided the sea by your might ... You crushed the heads of Leviathan ...

You cleft open springs and brooks . . . You fixed all the bounds of the earth' (vv. 12–17).

This theme of creation also appears in the prophets of Amos and Jeremiah, but most especially in Deutero-Isaiah, 40–55, written around the end of the exile in Babylon. The theme of New Creation is prominent in Deutero-Isaiah and is used as a point of comparison to the Exodus theme that brought Israel into existence – not therefore in contrast to the act of creation found in Genesis.[9] When Deutero-Isaiah talks about the first creation, he is talking about the creation of the Jewish people through the exodus experience. A second but new coming into existence will take place with the return of the chosen people to the land of Canaan. The underlying supposition of Deutero-Isaiah is that creation is not simply an act of God in the beginning but an ongoing reality in history:[10]

> Thus says Yahweh
> Who makes a way in the sea . . .
> Who brings out the chariot and the horse . . .
> I am about to do a new thing,
> I will make a way in the wilderness and rivers in the desert.
>
> (Isa. 43:16–21)

In the Wisdom literature of the post-exilic period covering such books as Proverbs, Job, Qoheleth, Sirach, Wisdom, some of the Psalms, Yahweh is presented primarily as the creator God. Indeed Wisdom tradition is very much a creation-based theology.[11] Many argue that there is considerable evidence in the Hebrew Scriptures to suggest that at least a functional equivalency exists between the deeds of Wisdom and those of the biblical God and that Wisdom is the female personification of God.[12] The Wisdom of God is intimately involved in creation – not only at the beginning of creation (Prov. 8:22–31) but also continuously throughout creation as the One who 'pervades and penetrates' (Wisdom 7:24), 'orders' (Wisdom 8:1) and 'renews all things' (Wisdom 7:27) within creation.

A further powerful portrayal of God's personal involvement with creation at the beginning of time and subsequently throughout time can be found in the Book of Job. God's response to Job's questions in chapters 38 to 41 are explicit reminders to Job of the extraordinary order and complexity of creation itself: 'Were you there when I laid the foundations of the earth?' (Job 38:4); 'Do you know when the mountain goats give birth?' (Job 39:1).

Turning now to the Book of Genesis, the first story in Genesis 1:1 to Genesis 2:3 outlines the history of creation. The climax of this story is the seventh day on which God rests. A contrasting parallel exists between days one to three, and days four to six, with darkness and light being the focus of days one and four, waters being the point of days two and five, and two events taking place on days three and six. A key moment in this priestly story of creation is the making of humanity by God 'in his image, in the image of God he created them' (v. 27). The uniqueness of human beings consists in their likeness with and relationship to God.[13] The point of this creation account in Genesis 1 seems to be the restoration of confidence in God among the people of Israel at a time, namely the Babylonian exile in the sixth century, when everything seemed to be lost. The significance of this creation story is that the God who brought order out of chaos at the beginning of time is the same God who will rescue the people of Israel from the chaos of their captivity. Creation faith, faith in the God who 'created the heavens and the earth' is the basis of hope in the future. A further point within this account of creation is the presence of a reaction against current views of creation, especially as these were influenced by the Babylonian epic poem 'Enuma Elish' which many claim is a part of the prehistory of Genesis 1.

The second creation story in Genesis 2:4b to Genesis 3:24 is much older, being located in the tenth century BCE. This story is associated with the Yahwist tradition and is influenced by the kingdom of David ideology. The purpose of this account of creation is not to give an explanation of the historic origins of the world but rather to explain the present experience of the human condition which is one of intimacy and estrangement with God at one and the same time.

This second creation story is believed by many to be a combination of two stories – one about the creation of the human from the earth, and the other about the completion of humanity in the creation of woman. From our point of view what is significant is verse 7 which says: 'then the Lord God formed man from the dust of the ground, and breathed into his nostrils the breath of life; and man became a living being'. At least two important points emerge here. The verse 'the Lord God formed man from the dust of the ground' contains a play on words which is not self-evident in most English translations. In the original Hebrew, *Adam*, the human, is made, better shaped from *Adamah*, the earth, prompting commentators to translate humanity as 'earth-creature', or 'earthling', or 'groundling' in order to highlight the intrinsic connection between humans and the earth. The primary point here is the creature's connection with the earth and not the so-called priority of the male which, all too often, is the way the story has been handed down. Adam, that is the earth-creature, it should be remembered, at this stage is sexually undifferentiated.[14]

The second point worthy of note here is that the activity of God in fashioning *Adam* from *Adamah*, that is, making the human from the earth, echoes the story of the potter moulding the clay which is one of the foundational images for the activity of God in the Hebrew Scriptures.[15]

Within the rest of this creation story it becomes evident that the human is completed only when woman is created, at which point the earth-creature is differentiated as male and female. It is also clear that a special relationship of equality and mutuality between woman and man is intended. Genesis 2 is unique among creation myths of the ancient Near East in its appreciation of this equality between woman and man.[16] The remainder of this creation story is given over to the fall which affects not only humanity but also the ground from whence they have come. Male and female are estranged from God, from one another and from the earth. What begins to emerge from this overview of creation faith in the Hebrew Scriptures are the following points:

- The God of Judaism is a creator God who is at once transcendent and immanent, transcendent to creation and yet immanent within it.
- The God of Judaism is dynamically involved not only in initiating creation but also in sustaining creation and the history of Israel.
- That creation in the eyes of God is good in itself.
- That a close relationship of origin and continual dependency exists between the creator, earth and humanity.
- That in spite of a close relationship between God the creator and the creature there also exists a sense of estrangement between God, humanity and the earth.

CREATION IN THE LIGHT OF CHRIST

It is against this background of the Hebrew understanding of creation that we now turn to Christ. Our approach will follow the general direction given by Irenaeus, Scotus and de Chardin who saw Christ as the goal and summit of creation in contrast to Aquinas who presented Christ primarily in terms of redemption from sin. The former proposal presupposes an underlying unity between creation and incarnation, that incarnation therefore is not some divine 'afterthought', whereas in Thomistic theology there appears to be a dualism between creation and redemption. For Aquinas salvation is primarily human-centred with very little reference to the salvation of creation.

Edward Schillebeeckx captures this preferred approach when he suggests that the study of christology be approached as 'concentrated creation'.[17] By this he means that what happened in the life, death and resurrection in Jesus is a microcosm of what will happen in the macrocosm of creation. An underlying unity exists between the reality of creation and the reality of Christ. The salvation brought by Christ affects not only the human and the historical but also creation itself. In effect salvation embraces the human, the historical, and the cosmic as a unity. Christ is the centre and goal of creation. The potential and promise of creation comes to full term in the life, death and resurrection of Christ. If we want to know about the future of creation, then we must look to the Christ-event. This means that we must move beyond the dualism of classical theology which separated creation and redemption.[18] As Rahner puts it as far back as the early 1960s:

> We are perfectly entitled to think of creation and of the incarnation, not as two disparate, adjacent acts of God *'ad extram'* which in the actual world are due to two quite separate original acts of God, but as two moments and phases in the real world of the unique . . . process of God's self-renunciation and self-expression into what is other than himself.[19]

In the last ten years we have begun to hear more and more about the cosmic Christ. However, what has not always been clear in discussions about the cosmic Christ is the justification for moving from the human and historical Jesus to the 'cosmic Christ'. To simply jump from the historical Jesus to the cosmic Christ, or even from the risen Christ to the cosmic Christ without explanation, can be misleading and seem like theological opportunism. Instead the grounds justifying this move must be explored if the shift is to succeed. I suggest that these grounds are primarily anthropological, or more accurately the recovery of a cosmo-centred anthropology outlined in Chapter 3. More specifically the cosmic Christ will only be fully recovered in theology, and in particular in eschatology which is our concern here, when we have rediscovered the cosmic dimensions of what it means to be human. The cosmic Christ disappeared from theology with the scientific rise of a mechanistic cosmology during the Enlightenment and the consequent emergence of an excessive anthropocentrism in theology. The first step therefore in retrieving the cosmic Christ is to move towards a renewed anthropology, and by this I mean a more cosmo-centred anthropology. The second step in recovering the cosmic Christ will be a re-reading of the New Testament christologies in the context of this cosmo-centred anthropology.

Anyone looking at the state of anthropology today will realise very quickly as we have already seen in Chapter 3 that it is in a situation of crisis. To recap a little, calls to 're-invent the human',[20] to 'replace a narrow anthropocentric sensibility',[21] to rethink the 'modern notion of the self',[22] to develop a more 'chastened anthropocentricity',[23] are the order of the day. Responses to these calls are coming from areas as diverse as psychology, feminism, ecology, philosophy and cosmology. We will limit ourselves here to impulses coming from contemporary cosmologies already summarised in Chapter 3.

By far the most significant impulse from cosmology is the emergence of a common-creation story – a story about the origin of the universe that goes back some 15,000 million years to an initial singularity which is commonly called the Big Bang. This initial explosion is understood to be the source of all matter, space and time. As a result of this new understanding of origins cosmologists are generally agreed that the universe as we know it can be treated as a single organic entity that is continually evolving and expanding.[24] Everything within this expanding universe can be traced back – somewhat like a film run backwards – to an initial explosion. The existence of microwave radiation throughout the universe – one of the many pieces of evidence for the Big Bang hypothesis – is interpreted as a kind of 'afterglow of the Big Bang'.[25]

Discernible links within cosmology are perceived to exist between the macro-astrophysics of swirling galaxies; the evolutionary biology of extraordinary complexity on the planet earth and the micro-physics of matter made up of dancing particles at sub-atomic levels. The universe as we know it, in terms of the cosmos, the earth and human existence is a single though highly differentiated organic reality which is understood to be inter-related, interconnected and interdependent.

Within this extraordinary unfolding of life from the earth and the earth from the galaxies, and the galaxies from the original explosion of energy, there is the emergence of human existence. The human person is understood to be matter in a mode of self-conscious freedom. According to Carl Sagan, human beings are 'the local embodiment of a cosmos grown to self-awareness'.[26] Arthur Peacocke points out that 'in human beings part of the world has become conscious of itself'.[27] Thomas Berry suggests that 'we carry the universe in our being (just) as the universe carries us in its being'.[28] In the words of John Polkinghorne 'we are all made of the ashes of dead stars'.[29] Teilhard de Chardin sums up these perspectives by suggesting that 'The human person is the sum total of fifteen billion years of unbroken evolution now thinking about itself.'[30]

The point of these more than poetic statements about the human person is that they all highlight the fundamental continuity between matter and spirit in our world. Instead of thinking that the human person is somehow separate and independent from the earth we now begin to rediscover the close affinity that exists between humans and the earth without however reducing the human to the purely biological as certain forms of deep ecology do. The human is 'clay grown tall'[31] or as Karl Rahner likes to put it 'The human spirit "subsists" in matter.'[32] The human person therefore is earthbound, indeed 'an earthling', and cannot be understood without reference to cosmic origins. The human is a cosmic-based centre of self-awareness or, better, embodied self-consciousness. Instead of thinking that the earth belongs to the human we must begin to realise that the human belongs to the earth.

It is this cosmo-centred anthropology that must now be applied to the person of Jesus. Everything we have said so far about the human should embrace Jesus of Nazareth who is fully human, who in the words of the Council of Chalcedon is *homo-ousios* (of one being) with humanity. This means that we must begin to see Jesus as someone within cosmic history, who, like the rest of humanity, is the universe, that is material creation, in a state of self-conscious freedom. Jesus like the rest of humanity 'is made up of the elements forged inside the fiery centre of stars. He too is made of stardust.'[33] In other words, Jesus of Nazareth is at least part of the evolutionary outcome of the Big Bang, at least an essential and significant element within cosmic history, at least a child of the earth.

Thus when we talk about the humanity of Jesus in the history of salvation we must remember that we are talking about a humanity not over or above or beyond cosmic history but a humanity deeply immersed in the history of the cosmos and its galaxies, a humanity derived from the earth and its life-forms, a humanity rooted in the history of humans and their radical relationality. It is only from within this larger cosmic and anthropological panorama that we can identify the human and historical Jesus with the cosmic Christ, that is the Christ who represents not only humanity but also embraces cosmic history and embodies the earth in a unique state of self-awareness.

A question that may arise for some at this stage is whether there is any historical warrant in the life of Jesus for these claims? I think the way we understand this question is important. If we are looking for something of a parallel between our present understanding of what it is to be human and the teaching of Jesus two thousand years ago, then I suggest we are misunderstanding the question and will end up looking in vain. Every generation will have its own unique self-understanding of what it means to be human and this will change culturally and scientifically. On the other hand, if we are asking did Jesus have a sense of unity with the earth and the cosmos, then a modest case can be made to suggest that Jesus had a remarkable awareness of the fundamental unity of all things in God's creation. But on what grounds?

In the first instance Jesus as a Jew would have been familiar with the Hebrew understanding of creation already outlined in part one of this chapter. Jesus as a son of Israel would have believed in the Genesis story which perceived the human 'as formed from the dust of the earth' (Gen. 2:7), that is more properly as an earth creature or 'an earthling', Adam from *Adamah*. Further, Jesus would have been aware also of the Hebrew prophetic tradition which saw creation as bound up with salvation and even described that salvation as a New Creation. Equally Jesus would have been acquainted with the Wisdom tradition which perceived God as active and present within the ongoing dynamic of creation itself. Finally, it must be remembered that when Jesus came to image the reign of God he did so pre-eminently through the use of images drawn from the earth and the cosmos: the birds of the air, the lilies of the field, the sowing of seeds, harvesting, vineyards, trees, the salt of the earth, yeast and flour, and bread as the fruit of the earth.

What is perhaps even more significant is the way the early Church interpreted the Christ-event in terms that are explicitly cosmological. Most commentators suggest that the earliest christologies were cosmological in content. For example, Edward Schillebeeckx argues that 'belief in creation "is" the all-supporting basis for the Jewish Christian kerygma'.[34] This perception of creation as the primary context for the proclamation of the Christ-event in the early Church is also borne out by the claim that the earliest christologies of the New Testament are Wisdom christologies.[35]

We need only turn to the early Pauline christologies to see how creation-centred they are and to discover the privileged position given to Jesus as the Wisdom of God. We must be selective here. In his letter to the Colossians Paul, quite clearly and explicitly, presents Christ as the centre of creation: 'He is . . . first born of all creation; For in him all things in heaven and on earth were created, all things have been created through him and for him . . . In him all things hold together' (Col. 1:15–17).

In a similar vein the letter of Paul to the Ephesians talks about the plan of God: 'set forth in Christ, as a plan for the fulness of time, to gather up all things in him, things in heaven and things on earth' (Eph. 1:9–10). Clearly Christ is perceived to be centrepiece of God's plan.

Likewise the early confession of Jesus as the Wisdom of God found in 1 Corinthians has cosmic connections: 'We proclaim Christ crucified, a stumbling block to the Jews and foolishness to the Gentiles but to those called, both Jews and Greeks, Christ the power of God and the wisdom of God' (1 Cor. 1:23–4).

Here we need only recall, as already seen in the Hebrew theology of creation, that wisdom has a creative, caring and ordering role within creation and the affairs of the world; this role is now given to Christ, especially the crucified Christ – a point we will return to in the next section. Further, many of the christological titles such as Jesus as Lord and Logos take on cosmic connotations within the culture of first-century Christianity. The Lordship of Jesus, especially in the light of the resurrection, assumes cosmic dimensions. This is brought out for example in the christological hymn of Philippians which is structured according to the cosmology of the day: 'at the name of Jesus every knee should bend in heaven, and on earth and under the earth, and every tongue confess that Jesus Christ is Lord to the glory of God the Father' (Phil. 2:10–11).

In an equally significant way the prologue of John's Gospel, 'In the beginning was the Word' is intended to parallel the opening words of the Book of Genesis: 'In the beginning God created heaven and earth' – thus establishing a clear connection between creation and the incarnate Word.[36] This bare outline of early New Testament christology highlights in part the clear connection between creation and Christ and signals a real appreciation of the cosmic Christ within early Christianity. It should be noted that this emphasis on the cosmic Christ is continued throughout the Patristic period up to the seventh century.

THE FUTURE OF CREATION

In the light of this recovery of the cosmic Christ via a renewed anthropology and our brief outline of a creation-centred christology we are now at last in a position to address the question of this chapter, namely the future of creation. Does creation as we know it have a future; does the material world have a destiny or is it programmed to burn out in the evolutionary spiral of cosmic expansion or contraction; is the human merely a transient episode in cosmic, historical and cultural evolution? Are not such awkward questions perhaps better answered by simply affirming that the world is a valley of tears, a testing ground, a prelude to some form of post-mortem spiritual fulfilment. Is not the next life really some kind of other-worldly existence shorn of contact with material creation?

In framing the question in these terms it should be clear I am assuming that the destiny of the individual is bound up with the destiny of the whole and that therefore the macro-question about creation will influence the way we approach questions about human destiny. Further, I am implying in the light of our cosmo-centred anthropology that questions about the future of creation must move back to the centre of the theological stage from which they disappeared since the time of the Enlightenment. Since these questions about the future of creation are ultimately eschatological questions it becomes necessary to recap some of the perspectives of our earlier chapters on the scope of eschatology.

It is important to bear in mind continually what eschatology is not. For example eschatology needs to be clearly distinguished from evolution which posits some kind of endless progress from lower to higher forms. Mary Midgley has performed a singular service to theology by critiqueing modern scientists who insert a happy-ever-after final chapter into their scientific treatises on cosmology.[37] In contrast to this science fiction view of the future and the different theories of evolutionary optimism that inspire them, eschatology posits a future point of finality and fulfilment for the world brought about by God in the fullness of time. Closely related to the evolutionary outlook is the teleological perspective on life. Teleology sees the future in terms of working out what is already there, a bringing to fruition of what is already given in life. Eschatology on the other hand proposes an understanding of the future in terms of *adventum*, that is the arrival of the future as something new and unexpected out of the present coming ultimately as gift and promise from God. In classical eschatology there has been too much *telos* and not sufficient *adventum*, too much optimism and insufficient hope. A third distortion of eschatology is the suggestion that the future is about some form of mystical union or re-absorption into God that by-passes material creation. Christian eschatology, as we have emphasised already, should embrace a more wholistic, inclusive and embodied vision of the future. A fourth misunderstanding about eschatology is the impression that it is only about the next life, concerned only with other-worldly realities. Again it must be re-stated that Christian eschatology is as much about this life as it is about the future. If there is no meaning to life in the present, if there are no anticipations of the future in the present, if there are no glimpses of wholeness in this life, then it will be difficult to talk meaningfully about a future life.

For too long and for too many people eschatology has been narrowly conceived in terms of the four last things: death, judgment, heaven and hell. Against this it must be countered, as we have argued throughout this book, that the *eschata* will only make sense in the light of the advent of the *Eschaton* in Christ. The primary focus of eschatology therefore should be the *Eschaton* in Christ[38] as present reality and future promise. As noted in previous chapters eschatology can be constructively conceived as the application of christology to the self, society and the world in a mode of fulfilment. It is against the background of these suppositions that we can now look at the future of creation in the light of the christological doctrines of the incarnation, the resurrection, the *Parousia* and the Cross.

The theological centre of Christianity is the doctrine of the incarnation. As already noted the incarnation is the fulfilment of creation, the realisation of the inner dynamic and orientation of the Hebrew understanding of creation. The theological significance of the incarnation, more specifically the eschatological implications of the incarnation for the future of creation, must now be addressed. The Christian claim that God became human in Jesus, that the Word was made flesh, implies that God assumed not only the particular humanity of Jesus but also the flesh of the whole of humanity. The theologian who has captured this aspect of the incarnation most persuasively is Karl Rahner. For Rahner the incarnation is 'the beginning of the divinisation of the world as a whole'[39] because 'God lays hold of matter when the Logos becomes flesh'.[40] In laying hold of matter we must remember that the matter in question is always a part of the reality and history of the cosmos.[41] In other words, given what we have said about the relationship of the human to the earth and of the earth to the cosmos, God in Christ has assumed in principle the whole of material creation. As Ernan McMullin points out: 'When Christ took on human form, the DNA that made him Son of Mary may have linked him to a more ancient heritage stretching far beyond Adam to the shallows of unimaginably ancient seas.'[42]

These particular claims makes little or no sense in an exclusively anthropocentric universe nor do they make much sense in the context of modern mechanistic cosmologies but they can make sense in the context of a renewed understanding of the human person as cosmic along the lines indicated in Chapter 3. They also make particular sense in the context of the Hebrew theology of creation which sees the human as the off-spring of the earth, that is, as an earth-creature/earthling/groundling.

The incarnation commits God to the whole of humanity in the flesh of Jesus and to creation in virtue of the fact that Jesus in his humanity is, like every human being, the cosmos in a state of self-conscious freedom. Because Jesus is a child of the cosmos, there is an important sense in which we can say God has taken hold of the whole of creation in Jesus. The God who created heaven and earth, the God who created the human as an earthling is the same God who became incarnate in Jesus of Nazareth as a child of the cosmos. As Tertullian remarked: 'Whatever was the form and expression which was given to the clay (by the creator), Christ one day to become man, was in his thoughts.'[43]

Vatican II talks about a fundamental solidarity between the Incarnate Word and the rest of humanity.[44] This solidarity between God and humanity must be extended to the whole of creation in the light of a renewed cosmocentric anthropology.[45] It is this unity and solidarity between God and the human in Jesus of Nazareth that gives us grounds for claiming that creation does have a future.

Closely related to this perspective on the incarnation and following from it is the eschatological import of the resurrection of Jesus from the dead for the future of creation. The bodily resurrection of Jesus from the dead does not mean simply some kind of physical resuscitation or restoration or re-animation of the body of Jesus. Instead the resurrection of Jesus points us in the direction of the transformation of the material body of Jesus into a New Creation. The language of resurrection must be safeguarded from a literalistic understanding and this can be done when it is accompanied by the equally important New Testament symbols of exaltation, glorification, ascension and Pentecost.[46] In the words of Paul Ricoeur, 'the symbol gives rise to thought' and it is the configuration of these different symbols concerning the death of Jesus around an eschatology of the human and the cosmic, history and creation, the world and people.

The resurrection of Jesus, like the incarnation, embraces not only the human but also the reality of material creation as embodied in Jesus. To quote Rahner again the bodily resurrection of Jesus from the dead is 'the beginning of the transformation of the world' and 'in this beginning the destiny of the world is already in principle decided and has already begun'.[47] In other words, the bodily resurrection of Jesus from the dead prefigures not only the destiny of all human beings but also the future of creation. The resurrection of Jesus from the dead assures us that material creation is included in God's plan of salvation: it is something of a preview of the future of creation, a preview providing meaning more by way of negation than affirmation.

There is no salvation without the participation of creation, no redemption that by-passes the world, no heaven without earth. Christian salvation is never purely a spiritual affair, never simply a mystical union with God, never just anonymous absorption into the divine. The resurrection of Jesus from the dead affirms that the individual whole person and material creation are directly involved in the coming-to-be of God's final gift of salvation. It is precisely for this reason and other reasons like the sacramentality of the world that Christianity cannot accept the immortality of the soul *per se* as a satisfactory answer to the question about the future of creation.

A further point corroborating this affirmation about the future of creation as rooted in the resurrection of Jesus from the dead is the christological symbol of the empty tomb. While the empty tomb can hardly be said to provide the primary evidence for resurrection, it does nonetheless indicate that the material reality of Jesus' body has been caught up in the transformation that is resurrection. The empty tomb is an important reminder that a part of creation has already been transfigured and transformed. To this extent both the empty tomb and the bodily resurrection of Jesus are important indicators, each in their own different way, that material creation does have a future destiny and is not something therefore that can be cast aside as inconsequential.

It is surely more than a coincidence that many of the resurrection narratives in the Gospels are closely associated with the Eucharist. Important links exist between the bodily resurrection of Jesus, the transformation of bread and wine that takes place in the Eucharist and the future of creation. In a symbolic and sacramental sense the Eucharist is the link/bond/pledge between the resurrection of Jesus and the future transformation of creation. The Eucharist represents the ongoing transformation of material reality in anticipation of the future glorification of creation. In the words of the agreed statement on the Eucharist by the Anglican-Roman Catholic International Commission of 1971: 'elements of the first creation become (in the Eucharist) pledges and firstfruits of the new heaven and new earth'.[48]

A third christological symbol important to our question about the future of creation is the *Parousia*, or as it is often called the second coming of Christ. This much-neglected Christian doctrine is part of the Nicene Creed which talks about the One who 'will come in glory to judge the living and the dead'. The *Parousia* is about the public manifestation of the completion and perfection of the work of Christ embracing the history of humanity and the world. The symbol of the *Parousia* has several different theological functions within the Christian vision: it highlights the finality of God's work of salvation, it points up the social character of salvation, and it reminds us of the place of creation within salvation. Without wishing to diminish the importance of the first three categories I want to concentrate here on the place of creation within salvation. Christian scriptures quite explicitly refer to the inclusion of creation in salvation. The Book of the Apocalypse talks about 'a new heaven and a new earth at the end of time' (Apoc. 21:1–5). The Letter to the Ephesians refers to 'a plan for the fulness of time, to gather up all things in Him, things in heaven and things on earth' (Eph. 1:10). It is the Letter to the Romans, however, that is most significant for our theme. It says:

> For the creation waits with eager longing for the revealing of the children of God; We know that the whole creation has been groaning in labour pains until now; and not only the creation but we ourselves, who have the first fruits of the spirit, groan inwardly while we wait for adoption, the redemption of our bodies.

Several points must be noted here. First of all, the reference to creation being subjected to futility is a clear allusion to the fall of creation described in Genesis 3:17. Secondly there is a suggestion that when human beings obtain the full freedom of the children of God that creation itself will be set free from its bondage to decay. Thirdly a close parallel is proposed between the groaning of creation and the groaning of humanity. These three points highlight the unity that exists between humanity and creation and confirm what we have been saying about the implications of the incarnation and the resurrection for the future of creation – namely that what happens to humanity happens to creation. In effect the future of creation is closely bound up with the destiny of humanity. A fundamental solidarity exists concerning the future of the earth and earthlings, the destiny of the cosmos and the *humanum*, the re-creation of humans and the transformation of the world within God's plan of salvation.

Having suggested therefore that creation does have a future and that this future is one of transformation, it is important at the same time to affirm that we do not know how this transformation of the cosmos will take place – no more than we know how the resurrection of humanity will take place. It is imperative for theology to acknowledge openly what it does not know about the future and in this instance that means affirming that we do not know the time or the manner of the future consummation of the world. Theology has an important role to play 'as the guardian of the *docta ignorantia futuri*'.[49] The details of the future transformation of creation are beyond human understanding, yet this must not prevent us from making some theological statements about the future of creation.

For example, it is important to be able to say at least that the key to the future of creation is the Cross. This link between the Cross and creation is brought out quite dramatically by Matthew in his cosmic interpretation of the death of Jesus: darkness over the earth, the tearing of the veil in the Temple, the shaking of the earth, the renting of rocks and the opening of the tombs (Matt. 27:45–53). Just as the Cross gives us some inkling of what resurrection involves, so the Cross of Christ gives some clue to the future of creation. It can be said at least that the future of creation in God's plan is cruciform, involving the paschal process of death and resurrection, of disintegration and re-creation. The reality of death that embraces the future of the individual is also a reality that embraces the future of creation. The Cross of Christ stands out as a necessary but realistic reminder that the future of humanity and creation is one of a 'bright darkness', one in which sadness and joy coincide. R. S. Thomas, the Anglican poet, captures some of this sad-joy in the following words:

> You have answered us
> with the image of yourself
> as a hewn tree, suffering injustice, pardoning it ... horrifying us
> with the possibility of dislocation.[50]

The future of creation does involve a dislocation – a painful dislocation leading to joyfilled relocation. In this way the Cross also serves as an important control and check on fanciful projections about the future – quite common among scientists and some theologians.

Further, the advent of the New Creation is not simply a repeat of the first creation which was a *creatio ex nihilo*. Instead the New Creation is in part a *creatio ex vetero*. What is taken up, transfigured and transformed in the New Creation is the old creation in all its potential to reflect the glory of God. The first creation is redeemed and transformed in the New Creation.

Thirdly, the transformation of creation in the future is the work of the Holy Spirit. It was the breath of God, the Spirit of God, that brought life into the dust of the earth in Genesis (2:7). It is that same Spirit of God that continually holds creation together throughout history as we have already seen in the Hebrew theology of creation. For instance, Psalm 104:29 reminds us that when God takes away the breath of living things they wither but when God sends forth his Spirit they are created and the face of the earth renewed. It is this Spirit of God poured out into the world through the Christ-event that will bring creation to perfection in the future.

By way of conclusion, I propose an image of the divine activity that brings creation to completion. Some of the early Fathers described what happens in death in the following way. They likened the human condition as sinful to a flawed piece of art that needs to be reduced to its raw state so that it may be restored to perfection. Theophilus writing about the fall some time around the year AD 180 gives the following example:

> Take some sort of vessel that is discovered to have a particular defect after its completion. It is recast and refashioned so that it becomes new and perfect. A similar thing happens to man through death: he is, if I may put it that way, broken in pieces that he may be found whole and sound in the resurrection.[51]

A similar perception of death can be found in Methodius writing towards the end of the third century in a work on resurrection:

> God through death dissolved man into his primeval matter, in order that, by a process of remodelling, everything blameworthy in him might melt away ... for the melting down of the statue ... corresponds to the death ... of the body while the refashioning and restoration of the original material finds its parallel in the resurrection.[52]

It seems reasonable to hold that something similar will happen in relation to the future of creation. God's salvific work of recreating the world precisely because it is flawed like humanity will involve a process of being broken down in death before it can be transfigured into the New Creation. There is a process of disintegration so that there may be reintegration, a process of breakdown so that there can be re-creation.

What is suggestive about this analogy is that the activity of God in bringing life out of death is somewhat akin to the activity of the human artist. The image of God as artist, more particularly as the potter, is prominent in Jewish Scriptures. Jeremiah 18:2 tells us that the word of God is like the activity of the potter who reworks the flawed vessel into another vessel. The Hebrew term used in Genesis to describe the creation of humanity from the dust on the ground 'is a verb which denotes the activity of the potter'.[53] Is it not reasonable to claim that the activity of God as potter in the creation of humanity prefigures the activity of God to come in effecting the New Creation at the end of time – an activity which involves the artistic process of breakdown for the sake of creative breakthrough, a process symbolising the paschal event of death and resurrection? If the first creation is the work of a divine artist can we not dare to assume that the advent of the New Creation will also be an artistic work bearing the paschal hallmark of the Christ-event?

I began this chapter with the fairytale expression 'Once upon a time'. Most fairytales end with 'and they all lived happily ever after'. Is the

Christian story about the future of creation simply a happy-ever-after ending? The thrust of this chapter has been in the direction of a clear 'No' to this question! The future of creation is an ending stamped with the sign of the Cross, marked by the void of the empty tomb, and prefigured by the reality of the resurrection as God's gift to the whole of creation.

12

THE EUCHARIST AS SACRAMENT OF THE *ESCHATON*

In the earthly liturgy, by way of foretaste, we share in that heavenly liturgy which is celebrated in the holy city of Jerusalem towards which we journey as pilgrims.

(S.C., 1963)

IN THIS CONCLUDING CHAPTER I want to suggest that a close though largely under-emphasised connection exists between eschatology and the Eucharist. It is within the celebration of the Eucharist that the historical drama of Christian eschatology unfolds uniting past, present and future; it is in the Eucharist that the eschatological significance of the death and resurrection of Christ is represented; it is in the Eucharist that the *Eschaton* becomes sacramentally operative in the lives of individual communities. Above all it is the celebration of the Eucharist that keeps hope alive within the Christian community and the world.

To illustrate this thesis we will seek to recover some of the eschatological aspects of the Eucharist in the New Testament. This in turn will be followed by showing that it is in and through the liberating power of memory that the Eucharist embodies the *Eschaton* in the world today. Lastly this chapter will close by suggesting that the Eucharist celebrates not only the past but also the future. Of course there are many other equally important dimensions to the Eucharist such as sacrifice, *koinonia*, covenant and thanksgiving that could be highlighted. However, the selective focus of this chapter is intended to retrieve some of the neglected eschatological aspects of the Eucharist.

ESCHATOLOGICAL DIMENSIONS OF THE EUCHARIST

The origin of the Eucharist is usually associated with the so-called Institution Narratives of the Synoptics (Mark 14; Matt. 26; Luke 22) and Paul

(1 Cor. 11). Without diminishing the significance of the Last Supper accounts, recent biblical scholarship has 'loosened our hold on the upper room as the origin for the Lord's Supper in Christianity, at least as a single direct cause'.[1] Also important are the many meals celebrated by Jesus in his ministry which have come to the fore in the 'second quest' of the historical Jesus in the 50s and 60s as well as the 'third quest' of the 80s and 90s. The Last Supper therefore is more appropriately approached as the final meal in a series of significant meals in the life of Jesus.

Norman Perrin claims that table fellowship with sinners was a key feature of the ministry of Jesus.[2] The four Gospels contain many meal-stories in the ministry of Jesus. For example the Gospel of Luke has ten different meal-stories in the life of Jesus, among which the Last Supper stands out as the one summing up all the others.[3] Coming at the end of the life of Jesus the Last Supper in Luke 'looked back to the beginning, recapitulated all previous meals with Jesus, and fulfilled Israel's historic Passover'.[4] Given this link between the Last Supper and the other meals in the life of Jesus, commentators now prefer to talk about the origins of the Eucharist in the life of Jesus in contrast to seeing the institution of the Eucharist as an isolated event coming at the conclusion of his life.[5]

To situate the Last Supper within the context of the meals in the life of Jesus is not to relativise the importance of the Last Supper but rather to widen the horizon within which to appreciate the full meaning of the Eucharist. The Last Supper belongs to the whole life of Jesus and not just the end of his life.

The life of Jesus, as we have seen in Chapter 6, is eschatological, embracing both prophetic and apocalyptic elements, uniting the past and the future in the present, bringing together the hopes of Israel and humanity into the present. The life of Jesus is determined by the horizon of the reign of God proclaimed in word and deed as both present and future. For Jesus the reign of God is the object of his mission and ministry; it is already partially present in certain liberating activities such as heal-ings and exorcisms; it is also experienced as symbolically present in a new open table-fellowship initiated by Jesus among 'tax-collectors and sin-ners', prostitutes and outcasts. These meals are inclusive, embodying a new offer of unconditional forgiveness and acceptance; they defy the purity regulations governing table-fellowship within Judaism;[6] they break down the social and religious boundaries that existed in Palestine. The purpose of these meals is to give a glimpse of what the kingdom of God will be like. When Jesus does describe the future of Israel he employs the image of a meal: 'many will come from the east and west and will eat with Abraham, Isaac and Jacob in the kingdom of heaven' (Matt. 8:11).

These many meals of Jesus provoke considerable criticism: 'Why does he eat with tax collectors and sinners?' (Mark 2:16; see also Luke 15:2): 'He has gone to be the guest of one who is a sinner' (Luke 19:7); 'Look a glutton and a drunkard, a friend of tax collectors and sinners' (Luke 7:34). There can be little doubt that these meals of Jesus were what we today would describe as 'counter-cultural' experiences; they offered an alternative vision of life that had radical, social and religious implications. These meals of Jesus were a serious challenge to the social divisions obtaining in Palestine and to the religious rules governing holiness. In the words of Marcus Borg:

> ... the simple act of sharing a meal had exceptional religious and social significance in the social world of Jesus. It became a vehicle of cultural protest, challenging the ethos and politics of holiness, even as it also painted a different picture of what Israel was to be, an inclusive community reflecting the compassion of God.[7]

These meals also, and especially the feeding miracles, point towards the eschatological banquet described in the Hebrew Scriptures as representing the fulfilment of the reign of God.[8] Situated in the context of the preaching and praxis of Jesus concerning the reign of God it is difficult to ignore, as Marcus Borg does, the eschatological import of these inclusive, festive and open meals. For this reason some commentators describe these meals as 'messianic'.

It is against the background of these meals in the ministry of Jesus that we should approach the accounts of the Last Supper in Paul and the Synoptics. Before looking at these accounts there are three other surrounding influences that should be taken into consideration in any discussion of the Last Supper. These are Jesus' self-understanding of his own death, the cleansing of the Temple, and the Passover.

It is important to remember that the Last Supper takes place within the context of the growing awareness of Jesus that his imminent death is bound up with the coming reign of God. The only way in which the reign of God proclaimed as present and future can now be realised is in and through the awesome reality of his own death. This positive interpretation of imminent death by Jesus is made possible through the association of his ministry with the fate of previous prophet-martyrs. Further, Jesus would have been familiar with the Jewish conviction that though the righteous suffer, God will vindicate them – a theme that is quite prominent in the Psalms.[9] In addition, much of the ministry of Jesus is closely aligned with the servant songs of Isaiah. This emerging link between the death of Jesus and the coming reign of God should not be construed as a lessening in any way of the personal crisis for Jesus provoked by his impending death.

A second surrounding influence is the cleansing of the Temple. While it is extremely difficult to determine the details of this prophetic action and its full meaning it does seem 'to call for a radical break with the past'.[10] The life of Jesus in word and deed implies a critique of the Temple, its cult and priesthood, offering an alternative vision which is inclusive and universal. The prophetic action of cleansing the Temple implies the nearness, that is the coming into being, of an alternative kingdom-centred vision form of worship.

A third influence providing an important context for understanding the Last Supper is that it took place around the time of Passover. The debate about whether the Last Supper was (according to the Synoptics) or was not (according to John) a Passover meal is something of a distraction from the eschatological significance deriving from the fact that the Last Supper occurred around the time of Passover. The Jews journeyed up to Jerusalem once a year to celebrate God's action of deliverance from the Egyptians as well as all the other subsequent occasions that God had rescued Israel. This annual event was a deeply religious experience, not only recalling the past but also evoking hope that God would deliver Israel in the near future. During Passover time messianic hopes and eschatological expectations would have been raised. The minds and hearts of the Jews would have focused not only on past deliverance but also on the future, not only on the gift of creation but also on hopes for a New Creation. Thus an important part of the atmosphere surrounding the celebration of the Last Supper was the context of Passover.[11]

Given this background of meals in the life of Jesus, the emerging self-understanding of Jesus concerning the significance of his own death, the actions of cleansing the Temple, and the Passover setting, it is hardly surprising to discover that the Last Supper accounts are laden with eschatological symbolism and meaning. It should be acknowledged immediately that there is considerable variation among the four accounts of the Last Supper and that what we are given are interpretative narratives containing different liturgical usages operative within different communities. In spite of this variation in accounts there is a common eschatological motif running through the narratives. This motif is present in varying degrees through the emphasis on memory, references to the covenant, statements about drinking the new fruit of the vine in the kingdom of God (Mark 14:25; Matt. 26:29; Luke 22:18), and the link made between the death of Jesus and his coming again.

It is generally agreed that the Last Supper is 'a meal within a meal', that is the immediate framework of the Last Supper is a meal: 'When they had taken their places and were eating' (Matt. 26:21, 26; Mark 14:18, 22). There are two actions within the Last Supper, one concerned with the bread and the other with the cup. In the first action Jesus takes the bread, says a blessing, breaks the bread and gives it to his disciples. In the second action Jesus takes the cup, offers thanks, and gives the cup to his disciples. These actions are accompanied by four statements addressed by Jesus to his disciples. These statements are about connecting the bread with his body, linking the cup with his blood and the covenant, commanding the disciples to do this in memory of me, and talking about drinking the fruit of the vine in the kingdom of God.

Mention of the covenant at the Last Supper would have resurrected recollections of the Jewish covenant already established between God and Israel in history. The language of covenant has eschatological connotations: it evokes not only the covenant of the past between God and Israel but also carries within itself the pledge of God's fidelity to his people in the present and the future. In the Hebrew Scriptures it is Yahweh in the first instance who remembers the covenant in the past in a manner that also embraces the present and the future. The association of covenant with blood at the Last Supper parallels in particular the covenant sacrifice offered by Moses on Mount Sinai (Ex. 12:14). In addition the language of covenant would also recall the many other covenants established between God and Israel in the course of history which were understood to include the overarching covenant established by the gift of creation itself. To this extent, covenant goes back beyond the God of the Sinaitic covenant to the God of all creation who continues to be faithful to Israel in the present and will remain faithful into the future.

Reference to the covenant is followed immediately with the command 'Do this in memory of me' found in Paul (1 Cor. 11:24, 25) and Luke (Luke 22:19). There was within Judaism a strong link between covenant and memory. The full import of the word 'memory' within Hebrew thought will be taken up in the next section. Suffice it to say here that the command to 'do this in memory of me' parallels a similar command relating to the Jewish Passover meal before the Israelites' exodus from Egypt: 'This day shall be a remembrance for you. You shall celebrate it as a festival to the Lord' (Ex. 12:14). In both instances the event being celebrated, one through the Passover meal and the other by the Lord's Supper, while belonging to the past is also at the same time a pledge of a new and definitive future. There is however a difference between the event being remembered at the Last Supper insofar as it is identified explicitly with the personal life of Jesus. In both instances the effect of memory is to make active in the present the power and significance of what has happened in the past.

It is in the statement concluding the Last Supper account in Mark 14:25, Matthew 26:29, Luke 22:18, that is most formally eschatological: 'Truly, I tell you I will never drink again of the fruit of the vine until that day when I drink it new in the Kingdom of God' (Mk. 14:25).[12]

This eschatological perspective makes explicit what is implicit in the reference to covenant and memory. Though the focus in the Last Supper account is on what is to take place in the imminent death of Jesus, there is also at the same time a fundamental confidence that what is about to happen will lead to the participation of Jesus in the eschatological banquet of the end of time. This expression of eschatological faith links the Last Supper with the heavenly banquet. In his earthly ministry Jesus had referred to and at times prefigured the messianic banquet (e.g. Luke 14:1–24; Matt. 8:11; Matt. 22:2–14); he now formally connects his Last Supper with the master symbol of the *Eschaton*, namely the reign of God. Within the Last Supper and the communion effected between himself and his disciples, Jesus glimpses the eschatological banquet of the king-dom of God. In this way the Last Supper, which gathers up the mission and ministry of Jesus as well as his death and destiny, establishes in word and sacramental action the eschatological banquet of the reign of God.

It should be noted that the wine he will drink in the kingdom of God is 'new' and the Greek word used here is '*kainon*' which is something radically different from the wine of this life; it is a newly created and unexpected wine, just like the radically new of the new heaven and the new earth.[13] The word 'new' used in reference to the wine in the reign of God is also the same word used to describe the new covenant in Paul's account of the Last Supper.

A final eschatological motif on the Last Supper account is found in Paul: 'For as often as you eat this bread and drink the cup, you proclaim the Lord's death until he comes' (1 Cor. 11:26). This statement is regarded by many as more of a commentary on the meaning of the Last Supper than a record of the actual words of the original event. The reference to 'until he comes again' suggests that the Last Supper will find its fulfilment in the second coming of Christ and that in the meantime the celebration of the Lord's Supper anticipates that final coming of Christ. In effect the Last Supper puts the participants in touch with the future, reminding them that the death of Jesus and participation in the death of Jesus through the Eucharist links people with the future coming of Christ. This link between the historical death of Jesus and the second coming is further highlighted by Paul in his use of the prayer, 'Come, Lord Jesus', *Maranatha*.

This double action of Jesus over the bread and wine at the Last Supper will only make sense when it is kept within its Jewish context. The behaviour of Jesus at the Last Supper is a 'behaviour peculiar to the prophets of the Bible'.[14] The prophets of old often mime their message in a manner that is at once symbolic and efficacious. For example, Ezekiel who wishes to announce the impending deportation of the inhabitants of Jerusalem engages in the prophetic action of shaving his head and scattering the hairs to the wind with the comment: 'Thus says the lord, "this is Jerusalem"' (Ezek. 5:5). In a somewhat similar way Jesus' Last Supper is the performance of a prophetic act which prefigures his own immediate future of death and its significance for the future of Israel. In other words the future is represented symbolically in the actions of Jesus with his disciples at the Last Supper.

THE EUCHARIST AND THE POWER OF MEMORY

The question that arises today is whether it is possible to recover this rich relationship between eschatology and the Eucharist. Does the celebration of the Eucharist evoke any connection with eschatology that has practical implications for the way we live in the present and the future? Given the overall thesis of this book that eschatology is as much about relationships in this life as the next life, is it possible that the celebration of the Eucharist might creatively embody this unified eschatological perspective? More particularly, it must be asked does our eschatological understanding of the Eucharist have anything to say to the existence of so much suffering and death in our world, especially the presence of mass suffering and death in the twentieth century: the Jewish holocaust, Hiroshima, the Gulf War, Somalia, Rwanda, and the ongoing holocaust in so many other parts of the Third World? The single most serious challenge to eschatology comes from the reality of human suffering and death followed closely, as we have already pointed out at the beginning of this book, by the imminent threat to the life of the planet from nuclear destruction and ecological collapse. Is it possible that the concentration of eschatology within the Eucharist and of the Eucharist within eschatology could provide something of a counter-cultural sign to the presence of so much fatalism and cynicism that many of these issues all too often engender today.

Obviously an adequate response to these questions is beyond the limited parameters of this work. At most we can provide only pointers as to how these questions might be addressed within an eschatological understanding of the Eucharist.

In spite of these obvious limitations I want to suggest that one of the keys to a retrieval of an eschatological appreciation of the Eucharist is the category of memory. Recent studies in philosophy, political theology and biblical scholarship have begun to rediscover the redemptive power of memory within history. In particular the work of Walter Benjamin (1892–1940), already touched upon in Chapter 8, raises searching questions about the nature of history, about the forgotten suffering of the victims of history, and the possible influence of the dead upon the present. The questions of Benjamin are our questions today and are ultimately eschatological.

Seeking to resolve these issues Benjamin invokes the liberating power of memory. Though his answers are highly suggestive they are in the end unsatisfactory from a theological point of view. Yet there are elements of his philosophy that can be used at least dialectically in retrieving an eschatological understanding of the Eucharist. The theologian who has developed Benjamin's ideas most creatively is Johann Baptist Metz in his well-known political theology.

Benjamin in his dialogue with Horkheimer and in his further refinement of that dialogue in his famous historical-philosophical thesis 'On the concept of history' is passionately concerned to keep history open, resolutely refusing to see history as closed and finished.[15] To achieve this aim Benjamin proposes that it is necessary to read history against the grain. By this he means we must look at history from the perspective of the victims of history, especially their forgotten sufferings, and not, as is usually the case, from the perspective of the victors.

For Benjamin the so-called progress of history appears as 'one single catastrophe which keeps piling wreckage upon wreckage' and the 'pile of debris' is so vast that it 'grows skyward'.[16] According to Benjamin every great work of civilisation is at the very same time a work of barbarism. Against this background the fundamental issue for Benjamin is: How can the dead victims of history exercise an influence on history today? His answer as an historical materialist is twofold: through the power of memory and by enlisting what he calls 'the services of theology'. He argues:

> The corrective of this line of thought [namely that history is closed] lies in the reflection that history is not only a science, but equally a form of remembrance. What has been 'established' by science can be modified in remembrance. Remembrance can make the incomplete (happiness) complete, and render the complete (suffering) incomplete. That is

theology; but remembrance gives us an experience which forbids us to regard history completely without theology, any more than we should record it directly in the form of theological concepts.[17]

Benjamin, of course, distinguishes between false memory and authentic memory, between memory that merely recalls the past as it is and memory that wrests tradition from conformism in the present, between memory that repeats the history of oppressors and memory that records the history of the oppressed. The creative power of memory is to disrupt historical continuity. Like his colleague Marcuse, Benjamin held that the recovery of the capacity to remember could become a vehicle of liberation. In the end it is memory that keeps the spark of hope alive. In a most poignant remark Benjamin points out: 'It's only for the sake of those without hope that we have been given hope.'[18] Elsewhere he states: 'There is a secret agreement between past generations and the present one. Our coming was expected on earth.' By this he means that the past has a claim on us in the present and that this claim for the historical materialist cannot be settled cheaply.[19] Memory, especially the memory of the suffering of the oppressed in the past, has the power to disrupt the flow of history in the present; in effect the memory of enslaved ancestors can transform present history.

It is Johann Baptist Metz who expands these dense theses of Benjamin about memory and history. Metz describes memory as 'a category of resistance to the passage of time (interpreted as evolution) and, in this sense as the organon of apocalyptic consciousness'.[20] The exercise of memory can become a protest against existing conditions and a way of overcoming the omnipresent power of the established facts. Memory enables people to realise that the way we are is not the way we have to be and in this regard memory has the power to activate a new praxis that breaks through the prevailing historical consciousness. This exercise of memory operates out of a fundamental solidarity with the dead and this solidarity with the dead from the past allows the victims of the past to effect a change on history in the present. The past, therefore, need not be past but an effective leaven operative in the present.

This philosophical recovery of the power of memory by Walter Benjamin and Johann Baptist Metz must be complemented by an equally significant rediscovery of memory within biblical studies. John Reumann sums up this rediscovery by pointing out that

> biblical theology in the last sixty years has emphasised that in the *Old Testament* (and hence here in the New) the term 'remembrance'

suggests not so much *our* calling something to mind as an action that where *God* as subject makes concretely present something out of the past so that it speaks afresh to the contemporary situation.[21]

Most biblical commentators begin their reflection on memory by pointing out it is God in the first place who remembers and that it is in virtue of God remembering that Israel is able to give praise to God in the present. God in many instances is the subject of the verb 'to remember' and the most frequent use of this verb is God remembering his covenant with his people (Gen. 9:15; Ex. 2:24; Lev. 26:42; Ezek. 16:60). The memory of God for God's people determines Jewish identity and shapes human conduct.[22]

The Hebrew verb 'to remember' – *zikkaron* – carries with it a resulting action so that when God remembers the covenant, he effects a blessing upon the people of the covenant. Memory and action go together in Hebrew thought so that memory is not simply calling a person to mind but also involves acting in a particular way in virtue of that memory. Further, the memory of God embraces not only God's covenant but also the primordial covenant of creation itself. In addition, within Judaism memory is bound up very closely with cult: 'This day shall be a remembrance day for you. You shall celebrate it as a festival to the Lord' (Ex. 12:14). Though the memory of God primarily embraces the covenant it also includes God's love and forgiveness (1 Sam. 1:11; 2 Chr. 6:42) as well as the memory of creation and Passover.

At the same time God also calls on the people of Israel to remember the Passover, the covenant, the Sabbath day and the Commandments (Ex. 12:8; Mal. 4:4). Moses challenges the people of Israel especially in the Book of Deuteronomy to remember God, the deeds of God in history, their liberation from slavery in Egypt, and the desert journey. Likewise the role of the prophets is to jog the memory of the people of God. It is memory that makes the past operative in the present and in doing so holds out promises for the future. The memory of the liberating action of God in the past through Passover and the creation is the basis of promises for the future. It is the memory of the past that is the foundation of Israel's hope in the future; in effect the memory of past experience generates a confident hope in the future.

This distinctively Jewish theology of memory is an important part of the context and atmosphere surrounding the Last Supper. Jesus the Jew, in his farewell supper with his disciples around the time of the Passover, resurrects this rich background when he invites them 'do this in memory of me'. The action of Jesus at the Last Supper is not only prophetic in terms of his own personal destiny that is about to take place but is also eschatological insofar as it prefigures his own future and the future of humanity.

It would be incorrect to create a mutual exclusive opposition between Benjamin's philosophy of memory and the Jewish theology of memory. It should not be forgotten that Benjamin himself was Jewish and even though he had severed his connections formally with Judaism, it nevertheless left an indelible mark on his thinking, especially in relation to memory. Benjamin is probably best understood in the words of his life-long Jewish friend and Hebrew scholar Gershom Scholem 'as a scribe cast into another world' and something of 'a theologian marooned in the realm of the profane'.[23] Instead of opposing these two streams of thought it is much more desirable to see them as complementary. God and humanity must not be presented in opposition or competition with each other, but rather in covenant (as Judaism puts it) and in communion (as Christianity claims). It is a false theology and ultimately a wrong-headed eschatology that separates the sacred and the secular, divorces time and eternity, or divides endings and beginnings.

We must, however, distance ourselves from Benjamin's philosophy in at least two specific areas from an eschatological point of view. On the one hand Benjamin subordinates the services of theology to the dictates of historical materialism. It is Benjamin's philosophy of historical materialism that takes control of theology, reducing it simply as a means to the services of a purely human utopia. The second difficulty follows from the first. Benjamin's historical materialism gives the impression that humanity can save itself, forgetting that true freedom in this life comes as a gift from outside oneself and that ultimate salvation comes as absolute gift from God. The only real heresy in eschatology is the dangerous illusion that the individual can save himself or herself and the rest of the world both in this life and the hereafter. Perhaps the real value of Benjamin's philosophy is to remind eschatology once again of the importance and the possibility of keeping history open, of uniting the living with the dead in the struggle for freedom, and of highlighting the challenge imposed on this generation by the suffering of past generations in and through the liberating power of memory. In doing this, Benjamin has provided significant resources for developing an eschatological understanding of the Eucharist which can bring about changes in the present for the sake of the coming reign of God. In addition, Benjamin's philosophy of memory and the renewal of a biblical theology of memory together provide a more dynamic perspective in which the Eucharist as memorial may be appreciated.

THE EUCHARIST AS A MEMORIAL OF THE PAST
AND A CELEBRATION OF THE *FUTURE*

The existing links between Eucharist and *anamnesis* within the Christian liturgy can be renewed through this new appreciation of memory. In particular the liberating power of memory brought to the fore by philosophy and biblical theology can help to bring out the eschatological potential of the Eucharist and how this might be connected to the perennial questions of suffering and death as well as the challenges coming from nuclear and ecological issues. Through the power of memory, especially the faithful memory of God active in Christ and now among his disciples, the Eucharist stands out as a celebration of eschatology uniting the past and the future in the present. The Eucharist gathers up all that Christ stood for, symbolised in his meals, prophetically formalised at the Last Supper and the washing of the feet, and eschatologically realised in his death and resurrection. However for many, according to David Power 'The relation of the remembered event to the present and its continued influence on history is the crux of a current Eucharistic theology.'[24] To help overcome this crux we will draw on the insights of Benjamin and Judaism concerning the redemptive power of memory.

If divine memory is about making the past active in the present and if human memory is about being faithful to the agreement of solidarity that exists between past and present generations, then the celebration of the Eucharist becomes that event which makes the eschatological work of Christ available in the present. By making the work of Christ active in the present, the celebration of the Eucharist challenges and disrupts the secular course of history. If, as Benjamin insisted, authentic memory is about reading history against the grain, then keeping the memory of Christ alive in the world is about reading history against the grain of accepting so much oppression, suffering and death. Christ in the past and the present stands out prophetically against all dominating forms of oppression, suffering and death. In this way the celebration of the Eucharist which makes Christ present is a counter-cultural sign just as Christ was a counter-cultural sign in Palestine bringing through his meals and the Last Supper, good news to the poor, release to captives, sight to the blind and freedom to the oppressed (Luke 4:18). The celebration of the Eucharist as a memorial of the past in the present is counter-cultural insofar as it offers an alternative way, opens up a new world, represents a privileged moment of divine presence (*kairos*) in contrast to the boredom of endless time (*chronos*), critiques the individualism of the modern world, and challenges the reigning culture of contentment. Because the Eucharist is essentially a community-event representing in word and sacrament the newly established eschatological order of the reign of God, it disallows unfair distribution, refuses individualism and division, negates the self-interest of so much political and worldly power, opposes all relationships of domination, and disrupts the empty flow of secular history. In effect the Eucharist is 'the sacrament of equality in an unequal world'.[25]

But the Eucharist is also a counter-cultural sign insofar as it connects all those in the assembly with the suffering and death of Christ as well as the forgotten suffering and death of all who have gone before us.[26] The Eucharist through the dynamic power of memory represents the suffering and death of Christ, making it effective once again for those who are willing to follow the way of the crucified Christ. The story of the suffering and death of Christ challenges the ongoing historical forces of darkness and evil in the world, reminding us prophetically that injustice and death do not have the final word and that therefore history remains open and incomplete and unfinished 'until he comes again'. Likewise the ongoing presence of so much innocent suffering and death in our world since the Christ-event is also represented in the Eucharist insofar as the memory of the dead is formally invoked as an integral part of every celebration of the Eucharist. The fundamental solidarity of the living with the dead in Christ is announced in the celebration of the Eucharist in a way that creatively links the past with the present. This unity of the dead with the living in Christ challenges the continuation of so much suffering and demands what Benjamin describes as the discontinuity of such a history of suffering. This memory of suffering and death has the power to evoke a new praxis of liberation in present history. Memory without action addressed to the sources of suffering and death runs the risk of becoming mere routine – a temptation that is present in every celebration of the Eucharist. It was this particular temptation within Jewish worship that was the object of outspoken criticism by the prophets of old and was similarly the object of critique in the preaching and praxis of Jesus.[27] Action for justice and the praxis of liberation from social and cultural idolatry is an imperative intrinsic to every celebration of the Eucharist. This creative link between the celebration of the Eucharist and the requirement of a new ethical praxis is brought out explicitly by Paul in his instruction to the Corinthians and how they should conduct themselves when they gather to eat the bread and to drink the cup of the Lord. Paul in particular complains that the meal in which the Eucharist is celebrated is marked by divisions, with some remaining hungry and others becoming drunk (1 Cor. 11:17–34). Paul, one suspects, would be equally critical of many eucharistic assemblies today.

The eschatological meals of Jesus, the Last Supper, and the commentary by Jesus on the Last Supper through the prophetic action of washing the feet of his disciples were disruptive of social and cultural history in first-century Palestine. Insofar as the celebration of the Eucharist today fails to critique or disrupt social and cultural history, it loses its eschatological significance. It is for this reason that many theologians today describe the memory of the Passion, death and resurrection of Christ as 'dangerous', 'subversive' and 'liberating'.[28] To be sure the celebration of the Eucharist also involves a celebration of unity, peace and reconciliation. But these particular descriptions of the Eucharist are in danger of becoming vacuous if the memory of Christ celebrated in the Eucharist is not accompanied by a new praxis of liberation challenging the historical social and cultural distortions of the present.

The other side to every celebration of the Eucharist is that it is also an announcement and celebration of the future. We have become so accustomed to understanding the Eucharist as a celebration of the past and the present, that we have lost sight of its prophetic significance as also a celebration of the future in the present. Yet the earliest celebrations of the Eucharist available in Corinthians and in the *Didache* 10:6, were deeply conscious of the link with the future, symbolised in the prayer of *Maranatha*, 'Come, Lord Jesus'. This prayer of the early Church accompanying the celebration of the Eucharist is understood by many to have had a double point of reference, namely a prayer for the *Parousia* ('Come, Lord Jesus') as well as a confession of faith recognising the eschatological advent of Christ in the Eucharist (The Lord has come).[29] What is perhaps even more significant is that very early on *Maranatha* is replaced by the formula 'Blessed is he who comes in the name of the Lord' – a statement suggesting that the celebration of the Eucharist is also about recognising the advent of the future in the present. It is the perception of the risen Christ as already present in the Eucharist that gave rise subsequently within the Patristic period to descriptions of the Eucharist as an anticipation of the future and a prefiguration of what is to come.[30] In this way the celebration of the Eucharist was understood as much as a celebration of the future as it was a celebration of the past in the present.

This focus on the Eucharist as an anticipation of the future is present quite explicitly in the sacramental theology of Aquinas who describes a sacrament as a *'signum prognosticum'*, a sign that foretells what is to come: 'A sacrament is a sign which recalls a past event, the passion of Christ, indicates the effect of the passion of Christ in us that is grace, and foretells, that is, heralds the glory that is to come.'[31] This principle is applied in a special way in the well-known verses attributed to Aquinas that sum up the Eucharist:

> O Sacred banquet in which Christ is received
> the memory of his passion is recalled
> the mind is filled with grace,
> and a pledge of future glory is given to us.

This emphasis on the Eucharist as anticipating the future is also found in various Councils and church documents down through the centuries. The Council of Trent describes the Eucharist as 'a pledge of future glory and everlasting happiness'.[32] The Second Vatican Council talks about the Eucharist as a foretaste of the heavenly banquet,[33] and the new *Catechism of the Catholic Church* refers to the Eucharist as 'an anticipation of heavenly glory' and 'a sign of hope in the new heavens and the new earth'.[34] Perhaps even more significant is the presence of this theme of the Eucharist as a foretaste of the future in recent ecumenical statements. For example, the document *Baptism, Eucharist and Ministry* published by the World Council of Churches in 1982 declares:

> The Eucharist opens up the vision of the divine rule which has been promised as the final renewal of creation, and is a foretaste of it . . . the Eucharist is the feast at which the church gives thanks to God for these signs and joyfully celebrates and anticipates the coming of the kingdom in Christ.[35]

In what sense can we say that in the Eucharist we anticipate the future and are given a foretaste of things to come? To answer this question we must keep in mind the origins of the Eucharist going back to the life and ministry of Jesus. The meals celebrated by Jesus with sinners and outcasts were intended to symbolise the new life of the coming reign of God: the unconditional offer of forgiveness, the establishment of new relationships, the reversal of the old order, and the creation of a new inclusive community. These meals are given particular eschatological focus and expression at the Last Supper celebrated at Passover time, renewing the covenant of God with creation and history, and at the same time linking the imminent death of Jesus with the dawning of the reign of God. This eschatological advent of the reign of God is experienced by the disciples to have taken place in and through the historical death and resurrection of Jesus so that from now on 'the breaking of the bread and the sharing of the cup' is linked with the already established reign of God in Christ. The Eucharist mediates the future reign of God by incorporating within its celebration the fundamental qualities of the *Eschaton*: the praise of God, the corporate solidarity of humanity in Christ, the unity between past, present and future effected by the Spirit, and the transformation of the material elements of bread and wine into the New Creation of the Body of Christ.

Every Eucharist is about giving praise to God and therefore this experience reminds us of our future destiny 'in Christ'. The celebration of the death and resurrection of Christ in the Eucharist re-enacts individual and corporate destiny, reminding us that every individual is faced with the dark but bright prospect of personal death and resurrection 'in Christ'. In the Eucharist a fundamental communion, foreshadowing the future, is brought about between the living and the dead, between the individual and the community, between the human (*anthropos*) and the cosmic (*cosmos*) – and all of this is symbolised in the transformation of the bread and wine into the Body and Blood of Christ.

In particular the Eucharist captures *in embryo* the future transformation of the cosmos into a New Creation. The material elements of bread and wine are transformed into the Body of Christ, reminding us that material creation itself is destined to be part of the New Creation in Christ. This important but neglected aspect of the Eucharist ought to be brought out more imaginatively in the way we celebrate the Eucharist in view of the presence of so much ecological degradation and destruction of God's creation. The celebration of the Eucharist ought to be seen and experienced as a counter-cultural sign of ecological wholeness, an ecological integrity protesting against the mindless destruction of God's material creation by modern industry and technology. The ecological significance of the Eucharist cries out for attention in a world threatened by the ecological collapse of so many of the life-support systems in our world.

James P. Mackey has pointed out in an imaginative way that 'Eucharistic praxis . . . is the Christian alternative to war'.[36] The spirit of this original observation must be extended so that authentic eucharistic praxis can be seen to be not only the Christian response to war but also to the human, ecological and nuclear exploitation of the world in which we live. The Eucharistic Assembly is that particular historical location on earth that seeks to symbolise in word and sacrament the dreams and hopes released by Jesus for the future of humanity and creation.

These all too brief and merely schematic observations on the Eucharist as a sacrament of the *Eschaton* suggest that it is the Eucharist that keeps

Keeping Hope Alive

Christian hope alive within the community of faith and the world. The Eucharist keeps Christian hope alive by celebrating through the power of memory the fundamental unity that exists between past, the present and future 'in Christ'. By bringing the past into the present and by prefiguring our corporate Trinitarian future the Eucharist activates hope in the present. By previewing the future the Eucharist gives a sense of direction to a world that is in danger of losing sight of gifted origins and graced endings. Only when we have a sense of life as gift will we be able to celebrate that gift in the present through the Eucharist and at the same time dare to hope that what the Eucharist symbolises will come to eschatological fruition for the whole of humanity and creation in the fullness of God's time.

NOTES

Chapter 1

1 J. B. Metz, 'Theology Today: New Crises and New Visions', *Proceedings of the Catholic Theological Society of America* 40 (1985), 13.

2 K. Rahner, 'Possible Courses for the Theology of the Future', *Theological Investigations*, vol. 13 (London: DLT; New York: The Crossroad Publishing Company), 33.

3 See W. Pannenberg 'The Critical Function of Eschatology', *Harvard Theological Review* 77 (1984).

4 See *G.S.*, 43, 39, 38, 21, 57.

5 *G.S.*, 5.

6 Vatican Council 1, *Dei Filius* in *The Christian Faith in the Documents of the Catholic Church*. Edited by J. Neuner & J. Dupuis (London: Collins, 1983; New York: Alba House), 45.

7 See A. Kelly, *An Expanding Theology: Faith in a World of Connections* (Australia: E. T. Dwyer, 1993).

8 Barth, *The Epistle to the Romans*. Translated by Edwyn C. Hoskyns (London: Oxford University Press, 1933), 314.

9 J. Moltmann, *The Theology of Hope*, 16.

10 Peter Phan, who has written a significant study of Rahner's eschatology, points out that 'eschatology occupies a central place in Rahner's theology ... Thus it is indisputably clear that for Rahner all Christian theology is in a very genuine sense eschatology.' *Eternity in Time: A Study of Karl Rahner's Eschatology* (Selinsgrove: Susquehanna University Press, 1988), 22–3.

11 K. Rahner, *Foundations for Christian Faith: An Introduction to the Idea of Christianity* (London: DLT, 1978; New York: The Crossroad Publishing Company), 457.

12 On the place of eschatology within the patristic period see B. Daley, *The Hope of the Early Church* (New York: Cambridge University Press, 1991); J. R. Sachs, 'Apocatastasis in Patristic Theology', *Theological Studies* 54 (1993), 617–40.

13 G. Gutierrez is an exception to this generalisation. His *Theology of Liberation* does have a chapter on eschatology but it would need to take greater account of the place of creation and the criticisms of modern anthropology.

14 P. Land detects the presence of an eschatological orientation in the 1991 encyclical *Centesimus Annus* of John Paul II. See P. Land, 'God in Our World' *Center Focus* 113 (September 1993), 6–7. In a similar manner the universal phenomenon of human hope cries out for an eschatological interpretation.

15 G. Daly in *Creation and Redemption* (Dublin: Gill and Macmillan, 1988; Collegeville: Liturgical Press), acknowledges the presence of eschatological questions in the theology of creation.

16 *G.S.*, 5 & 39.

17 *G.S.*, 4 & 5.

18 *G.S.*, 36, *D.H.* 1, 8.

19 *D.V.*, 8 & 14; *G.S.*, 33.

20 *G.S.*, 4.

21 An outline of this more positive understanding of post-modernity can be found in S. Toulmin, *The Return to Cosmology: Post Modern Science and the Theology of Nature,* (Berkley: University of California Press, 1982), 94–100; D. Griffin (ed.) *The Re-Enchantment of Science: Post Modern Proposals,* (New York: Suny Press, 1988); D. Griffin, *God and Religion in the Post Modern World: Essays in Post Modern Theology* (New York: Suny Press, 1989).

22 *Time,* 28th June 1993, 21.

23 J. Schell, *The Fate of the Earth* (1982), 173.

24 U.S. Bishops 'The Challenge of Peace: God's Promise and Our Response', *Origins,* 19th May 1988, 30.

25 G. D. Kaufmann, *Theology in a Nuclear Age* (Philadelphia: The Westminster Press, 1985), Ch.1.

26 K. Rahner, *Theological Investigations.*

27 *G.S.*, a.10.

28 Bradford A. Smith, 'New Eyes on the Universe', *National Geographic,* vol. 185, no. 1 (January 1994), 10.

29 B. Russell, *A Free Man's Worship* (New York: Allen and Unwin, 1918), 46.

30 J. Monod, *Chance and Necessity* (New York: Vintage Books, 1972), 180.

31 'Message of His Holiness John Paul II' in *Physics, Philosophy and Theology: A Common Quest for Understanding,* R. J. Russell, W. R. Stoeger & J. V. Coyne (eds.) (Vatican City: Liberia Editrice Vaticana, 1988; Notre Dame, In.: University of Notre Dame Press), M. 12 and M. 11 respectively.

32 The Bishops of the Netherlands, *A New Catechism: Catholic Faith for Adults* (London: Burns and Oates, 1967), 9.

33 T. Altiser, *Genesis and Apocalypse: A Theological Voyage Toward Authentic Christianity* (Kentucky: W./J.K.P., 1990), 9.

34 H. Brown, *The Wisdom of Science: Its Relevance to Culture and Religion* (Cambridge University Press, 1986), 172.

Chapter 2

1 For an elaboration of the turn to human experience in theology see Dermot A. Lane, *The Experience of God: An Invitation to do Theology* (Dublin: Veritas Publications, 1981; New York: Paulist Press). This turn to experience in Catholic theology can be found in many of the documents of the Second Vatican Council as well as post-conciliar documents and papal encyclicals: *D.V.,* 8 & 14; *G.S.*, 33, *G.C.D.,* 74.

2   K. Rahner, *Foundations of Christian Faith*, 431.
3   A. N. Whitehead, *Science in the Modern World,*76.
4   Ibid., 72.
5   D. Tracy, *Blessed Rage For Order: The New Pluralism in Theology* (New York: Seabury Press, 1975), Ch. 5, esp. 105–6.
6   D. Tracy, 'Tillich and Contemporary Theology', *The Thought of Paul Tillich*, J. L. Adams, et. al. (eds.) (San Francisco: Harper and Row, 1985), 260–77. See also Dermot A. Lane, 'Faith and Culture' for an elaboration of this point which is available in *Religion and Culture in Dialogue: A Challenge for the Next Millennium*, Dermot A. Lane (ed.) (Dublin: Columba Publications, 1993; Mystic, Ct.: Twenty-Third Publications).
7   *G.S.*, a.39; see also a.21 which makes the same point.
8   Eph. 1:9–10; see also Col. 1:15–20; 1 Cor. 15:20–25.
9   See *G.S.*, a.5, 21, 34, 38, 39, 57; *L.G.*, a.48–51.
10 *G.S.*, a.45.
11 K. Barth, *Epistle to the Romans*, trans. by E. C. Hoskyns (London, 1933), 314.
12 K. Rahner, 'The Hermeneutics of Eschatological Statements', *Theological Investigations*, vol 4, translated by Kevin Smyth (London: DLT, 1966; New York: The Crossroad Publishing Company), 334.
13 W. Kasper, 'Hope in the Final Coming of Jesus Christ in Glory', *Communio*, Summer/Winter 1985. See also Rahner in *Theological Investigations*, vol. 4, 342–3.
14 Aquinas, *De Veritate*, q.22, a.2, ad1.
15 *Pensees*, vii, 553.
16 For an illuminating treatment of this aspect of Von Hugel's thought see J. Kelly, *Baron Frederick Von Hugel's Philosophy of Religion* (Belgium: Leuven University Press, 1983), esp. Pt. II, Chs. II & IV.
17 *Little Gidding*.
18 *Karl Rahner: Im Gesprach*, vol. 1, 301.
19 K. Rahner, 'The Need for a Short Formula of Faith', *Theological Investigations*, vol. 9 (London: DLT, 1980; New York: The Crossroad Publishing Company), 1–2. It is interesting to note how Rahner's emphasis on the co-experience and understanding of God is echoed in the theology of W. Pannenberg in *Theology and the Philosophy of Science* (London: DLT), 301. Other areas in Rahner's theology touching on this understanding of the mystery of God include 'Reflections on the problem involved in devising a short formula of the Faith', *Theological Investigations*, vol. 11 (London: DLT, 1980), 238; 'The Experience of God Today', *Theological Investigations*, vol. xi (London: DLT, 1974), 149–65; 'The Experience of Self and Experience of God', *Theological Investigations*, vol. xii (London: DLT, 1975), 122–32; *Foundations of Christian Faith: An Introduction to the Idea of Christianity* (London: DLT, 1978; New York: The Crossroad Publishing Company), Ch. II.
20 *G.S.*, 19; (see also *G.S.* 18, 21, 22; *L.G.*, 13).
21 See E. Yarnold, *The Second Gift: A Study of Grace* (Slough, England: St Paul Publications, 1974), 1–24.

22 1 John 4:19.
23 See the Hymn for Mid-day Prayer in the Breviary, week 4, Tuesday: 'O God-head, here untouched, unseen. All things created bear your trace, the seed of glory sown in man, will flower when we see your face'.
24 Aquinas, *S.T.,* Ia IIae, 106, 4.
25 *G.S.,* 18.
26 *G.S.,* 45; see also *G.S.,* 22; *L.G.,* 48.
27 Psalm 104:30.
28 Rev. 21:5.
29 These points are impressively developed by Elizabeth A. Johnson in *Women, Earth, and Creator Spirit* (Paulist Press, 1993), 41–60.
30 Quotation taken from E. A. Johnson, *Women, Earth and Creator:* 50. See Cyril of Jerusalem, *Catechetical Lectures,* 16, 12.
31 A. Peacocke, *Creation and the World of Science* (Oxford: Oxford University Press, 1979), 95.
32 *G.S.,* 45; see also *G.S.,* 22; *L.G.,* 48.

Chapter 3

1 *G.S.,* 3, 10, 12, 22.
2 K. Rahner, 'Theology and Anthropology', *Theological Investigations,* vol. 9 (London: DLT, 1972; New York: The Crossroad Publishing Company), 28–45.
3 Ibid., 45; *Foundations of Christian Faith: An Introduction to the Idea of Christianity* (New York: Seabury Press, 1978), 431.
4 Y. Congar, 'Fins dernies', *Revue de Sciences Philosophiques et Theologiques* 33 (1949), 463–84; Z. Hayes, *Visions of a Future: A Study of Christian Eschatology* (Delaware: M. Glazier, 1989), 71–80; J. Sachs, *The Christian Vision of Humanity: Basic Christian Anthropology* (Collegeville: Liturgical Press/M. Glazier Book, 1991), 75–102.
5 I am conscious of the ambiguity attaching to the term 'post-modern'. 'Post-modern' is used here to convey more a sense of dissatisfaction with modern anthropology than any clearly defined alternative. In other instances post-modern can connote either a process of negative deconstruction or a positive process of reconstruction.
6 See Charles Taylor, *Sources of the Self: The Making of Modern Identity* (Melbourne: Cambridge University Press,1989), 495–521 and *The Ethics of Authenticity* (Massachusetts: Harvard University Press,1991), 1–12.
7 See the helpful account of this shift given by Charles Davis, *Body as Spirit: the Nature of Religious Feeling* (New York: Seabury Press, 1976), 75–9.
8 C. Davis, op. cit., 79.
9 Different accounts of the relational, connected and processive self of feminism can be found in Carol Gilligan, *In a Different Voice: Psychological Theory and Women's Development* (Cambridge: Harvard University Press, 1982); R. R. Ruether, *Sexism and God Talk: Towards a Feminist Theology* (London: SCM Press, 1983; Boston: Beacon Press), 93–115; K. Keller, *From a Broken Web: Sepa-*

ration, Sexism and Self (Boston: Beacon Press, 1986), Ch. 4; Anne Carr, *Transforming Grace: Christian Tradition and Women's Experience* (San Francisco: Harper Publications, 1988), 117–33; Elizabeth A. Johnson, *She Who Is: the Mystery of God and Feminist Theological Discourse* (New York: Crossroad, 1992), 154–6; M. Grey, *The Wisdom of Fools: Seeking Revelation Today* (London: SPCK, 1993), 67–80; S. McFague, *The Body of God: An Ecological Theology* (London: SCM Press, 1993; Minneapolis: Augsburg Fortress Pubs.), 99–129.

10 See H. Paul Santmire, *The Travail of Nature: the Ambiguous Ecological Promise of Christian Theology* (Philadelphia: Fortress, 1985); H. Paul Santmire, 'Healing the Protestant Mind: Beyond the Theology of Human Dominion', *After Nature's Revolt: Eco-Justice and Theology*, ed. by D. T. Hessel (Minneapolis: Fortress Press, 1992), 57–78; T. Berry, *The Dream of the Earth* (San Francisco: Sierra Club Books, 1988), 36–49, 123–37; A. Primavesi, *From Apocalypse to Genesis: Ecology, Feminism and Christianity* (London: Burns & Oates, 1991; Minneapolis: Augsburg Fortress Pubs.), 7–23; C. P. Christ, 'Rethinking Theology and Nature', *Reweaving the World: the Emergence of Ecofeminism*, ed. by I. Diamond & G. F. Orenstein (San Francisco: Sierra Club Books, 1990), 58–69.

11 See S. Toulmin, *The Return to Cosmology: Post-Modern Science and the Theology of Nature* (California: University of California Press, 1982), 217–74; S. Toulmin, 'Cosmology as Science and Religion', *On Nature*, ed. by L. S. Rouner (Notre Dame: University of Notre Dame Press, 1984), 27–41; W. R. Stoeger, 'Contemporary Cosmology and its Implications for the Science-Religion Debate', *Physics, Philosophy and Theology: A Common Quest for Understanding*, ed. by R. J. Russell, W. R. Stoeger & G. V. Coyne (Vatican City: Liberia Editrice Vaticana, 1988; Notre Dame: University of Notre Dame Press), 219–47; B. Swimme & T. Berry, *The Universe Story: From Primordial Flaring Forth to the Ecozoic Era – A Celebration of the Unfolding Universe* (New York: Harper Collins, 1992), 199–200, 219–20, 266–8.

12 T. Berry, *The Dream of the Earth* (San Francisco: Sierra Club Books, 1988), 198. See also G. Daly, *Creation and Redemption* (Dublin: Gill and Macmillan, 1988; Collegeville: Liturgical Press), 2–3.

13 T. Berry, ibid., 132.

14 R. Rorty, 'The Priority of Democracy to Philosophy', *Virginia Statute for Religious Freedom*, M. D. Peterson & R.C. Vaughan, eds. (Cambridge: Cambridge University Press, 1988), 270.

15 These and other questions are powerfully asked of the deconstructionists by Vincent M. Colapietro, to whom I am indebted for this section of my chapter, in his important article 'The Integral Self: Systematic Illusion or Inescapable Task?', *Listening: Journal of Religion and Culture* ' (Fall 1990), 192–210.

16 R. Bellah, et. al., *Habits of the Heart: Individualism and Commitment in American Life* (Berkeley: University of California Press, 1986), 334.

17 Ibid., V111.

18 T. Berry, *The Dream of the Earth*, 21.

19 S. McFague, *The Body of God: An Ecological Theology* (London: SCM Press,

1993; Minneapolis: Augsburg Fortress Pubs.), 68.

20 David Tracy, 'God, Dialogue and Solidarity: A Theologian's Refrain', *The Christian Century*, 10th October 1990, 902.

21 B. Haring, *Free and Faithful*, vol. 3 (New York: Crossroad 1981), 16. See also D. Carroll, *Towards a Story of the Earth: Essays in the Theology of Creation* (Dublin: Dominican Publications, 1987), 173–5.

22 For a helpful discussion of this complex issue see M. Z. Rosaldo, 'The Use and Abuse of Anthropology: Reflections on Feminism and Cross-cultural Understanding', *Journal of Women in Culture and Society* 5 (Spring 1980), 389–417;Barbara Andolsen, 'Gender and Sex Roles in Recent Religious Ethics Literature', *Religious Studies Review* 11 (July 1985), 217–223; Richard Kahoe, 'Social Science of Gender Differences: Ideological Battleground', *Religious Studies Review* 1 (July 1985), 223–8.

23 See D. Toulmin, *The Return to Cosmology: Post-modern Science and the Theology of Nature* (California: University of California Press, 1982); *The Re-enchantment of Science: Post-Modern Proposals*, ed. by D. Griffin (New York: Suny, 1988).

24 V. M. Colapietro, art.cit., 203.

25 See W. Pannenberg, 'The Christological Foundation of Christian Anthropology' in *Humanism and Christianity*, C. Geffré (ed.), Concilium, vol. 86 (New York: Herder & Herder, 1973).

26 V. Colapietro, art.cit., 197.

27 T. de Chardin, *Human Energy* (New York: Harcourt Brace Jovanovich, 1936/1978), 63.

28 T. de Chardin, *The Phenomenon of Man* (New York: Harper and Row, 1965), 262.

29 See W. N. Clarke, 'The 'We Are' of Interpersonal Dialogue as the Starting Point of Metaphysics', *The Modern Schoolman* LX1X (March/May1992), 357–68.

30 See 'To Be is To Be Substance-in-Relation', *Metaphysics as Foundation: Essays in Honour of I. Leclerc,* edited by Paul A. Bogaard & Gordon Treash (New York: Suny, 1992).

31 See R. A. Connor, 'The Person as Resonating Existential', *American Catholic Philosophical Quarterly* LXVI (1992), 40.

32 R. A. Connor, art. cit. 42. Connor's position echoes the magisterial work of the Scottish philosopher John McMurray. According to McMurray in *Persons in Relation* (New Jersey: Humanities Press International, 1961/1991) it is necessary to go beyond the extremes of the isolated individual (p. 24) and organism (p. 46): 'The idea of an isolated agent is self contradictory. Any agent is necessarily in relation to the Other. Apart from this essential relation he does not exist. But, further, the Other in this constitutive relation must be personal. Persons, therefore are constituted by their mutual relation to one another.' 24.

33 This is the concern raised by Fr. W. Norris-Clarke in his discussion of the turn to relationality in modern philosophy in his article 'To Be is To Be Substance-

in-Relation', *Metaphysics as Foundation: Essays in Honour of I. Leclerc.* Edited by Paul A. Bogaard & Gordon Treash (New York: Suny, 1992).

34 Mary Grey in *The Wisdom of Fools: Seeking Revelation Today* struggles with the same kind of question in working out a theology of the connected self. Much of what she has to say about the connected self parallels our proposals concerning the relational self. See *The Wisdom of Fools: Seeking Revelation Today* (London: SPCK, 1993), 75–80.

35 P. Ricoeur, *Oneself as Another* (Chicago: The University of Chicago Press, 1992), 317.

36 Ibid.

37 Ibid., 318.

38 Ibid., 3.

39 Ibid., 3 & 16–18.

40 S. Hawking, *A Brief History of Time* (New York: Bantam Books, 1988), 121–2.

41 F. Dyson, *Disturbing the Universe* (New York: Harper and Row, 1979), 250.

42 S. McFague develops what she calls an 'embodiment anthropology' in *The Body of God: An Ecological Theology.* (London: SCM Press, 1993; Minneapolis: Augsburg Fortress Pubs.), 99–129.

43 B. Swimme, *The Universe is a Green Dragon: A Cosmic Creation Story* (Santa Fe, New Mexico: Bear and Company, 1984), 32.

44 J. Polkinghorne, *One World: The Interaction of Science and Theology* (London: SPCK, 1986), 56.

45 In appealing to the anthropic principle, whether 'strong' or 'weak', as evidence for the existence of an underlying natural solidarity within the world, we do not wish to imply that this principle can also be invoked to justify or affirm particular theological doctrines. At most the anthropic principle raises questions about the kind of world we live in; it does not provide theological answers. S. McFague is surely correct in proposing 'a retrospective view' of the unity within the cosmos as something which provokes wonder, surprise and gratitude. See S. McFague, *The Body of God: An Ecological Theology* (London: SCM Press, 1993; Minneapolis: Augsburg Fortress Pubs.), 75–6.

46 B. Swimme and T. Berry, *The Universe Story: From the Primordial Flaring Forth to the Ecozoic Era – A Celebration of the Unfolding Universe* (New York: Harper Collins, 1992), 45.

47 For a searching account of the pros and cons of the theological challenge implied in emerging bio-technologies of medicine see R. A. Brungs, 'Biology and the Future: A Doctrinal Agenda', *Theological Studies* 50 (1989), 698–717.

48 See the works of John Macmurray, especially *The Self as Agent* (New York: Harper and Brothers, 1957) and *Persons in Relation* (New York: Harper and Brothers, 1961).

49 A. Whitehead, *Models of Thought* (New York: The Free Press, 1968), 110.

50 Teilhard de Chardin, *Writings in Time of War* (London: W. Collins & Sons, 1968), 25, emphasis added.

51 Alice Walker, *The Colour Purple* (New York: Pocket Books, 1982), 178.

52 I have been unable to source this quotation in the Rahner corpus. Rahner may have been influenced by Francis Thomson who wrote:

> All things by immortal power, near or far,
> hiddenly to each other linked,
> Thou canst not stir a flower without troubling of a star
> (*Mistress of Vision XXII*).

53 K. Rahner, 'Theology and Anthropology', *Theological Investigations*, vol. 9 (London: DLT, 1972; New York: The Crossroad Publishing Company), 45; *Foundations of Christian Faith*, 431. This point is impressively developed by P. Phan in *Eternity in Time: A Study of K. Rahner's Eschatology* (Selinsgrove: Susquehanna University Press, 1988), 43–63.

54 This point is developed at greater length by Eugene Fontinell in *Self, God and Immortality: A Jamesian Investigation* (Philadelphia: Temple University, 1986), 165–217.

55 J. P. Kenny, *The Self*, The Aquinas Lecture (Milwaukee: Marquette University Press, 1988), 26.

56 I *ad Corinthios XV*, 1.11, ed. Cai, 924. See J. P. Kenny, *The Self*, 27, & 34 n.8, & M. Brown, 'Aquinas on the Resurrection of the Body', *The Thomist*, (1992), 165–207.

Chapter 4

1 Philip Larkin, 'Aubade', *Collected Works*, edited with an Introduction by A. Thwaite (London: Faber & Faber, 1988), 208.

2 L. Bregman, *Death in the Midst of Life: Perspectives on Death from Christianity and Depth Psychology* (Michigan: Baker Book House, 1992).

3 Ibid., 145–6.

4 D. Callahan, 'Cramming for your Finals: Making Death a Part of Life', *Commonweal* 16th July 1993, 14.

5 Leo Tolstoy, *The Cossacks, Happy Ever After, and the Death of Ivan Illich*. Translated with Introduction by Rosemary Edmonds (London: Penguin Books, 1960), 103.

6 Ibid., 102.

7 Ibid., 143.

8 Ibid., 153.

9 Ibid., 152.

10 Ibid., 160.

11 David Patterson, 'The Death of Ivan Illich' *Thought*, vol. 65 (19th June 1990), 143–54.

12 M. Heidegger, *Being and Time* , translated by John Macquarrie and E. S. Robinson (London, 1962), 279–311.

13 Ibid., 295.

14 Ibid., 289.

15 Ibid., 297.

16 Ibid., 302.

17 Ibid., 307.

18 J. Bowker, *The Meaning of Death* (Cambridge University Press, 1991).

19 Ibid., 211; see also: 220.

20 Ibid., 215.

21 Ibid., 220.

22 Louis Evely, *In the Face of Death* (New York: The Seabury Press, 1979), 1. A similar appreciation of the link between living and dying can be found in Otto Kaiser and Eduard Lohse who point out 'only the person who thinks about death is fully aware that his days are coming to an end and will also know how rightly to enjoy the pleasures of life' *Death and Life* (Abingdon Press, 1981), 95.

23 I am indebted to Bartholomew J. Collopy for his challenging article on death for some of the material that follows here. See Bartholomew J. Collopy, 'Theology and the Darkness of Death', *Theological Studies* 39 (1978), I:22–54.

24 K. Rahner, 'Ideas for a Theology of Death', *Theological Investigations*, vol. 13, translated by David Bourke (London: DLT, 1975; New York: The Crossroad Publishing Company), 169–86 at 179.

25 Ibid.

26 B. J. Collopy, 'Theology and the Darkness of Death', *Theological Studies*, 39 (1978) argues quite persuasively that most approaches to death today neglect the darkness of death itself.

27 Roger Troisfontaines, *I Do Not Die*, translated by Francis E. Albert (New York: Desclee Company, 1963), 135.

28 R. Troisfontaines, op. cit., 140.

29 See Lucy Bregman, *Death in the Midst of Life: Perspectives on Death from Christianity and Depth Psychology* (Michigan: Baker Book House, 1992).

30 Ibid., 200.

31 K. Rahner, 'A Theology of Death', *Theological Investigations*, vol. 13, 174.

32 Ibid., 174.

33 Ibid., 181 & 180.

34 Ibid., 181.

35 This particular formulation of the question is taken from James P. Mackey, *Modern Theology: A Sense of Direction* (Oxford: Oxford University Press, 1987), 186–7.

36 Ibid.

37 P. Ricoeur, in *Oneself as Another* (Chicago: University of Chicago Press, 1992), 317–18.

38 James P. Mackey, op. cit., 187.

39 Maurice West, *The Shoes of the Fisherman*.

Chapter 5

1 Message of His Holiness John Paul II, *Physics, Philosophy and Theology: A Common Quest for Understanding*, R. J. Russell, W. R. Stoeger & G. V. Coyne

(eds.) (Vatican City: Liberia Editrice Vaticana, 1988; Notre Dame: University of Notre Dame Press), 12 & M.11 respectively.

2   *New Dictionary of Theology*, J. Komonchak, M. Collins, Dermot A. Lane (eds.) (Delaware: Michael Glazer Books, 1987), 497.

3   J. Macquarrie, *Christian Hope* (New York: Seabury, 1978), 8.

4   Gabriel Marcel, 'Sketch of a Phenomenology and a Metaphysic of Hope', *Homo Viator: Introduction to a Metaphysics of Hope*, translated by Emma Graufurd (London: V. Gollancz, 1951; Magnolia, Ma.: Peter Smith Pub. Inc.), 36.

5   K. Rahner, 'The Question of the Future', *Theological Investigations*, vol. 12, translated by David Bourke (London: DLT, 1974; New York: The Crossroad Publishing Company), 181–201.

6   See Joseph Pieper, 'Hope and History', *At the Heart of the Real: Philosophical Essays in Honour of Archbishop Desmond Connell* (Dublin: Irish Academic Press, 1992), 407–19 and *Hope and History* (New York: Herder and Herder, 1969), 21–5.

7   G. Marcel, 'The Preface', *Homo Viator: Introduction to a Metaphysic of Hope* (London: V. Gollancz, 1951; Magnolia, Ma.: Peter Smith Pub. Inc.), 10.

8   E. Bloch, *Traces*, 390.

9   See William F. Lynch, *Images of Hope Imagination as Healer of the Hopeless* (Dublin: Helicon, 1965; Notre Dame: University of Notre Dame Press), 22–4, 243–56.

10 E. Schillebeeckx, *For the Sake of the Gospel* (London: SCM, 1989; New York: The Crossroad Publishing Company), 46; see also *God the Future of Man* (London: Sheed and Ward, 1969), 136, 154–5; *Jesus: An Experiment in Christology* (London: Collins, 1979; New York: The Crossroad Publishing Company), 621–2.

11 K. Barth, *Church Dogmatics*, IV/3 (second half), 938.

12 J. Moltmann, *The Theology of Hope*, translated by James W. Leitch (London: SCM, 1967; Minneapolis: Augsburg Fortress Pubs.), 289.

13 J. Moltmann, *God in Creation: A New Theology of Creation of the Spirit of God*, translated by Margaret Kohl (London: SCM Press, 1985; Minneapolis: Augsburg Fortress Pubs.), 137.

14 Ibid., 138.

15 C. Keller, 'Why Apocalypse, Now?', *Theology Today* XLIX (1992), 2, 183–95.

16 This proposal is developed more extensively in Dermot A. Lane, *Christ at the Centre: Selected Issues in Christology* (Dublin: Veritas Publications 1990), 53–79.

Chapter 6

1   E. Käsemann, 'The Beginning of Christian Theology', *Apocalypticism*, ed. by Robert W. Funk (New York: Herder & Herder, 1969), 40. J. Christiaan Beker, *The Triumph of God: the Essence of Paul's Thought* (Minneapolis: Fortress Press, 1990), X11. J. Christiaan Beker, *The Triumph of God: The Essence of Paul's Thought* (Minneapolis: Fortress Press, 1990), 135.

2   D. Aune, 'Eschatology (early Christian)', *The Anchor Bible Dictionary*, vol. 2, editor-in-chief: D. N. Freedman (New York: Doubleday, 1992), 595–6; G. W. E.

Notes

Nikelsburg, 'Eschatology (early Jewish)', ibid., 578; J. Collins, 'Old Testament Apocalypticism and Eschatology', 298–304 and A. Yarbro Collins, 'Eschatology and Apocalypticism', *The New Jerome Biblical Commentary* edited by Raymond E. Brown, Joseph A. Fitzmyer & Roland E. Murphy (New Jersey: Prentice Hall, 1990), 298–304 & 1359–64 respectively; P. D. Hanson, *The Dawn of Apocalyptic* (Philadelphia, 1975, 11–12).

3   P. D. Hanson, *The Dawn of Apocalyptic*, 11.
4   See A. Descamps, 'Réflections sur l'eschatologie de Jesus', 171.
5   P. D. Hanson, ibid., 11–12.
6   G. W. E. Nickelsburg, ibid., 576.
7   The literature on this subject is vast. In what follows we have been guided by Zacberry Hayes, *Visions of the Future: A Study of Christian Eschatology* (Delaware: M. Glazier, 1989), 31–41; Christopher Rowland, *Radical Christianity* (Cambridge: Polity Press, 1988; Maryknoll, NY: Orbis Books), Ch. 3; Brian K. Blount, 'Preaching the Kingdom: Mark's Apocalyptic Call for Prophetic Engagement', *Princeton Seminary Bulletin*, Supplementary Issue, no. 3, (1994), 33–56; John J. Collins, 'Apocalyptic Literature', *Early Judaism and its Modern Interpreters*, ed. by Robert A. Kraft & George Nickelsburg, (Atlanta: Scholars Press, 1986), 345–70.
8   John J. Collins, 'Towards the Morphology of a Genre', *Semeia*, 14 (1979), 9.
9   Brian K. Blount, art. cit., 35.
10 D. H. Russell, *The Method and Message of Jewish Apocalyptic* (London: SCM Press, 1964; Louisville: Westminster John Knox), 92–6.
11 See Brevard Childs, *The Book of Exodus* (Philadelphia: Westminster Press, 1974), 60–79; Bernhard Anderson, *Understanding the Old Testament* (New Jersey: Prentice Hall, 1986), 61–6; Norman Gottwald, *The Hebrew Bible: A Socio-Literary Introduction* (Philadelphia: Fortress Press, 1985), 211–13.
12 G. W. E. Nickelsburg, ibid., 577.
13 This line of evolution is analysed by Dermot A. Lane, *The Reality of Jesus* (Dublin: Veritas, 1975; New York: Paulist Press), 147–62.
14 Albert Schweitzer, *The Quest of the Historical Jesus: a critical study of its progress from Reimarus to Wrede* (New York, 1968), (German edition 1906),4. George Tyrrell makes the same point even more strikingly by suggesting that researchers at this time were coming up with reflections of themselves discovered at the bottom of the deep well of historical examination. See G. Tyrrell, *Christianity at the Crossroads* London: Longmans, Green & Co., 1909), 44.
15 E. Käsemann, 'The Beginning of Christian Theology', *Apocalypticism*, ed. by Robert W. Funk (New York: Herder and Herder, 1969), 17–46.
16 See Robert W. Funk, Roy W. Hoover, and the Jesus Seminar, *The Five Gospels: the search for the authentic words of Jesus* (New York: A Polebridge book, Macmillan Publishing Co., 1993).
17 See Burton L. Mack, *A Myth of Innocence: Mark and Christian Origins* (Philadephia: Fortress Press, 1988); John Dominic Crossan, *The Historical Jesus: The*

Life of a Mediterranean Jewish Peasant (San Francisco: Harper San Francisco, 1992).

18 M. Borg, 'A temperate case for a non eschatological Jesus', *Foundations and Facets Forum* (September 1986), 81–102. See also by M. Borg, 'Portraits of Jesus in Contemporary North American Scholarship', *Harvard Theological Review* (1991), 1–22; and 'Jesus and Eschatology: a reassessment' in *Images of Jesus Today* ed. by James H. Charlesworth & Walter P. Weaver (Philadelphia: Trinity Press International, 1994), 42–67.

19 M. Borg, 'Jesus and Eschatology: A Reassessment', *Images of Jesus Today*, 46–8.

20 Ibid., 43–4, 46.

21 Ibid., 45.

22 Ibid., 46.

23 *The Anchor Bible Dictionary*, vol. 3, 806.

24 M. Borg, 'Jesus and Eschatology: current reflections' in *Jesus in Contemporary Scholarship* (Philadelphia: Trinity Free Press, 1994), 88–9.

25 M. Borg, 'Reflections on a Discipline: a North American perspective' in *Studying the Historical Jesus; evaluations of the state of current research* ed. by Bruce Chilton & Craig A. Evans (New York: E. J. Brill, 1994), 9–31 at 21.

26 E. P. Sanders, *The Historical Figure of Jesus* (London/New York: Penguin Books, 1993), 260–2.

27 J. P. Meier, 'A Marginal Jew: rethinking the historical Jesus', *The Anchor Bible Reference* (New York: Doubleday, 1994, 289–506.

28 J. P. Meier, *A Marginal Jew* , vol. 2, 331. A similar position is expressed by J. P. Meier in 'Reflections on Jesus-of-history research today' in *Jesus's Jewishness: Exploring the place of Jesus within early Judaism*, ed. by James H. Charlesworth (New York: Crossroad, 1991), where he states: 'The historical Jesus seems to have no interest in the great political and social questions of his day. He was not interested in the reform of the world because he was prophesying its end', 1992.

29 Ibid., 7.

30 Robert L. Webb, 'John the Baptist and his relationship with Jesus', *Studying the Historical Jesus: Evaluations of the state of current research*, ed. by Bruce Chilton & Craig A. Evans (New York: E. J. Brill, 1994), 179–229 at 223ff; J. P. Meier, *A Marginal Jew*, vol. 2, 401.

31 Robert L. Webb, art. cit., 224.

32 J. P. Meier, *A Marginal Jew*, vol. 2, 404–23.

33 See Albert Descamps, 'Reflexions sur l'eschatologie de Jesus', *Jesus et L'Eglise: Etudes d'exégèse et de theologie* (Leuven: Leuven University/Presses Universitaires de Louvan, 1987), 169–84 at 176–81.

34 The sayings selected in what follows are indebted to the meticulous historical-critical work of J. P. Meier in *The Marginal Jew*, vol. 2, 289–397.

35 Ibid., 297.

36 Ibid., 298–9.

37 Ibid., 309–17.

38 Ibid., 317–36.

39 Ibid., 334.

40 See Richard A. Horsley, *Jesus on the Spiral of Violence: popular Jewish resistance in Roman Palestine* (San Francisco: Harper and Row, 1987) and Sean Freyne 'The Geography, Politics and Economics of Galilee and the Quest for the Historical Jesus', *Studying the Historical Jesus: Evaluations of the state of current research*, edited by Bruce Chilton & Craig A. Evans (New York: 1994), 75–121.

41 J. P. Meier, *A Marginal Jew*, vol. 2, 363 n.43.

42 Raymond Brown, *The Death of the Messiah: A Commentary on the Passion Narratives in the Four Gospels*, vol. 1 (London: G. Chapman, 1994; New York: Doubleday and Company), 507.

43 J. P. Meier, 'Jesus', *The New Jerome Biblical Commentary*, ed. by Raymond E. Brown, Joseph A. Fitzmyer & Roland E. Murphy (New Jersey: Prentice Hall, 1990), 1324.

44 Ibid., 1325.

45 R. Brown, *The Death of the Messiah*, vol. 1, 513.

46 Ibid., vol. 2, 1478 n.19.

47 R. Brown, *The Birth of the Messiah*, vol. 1, 514.

48 Ibid., 515.

49 See John R. Donaghue, 'The Parable of the Sheep and Goats: A Challenge to Christian Ethics', *Theological Studies* 47 (1986), 3–31.

50 See Dominic Crossan, *In Parables: Challenge of the Historical Jesus* (New York: Harper and Row, 1973), 35–6.

51 A more elaborate account of these two points concerning the reign of God can be found in Dermot A. Lane, 'Theological Reflections on the Reign of God', *Christ at the Centre: Selected Issues in Christology* (Dublin: Veritas Publications, 1990), 33–52.

52 See David B. Batstone, 'Jesus, Apocalyptic and World Transformation', *Theology Today*, October 1992, 383–97.

53 A more detailed analysis of Jesus' experience of God can be found in Dermot A. Lane, *Christ at the Centre: Selected Issues in Christology*, 33–41, and Bernard J. Cooke, *God's Beloved: Jesus' Experience of the Transcendent* (Philadelphia: Trinity Press International, 1992), Ch. 1.

Chapter 7

1 See Raymond E. Brown, *The Death of the Messiah: from Gethsemane to the Grave*, vol. 2 (London, G. Chapman, 1994; New York: Doubleday and Company), esp. 1118–40. Brown tells us in a footnote to his examination of the special phenomena surrounding the death of Jesus in Matthew's Gospel that 'the import of the phenomena is eschatological rather than christological, for God is the agent rather than Jesus', 1137 n.101. See also on the eschatological character of the death of Jesus, Dale C. Allison, *The End of the Ages has come: An early interpretation of the Passion and Resurrection of Jesus* (Edinburgh: T. & T. Clark, 1985), and Jurgen Moltmann, *The Crucified God: the Cross of Christ as the*

Foundation and Criticism of Christian Theology, translated by R. A. Wilson & J. Bowden (London: SCM Press, 1974; Minneapolis: Augsburg Fortress Pubs.), 160–99.

2   This translation and layout of verses is taken from Raymond E. Brown, 'Eschatological Events accompanying the Death of Jesus, especially the raising of the Holy Ones from their tombs (Matt. 27:51–3)', *Faith and the Future: Studies in Christian Eschatology*, ed. by John P. Galvin (New York: Paulist Press, 1994), 43–73 at 45.

3   Vincent Taylor, *The Gospel according to St Mark*, second edition (New York: St Martin's Press, 1966), 596. On this point see also Dale C. Allison, op. cit. 30–3.

4   Raymond E. Brown, *The Death of the Messiah*, vol. 2, 1121–2.

5   Eq. Zech. 14:4; 1 Kings 19:11–12. According to Nahum: 'The mountains quake before him, and the hills melt; the earth heaves before him, and the world and all who live in it' (Nahum 1:5).

6   Raymond E. Brown, *Death of the Messiah*, vol. 2, 1126.

7   Ibid., 1130.

8   Donald E. Gowan, *Eschatology in the Old Testament* (Philadelphia: Fortress Press, 1986), 91.

9   Similar expressions of belief in resurrection can also be found in Hosea 6:1–2; Ezekiel 37:1–14; and Isaiah 26:9.

10 An impressive and nuanced analysis of the evidence for the resurrection of Jesus can be found in John P. Galvin, 'Jesus Christ' in *Systematic Theology: Roman Catholic Perspectives*, vol. 1, ed. by Francis F. Fiorenza & John P. Galvin (Minneapolis: Fortress Press, 1991), 251–324 at 297–314. See also on the evidence for the resurrection Dermot A. Lane, *The Reality of Jesus: Essay in Christology* (Dublin: Veritas Publications, 1975; New York: Paulist Press), Ch. 4, and *Christ at the Centre: Selected Issues in Christology* (Dublin: Veritas Publications, 1990), Ch. 4.

11 Christopher Rowland, 'Interpreting the Resurrection', *The Resurrection of Jesus Christ*, ed. by Paul Avis (London: DLT, 1993), 78.

12 We are not implying here that the language of immortality is alien to the biblical tradition. James Barr is surely right in reminding us that the Hellenistic concept of immortality had become part of the Jewish tradition but as part of the Jewish tradition it was prevented from becoming purely spiritualistic reality because of the presence of a more wholistic anthropology within Judaism.

13 See Joseph Plevnik, 'The Centre of Pauline Theology', *The Catholic Biblical Quarterly*, 51 (1989), 461–78; J. Christiaan Beker, *Paul the Apostle: The Triumph of God in Life and Thought* (Edinburgh: T. & T. Clark, 1980; Minneapolis: Augsburg Fortress Pubs.), Ch. 2; Joseph A. Fitzmyer, 'Pauline Theology', *The New Jerome Biblical Commentary*, ed. by Raymond E. Brown, Joseph A. Fitzmyer & Rowland E. Murphy (New Jersey: Prentice Hall, 1990), 1388–9.

14 See Rudolph Schnackenburg, 'Christologie des Neuen Testaments', *Mysterium Salutis: Grunddriss heilsgeschictlicher Dogmatik*, 3/1, ed. J. Feiner & M. Lohrer (Cologne: Benzinger, 1970), 227–38.

15 Joseph A. Fitzmyer, 'Pauline Theology', *The New Jerome Biblical Commentary*, 1388.

16 J. Christiaan Beker, *Paul the Apostle*, 16.

17 See the excellent account of this debate and the arguments favouring a full resurrection interpretation in Ben F. Meyer, 'Did Paul's View of the Resurrection of the Dead undergo Development?', *Theological Studies*, 47 (1986), 363–87 at 376–7.

18 These two points are developed persuasively by Ben F. Myer, art. cit., 379–81.

19 See the important article by Ben Meyer in *Theological Studies*, 1986, art. cit., esp. 375–7 against the thesis of development within Paul's theology and support for Meyer's position by Joseph Plevnik, 'Paul's Eschatology', *Toronto Journal of Theology*, 6 (1990), 86–99.

20 Rudolph Bultmann, 'The Eschatology of the Gospel of John', *Faith and Understanding* (New York: Harper and Row, 1969), 165–83.

21 Ernst Käsemann, *The Testament of Jesus according to John 17* (Philadelphia: Fortress Press, 1968), 13–14.

22 See the constructive account of this story by Sandra Schneiders, 'Death in the Community of Eternal Life: History, Theology, and Spirituality in John 11', *Interpretation* (1985).

23 John T. Carroll, 'Present and Future in Fourth Gospel Eschatology', *Biblical Theology Bulletin*, 19 (1985), 63–9.

Chapter 8

1 Jurgen Moltmann, *The Crucified God: The Cross of Christ as the Foundation and Criticism of Christian Theology* (London: SCM, 1974, German edition; Minneapolis: Augsburg Fortress Pubs.), 1973.

2 Ibid., 185.

3 On the recovery and development of a theology of the Paschal Mystery at the Second Vatican Council see Dermot A. Lane, *Christ at the Centre: Selected Issues in Christology* (Dublin: Veritas Publications, 1990), Ch. 5.

4 Karl Rahner, 'Resurrection', *Encyclopedia of Theology: A Concise Sacramentum Mundi*, ed. by Karl Rahner (London: Burns and Oates, 1975; New York: The Crossroad Publishing Company), 1438.

5 See Gerard O'Collins in *The Easter Jesus* (London: DLT), where he develops three experiential correlates with the resurrection, and Dermot A. Lane, *Christ at the Centre: Selected Issues in Christology*, 94–9.

6 Karl Rahner, *Foundations of Christian Faith: An Introduction to the Idea of Christianity* (London: DLT, 1978; New York: The Crossroad Publishing Company), 274.

7 Karl Rahner, op.cit., 269.

8 Ibid., 269.

9 Ibid., 269, 273.

10 Ibid., 269.

11 Helmut Peukert, *Science, Action, and Fundamental Theology: Towards a Theology of Communicative Action* (Mass.: MIT Press, 1984), 206.

12 English-speaking readers can find references for this debate in H. Peukert, op. cit., 206–10, and a more elaborate analysis of this particular debate can be found in Dermot A. Lane, 'Theology and Science in Dialogue', *Irish Theological Quarterly*, nos. 1 & 2 (1986), 31–53; Charles Davis, *Theology and Political Society* (Cambridge: Cambridge University Press, 1980), 141–5; Gary Simpson, '*Theogia Crucis* and the forensically fraught world: Engaging Helmet Peukert and Jürgen Habermas', *Habermas, Modernity and Public Theology*, ed. by Don S . Browning & Francis S. Fiorenza (New York: Crossroad, 1992), 173–205.

13 See Peukert, op. cit., 206.

14 Ibid.

15 Ibid., 207.

16 Ibid.

17 Ibid., 208.

18 M. Horkheimer, 'Gedanke zur Religion', *Kritische Theorie*, 1 (Frankfurt: Fischer, 1968), 372.

19 Ibid., 375.

20 Christian Lenhart, 'Anamestic Solidarity: The Proletariat and its Manes', *Telos*, 25 (1975), 133–54.

21 Christian Lenhart, art. cit., 139.

22 Art. cit., 133.

23 Herbert Marcuse, *One Dimension Man: Studies in the Ideology of Advanced Industrial Society* (Boston: Beacon Press, 1964), 98.

24 See for example essays in *Habermas, Modernity and Public Theology*, edited by D. S. Browning & F. S. Fiorenza (New York: Crossroad, 1992).

25 Helmet Peukert, op. cit., 227.

26 See Wolfhart Pannenberg, *Jesus – God and Man* (London: SCM Press, 1968; Louisville: Westminster John Knox), Ch. 3; 'The Revelation of God in Jesus of Nazareth', *Theology as History*, ed. by J. M. Robinson & J. B. Cobb (New York: Harper & Row, 1967). For a constructive and impressive review of Pannenberg's thinking on the resurrection see Elizabeth A. Johnson, 'Resurrection and Reality in the Thought of W. Pannenberg', *Heythrop Journal* (1983), 1–18.

27 Michael Scanlon, 'Hope', *The New Dictionary of Theology*, ed. by Joseph A. Komonchak, Mary Collins & Dermot A. Lane (Dublin: Gill and Macmillan, 1987; Collegeville: Liturgical Press), 497.

28 Gerry O'Hanlon, 'May Christians hope for a better world', *Irish Theological Quarterly*, 3 (1988), 175–89.

29 Art. cit., 187.

30 Ann Thurston, 'The Transformation of the World' and Gervase Corcoran 'We Have Here No Lasting City', *Studies*, Winter 1994, 393–400 & 384–92 respectively.

31 See the treatment of this shift in Chapter 3 and the literature therein.

32 Walter Kasper, 'The Logos Character of Reality', *Communio* (Fall 1988), 281.

33 See Sally McFague, *Models of God*, and *The Body of God: An Ecological Theology*

(London: SCM Press, 1993); Minneapolis: Augsburg Fortress Pubs.; and Elizabeth A. Johnson, *She Who Is: The Mystery of God and Feminist Theological Discourse* (New York: Crossroad, 1992).

34 See David Tracy, 'Approaching the Christian Understanding of God', *Systematic Theology*, vol. 1, ed. by Francis S. Fiorenza & John P. Galvin (Minneapolis: Fortress Press), 131–48.

35 See Catherine LaCugna, *God for Us: The Trinity and Christian Life* (New York: Harper Collins, 1991).

36 See *G.S.*, a.19, 18, 22, and *L.G.*, a.13.

37 See Stephen Duffy, *The Dynamics of Grace: Perspectives in Theological Anthropology* (Collegeville: a Michael Glazier book/Liturgical Press, 1993, Ch. 4.

38 Alfred N. Whitehead, *Process in Reality*, corrected edition ed. by D. R. Griffin & D. W. Sherburne (New York: Free Press, 1978), 342.

39 Karl Barth, *Church Dogmatics*, 11/1, translated by T. H. L. Parker et al. (New York: C. Scribner's Sons, 1957), 495.

40 Walter Kasper, *Jesus the Christ* (London: Burns and Oates, 1976; New York: Paulist Press), 168.

41 David Calvert, *From Christ to God* (London: Epworth Press, 1983), 65.

42 Jon Sobrino, *Jesus the Liberator: An Historical Reading of Jesus of Nazareth* (London: Burns and Oates, 1993), 74; *Jesus the Liberator: An Historical-Theological Reading of Jesus of Nazareth*, trans. by P. Burns and F. McDonough (Maryknoll: Orbis Books).

43 *G.S.*, art. 21; see also a.34, 38, 39, 57.

44 *G.S.*, art. 38 & 39 respectively.

45 *G.S.*, art. 55.

46 'Introduction', *Justice in the World*, 1971.

47 Paul VI, *Evangelisation in the Modern World* (London: CTS, 1976), art. 30, see also art. 38; published as *On Evangelization in the Modern World* (Boston, Ma.: St Paul Books and Media).

48 Seamus Heaney, *The Curé at Troy* (London: Faber and Faber, 1990; New York: Farrar, Straus and Giroux, Inc.), 77.

49 Taken from *Cries of the Spirit: A Celebration of Women's Spirituality*, ed. by Marilyn Sewell (Boston: Beacon Press, 1991), 181–2.

Chapter 9

1 Zachary Hayes, 'Visions of a Future: Symbols of Heaven and Hell', *Chicago Studies* (1985), 147.

2 These exceptions include Ladislaus Boros, *The Mystery of Death* (Edinburgh: St Andrews Press, 1971; New York: Herder & Herder, 1965); Karl Rahner, *Theology of Death* (New York: Herder & Herder, 1973); and Eberhard Jüngel, *Death* (Edinburgh: T. & T. Clark, 1975). Jacques Pohier's critique of the traditional theology of death in *God in Fragments* (London: SCM, 1985; New York: The Crossroad Publishing Company) still remains to be addressed.

3   Werner Jeanrond, *Call and Response: the Challenge of Christian Life* (Dublin: Gill and Macmillan, 1995; New York: The Continuum Publishing Group), 54.

4   Ladislaus Boros, *The Mystery of Death,* translated by G. Bainbridge (New York: Herder and Herder, 1965).

5   Ibid., 84.

6   K. Rahner, 'Christian Dying', *Theological Investigations*, vol. 18, translated by Edward Quinn (London: 1984; New York: The Crossroad Publishing Company), 226–56 at 229; see also K. Rahner, 'The Liberty of the Sick, theologically considered', *Theological Investigations*, vol. 17, translated by Margaret Kohl (London: DLT, 1981; New York: The Crossroad Publishing Company), 100–13 at 105 n.6.

7   K. Rahner, *On the Theology of Death,* translated by Charles H. Henkey (New York: Herder and Herder, 1961), 39.

8   Karl Rahner, 'The Hermeneutics of Eschatological Assertions', *Theological Investigations* , vol 4, trans. by Kevin Smyth (London: DLT, 1966; New York: The Crossroad Publishing Company), 323–46 at 338.

9   Ibid., 340.

10 Hans Urs von Balthasar, *Theodrmamatik,* 4, 246–53, One wonders how happy would Jewish theologians be with the starkness of this statement, or indeed Christian theologians who espouse a single covenant theology. However, the point Balthasar is making is that the Christ-Event changes the conditions of humanity before God in favour of salvation and away from damnation.

11 *The Christian Faith in the Doctrinal Documents of the Catholic Church,* ed. by J. Neuner & J. Dupuis (London: Collins, 1983; New York: Alba House), 685.

12 Karl Rahner, 'The Eternal Significance of the Humanity of Jesus for our relationship with God', *Theological Investigations*, vol. 2, translated by Karl-H. Kruger (London: DLT, 1963; New York: The Crossroad Publishing Company), 35–46.

13 Karl Rahner, 'Why and How Can We Venerate the Saints?', *Theological Investigations*, vol. 8, translated by David Bourke (London: DLT, 1971; New York: The Crossroad Publishing Company), 12.

14 *G.S.,* a.39.

15 Unhelpful expressions used by Hans Kung in *Eternal Life,* translated by Edward Quinn (London: Collins, 1984), 135–8; 175–8; *Eternal Life? Life After Death as a Medical, Philosophical and Theological Problem* (New York: The Crossroad Publishing Company).

16 As suggested by Alfred Whitehead and Charles Hartshorne.

17 An excellent, carefully researched account of the origin of hell can be found in Alan E. Bernstein, *The Formation of Hell: Death and Retribution in the Ancient and Early Christian Worlds* (Ithaca: Cornell University Press, 1993).

18 *Catechism of the Catholic Church* (Dublin: Veritas, 1994; New York and Mahwah: Paulist Press), 145.

19 E. Schillebeeckx, *Church: The Human Story of God* (New York: Crossroad, 1990), 136–9.

20 John Sachs, 'Eschatology and Universal Salvation', *Theological Studies* (June 1991), 52, 227–54 at 235 and 252 respectively.
21 The Doctrine Commission of the Church of England, *The Mystery of Salvation: The Story of God's Gift* (London: Church House Publishing, 1995), 199.
22 On the doctrine of Purgatory see A. Michel, 'Purgatoire', *Dictionaire Theologie Catholique*, vol. XIII (1963), 1176ff; M. Schmaus, *Dogma Vol. 6: Justification and the last Things* (London: Sheed & Ward, 1977; Westminster, Md.: Christian Classics, Inc.), 240ff; Piet Fransen, 'The Doctrine of Purgatory', *Eastern Churches Quarterly* XIII (1959); Jacques Le Goff, *The Birth of Purgatory* (Chicago: 1984); Karl Rahner, 'Purgatory', *Theological Investigations* , vol. 19 (London: DLT, 1983; New York: The Crossroad Publishing Company), 181–93.
23 Text taken from Emmanuel Lane, 'The Teaching of the Catholic Church on Purgatory', *One in Christ*, 13–30 at 23–4; see also John Sachs, '*Apocatastasis* in Patristic Theology', *Theological Studies* 54 (Dec. 1993), 617–40 at 618–20.
24 Text and translation taken from Emmanuel Lane, *art. cit.*, 25.
25 *D.S.*, 856–7.
26 *L.G.*, a.51.
27 International Theological Commission, 'Some Current Questions in Eschatology', *Irish Theological Quarterly* 58 (1992), 3:231–2.
28 *Catechism of the Catholic Church* (Dublin: Veritas, 1994; New York and Mahwah: Paulist Press), a1030–2.
29 Karl Rahner, 'Purgatory', *Theological Investigations*, vol 19, 186.
30 See for example Peter Phan, 'Contemporary Contexts & Issues in Eschatology', *Theological Studies* 55 (1994), 3:507–36 and John Sachs, 'Resurrection or Reincarnation? the Christian Doctrine of Purgatory' *Concilium* (1993), 5:81–7.
31 Zachary Hayes, *Visions of a Future*, 114.
32 Joseph Ratzinger, *Eschatology*, 230.

Chapter 10
1 Congregation for the Doctrine of Faith, 'Letter of the Sacred Congregation for Doctrine of Faith on certain questions concerning eschatology', *The Christian Faith in the Doctrinal Documents of the Catholic Church*, ed. by J. Neuner & J. Dupuis (London: Collins, 1983; New York: Alba House), 691–2. It should be noted that this quotation is taken from the official version quoted in the *Acta Apostolicae Sedis*, 71 (1979), 939, whereas the version which appears in *Osservatore Romano* does not contain the words 'Though deprived for the present of the complement of its body'.
2 The Latin original is available in *Gregorianum* 73 (1992), and an English translation in the *Irish Theological Quarterly* 58 (1992), 209–43.
3 'Some Current Questions in Eschatology', *Irish Theological Quarterly* 58 (1992), 224.
4 One of the better parts of 'Some Questions in Eschatology' by the International Theological Commission is its presentation and justification of the importance of the *Parousia* of Christ on page 216.

5   *Catechism of the Catholic Church* (Dublin: Veritas, 1994; New York and Mah-wah: Paulist Press), paragraphs 988–1065.

6   For example see the work of G. Greshake and G. Lohfink, *naherwartun, aufer-stehun, Unstersblichkeit: Untersuchung zur christlichen eschatologie* (Friburg: Herder, 1976), 178, 1982.

7   Ratzinger, *Eschatology: Death and Eternal Life* (Washington DC: Catholic Uni-versity of America Press, 1988, the German edition was originally published in 1977). The English translation contains an 'Afterword', pp. 261–74, reviewing the debate since 1977 and reaffirming his opposition to the thesis of resurrection in death.

8   Walter Kasper, 'Hope in the final coming of Jesus Christ in Glory', *Communio* 12 (Winter 1985), 368–84 at 373.

9   Peter Phan, 'Current Theology: Contemporary Context and Issues in Escha-tology', *Theological Studies* 55 (1994), 507–36 at 527 n.68.

10 See for example the collection of essays edited by Krister Stendahl entitled *Immortality and Resurrection: Death in the Western World – Two conflicting cur-rents of thought* (New York: Macmillan, 1969). The contribution by O. Cull-mann, 'Immortality of the Soul or the Resurrection of the Dead' is particularly significant, 9–53.

11 Wolfhart Pannenberg, 'The Constructive and Critical Functions of Christian Eschatology', *Harvard Theological Review* 77 (1984), 119–39 at 128.

12 Quotation taken from the International Theological Commission, 'Some Current Questions in Eschatology', *Irish Theological Quarterly* 58 (1992), 224, which quotes Tertullian's work *De resurrectione mortuorum* 34, 3.

13 *Super Primam epistolam ad Corinthios c.15 ed.* Cai. 924. On this point in Aquinas see J. P. Kenny, *The Self*, The Aquinas Lecture (Milwaukee: Marquette Uni-versity Press, 1988), 26.

14 I.T.C., *art. cit.*, 226.

15 Karl Rahner, 'The Intermediate State', *Theological Investigations*, vol 17, translated by Margaret Kohl (London: DLT, 1981; New York: The Crossroad Publishing Company), 115.

16 Pierre Benoit, 'Resurrection at the end of time or immediately after death' appears in a book called *Immortality and the Resurrection, Concilium*, ed. by P. Benoit & Roland Murphy (New York: Herder & Herder, 1970), 103–14.

17 International Theological Commisison, art. cit., 219 and 213

18 This tension is the inevitable outcome of a document written in Committee!

19 Art. cit., 212.

20 Wolfhart Pannenberg in 'The Critical Function of Eschatology', *Harvard The-ological Review* 77 (1984), puts forward a similar position about communion 'in Christ' after death at 131.

21 See the summary of this debate in Joseph Ratzinger, *Eschatology: Death & Eternal Life*, translated by M. Waldstein (Washington D.C.: C.U.A. Press, 1988), Appendices I and II.

22 Quotation taken from Origen, *Seven Homilies on Leviticus* , no. 2, as cited by

Walter Kasper in 'Hope in the final coming of Jesus Christ in Glory', *Communio* (Winter 1985), 368–84 at 377.

23 Jurgen Moltmann, *The Way of Jesus Christ: Christology in Messianic Dimensions* (London SCM Press, 1990; Minneapolis: Augsburg Fortress Pubs.), 318.

24 *S.C.*, a.5, 6, 61, 104, 106, 107; *G.S.*, a.22, 38, 52; *A.G.*, a.14; *O.T.*, a.8.

25 *S.C.*, a.5.

26 *S.C.*, a.107; *A.G.*, a.14.

27 *S.C.*, a.104.

28 *G.S.*, a.22, 38, 52.

29 *O.T.*, a.8.

30 *S.C.*, a.5, 61.

31 *S.C.*, a.6, 47.

32 *S.C.*, a.81.

33 *S.C.*, a.104.

34 *L.G.*, a.49, see also article a.51.

35 This question will be taken up in Chapter 11.

36 For a most helpful review of the theology of universal salvation within the patristic period see John R. Sachs, *'Apokatastasis* in Patristic Theology', *Theological Studies* (December 1993), 54, 617–40.

37 See Frank A. Sullivan, *Salvation Outside the Church* (New York: Paulist Press, 1992).

38 *L.G.*, a.16.

39 See *G.S.*, a.18, 19, 22; *L.G.*, a.13.

40 See John R. Sachs, 'Current Eschatology: Universal Salvation and the Problem of Hell', *Theological Studies* (June 1991), 52, 227–54 and Carmel McEnroy, 'Hope for Us All? Karl Rahner's Theology of *Apokatastasis*', unpublished paper presented to the Karl Rahner Society at the 1995 CTSA Convention, 1–15.

41 Published by Ignatius Press, San Francisco 1988. See also by von Balthasar, 'Christian Universalism' and 'Some Points of Eschatology' in *Word and Redemption* (New York; Herder and Herder, 1965), 127–47 and 147–75.

42 Von Balthasar, *Dare We Hope*, 210. It should be noted that this particular understanding of the descent of Christ into hell is echoed in *The New Catechism of the Catholic Church* (Dublin: Veritas, 1994; New York and Mahwah: Paulist Press), Section 635.

43 K. Rahner, *Foundations of Christian Faith: An Introduction to the Idea of Christianity* (London: DLT, 1978; New York: The Crossroad Publishing Company), 116–20.

44 On the whole question of Theodicy see the ground-breaking work of Terence W. Tilley, *The Evil of Theodosy* (Washington: Georgetown University Press, 1991).

45 See Elizabeth A. Johnson, 'Jesus and Salvation', *Proceedings of the CTSA* (1994), 1–18 at 11.

46 Stephen Duffy, 'Justification by Faith: A Post Conciliar Perspective',*Church*

and Theology: Essays in memory of Carl J. Peter, ed. by Peter C. Phan (Washington DC: Catholic University Press of America, 1995), 182–214 at 210.

47 A helpful review of current discussion concerning reincarnation can be found in *Concilium*, 1993/5, entitled *Reincarnation or Resurrection,* ed. by Hermann Haring and Johann Baptist Metz.

48 See David S. Toolan, 'Reincarnation and Modern Gnosis', *Concilium*, 1993/5, 33–4.

49 Aloysius Pieris, 'Reincarnation in Buddhism: A Critical Appraisal', *Concilium*, 1993/5, 16–22.

50 Frederick Nietzsche, *Thus Spoke Zarathustra* (New York: Penguin Books, 1961/1977), 234.

51 Johann Baptist Metz, 'Time Without a Finale: A Background to the Debate on "Resurrection or Reincarnation"', *Concilium*, 1993/5, 124–31 at 124.

52 Matthew Lamb, 'Resurrection and Christian Identity as *Conversatio Dei*', *Concilium*, 1993/5, 112–23.

53 See David S. Toolan, 'Reincarnation and Modern Gnosis', *Concilium*, 1993/5, 32–45.

54 See Walter Kasper, 'Reincarnation', *Osservatore Romano*, 16th April 1990.

55 Augustine, *Confessions*, Book XI.

56 Paul Tillich, *Systematic Theology*, vol. 3 (Chicago: The University of Chicago Press, 1963), 395–6 and 'The Eternal Now' in *The Eternal Now: Sermons* (London S.C.M .Press, 1963; New York: Macmillan Publishing Co.), 103–11.

57 David Tracy, 'God of History, God of Psychology', *Concilium*, 1993/5, 101–11 at 102.

58 Matthew Lamb, 'The Resurrection and Christian Identity as *Conversatio Dei*', *Concilium*, 1993/5, 112–23 at 115.

Chapter 11

1 Denis Edwards, *Jesus and the Cosmos* (New York: Paulist Press, 1991), 3.

2 See Ian Barbour, 'Creation and Cosmology', *Cosmos as Creation: Theology and Science in Consonance,* ed. by Ted Peters (Nashville: Abingdon Press, 1989), 120–21.

3 Carl Sagan, *Cosmos* (New York: Ballantine Books, 1980), 188.

4 These different options are discussed by Stephen Hawking in *A Brief History of Time: From the Big Bang to Black Holes* (London: Bantam Press, 1988; New York: Bantam Books), 42–51.

5 Brian Swimme, 'The Cosmic Creation Story', *The Re-enchantment of Science: Post modern proposals,* D. Griffin (ed.) (New York: Suny Press, 1988), 52.

6 Bradford A. Smith, 'New Eyes on the Universe', *National Geographic*, vol. 185, Jan. 1994, 10.

7 See Anne M. Clifford, 'Creation', *Systematic Theology: Roman Catholic Perspectives,* vol. 1, Francis F. Fiorenza & John P. Galvin (eds.) (Minneapolis: Fortress Press), 197–8.

8   Richard J. Clifford, 'Creation in the Hebrew Bible', *Physics, Philosophy, and Theology: A Common Quest for Understanding*, Robert J. Russell, William R. Stoeger & George V. Coyne (eds.) (Vatican City: Vatican Observatory, 1988; Notre Dame: University of Notre Dame Press), 157.

9   See Richard Clifford, art. cit., 159.

10 See Anne M. Clifford, art. cit., 203–4.

11 Art. cit., 204 and 204 n19.

12 See Elizabeth A. Johnson, *She Who Is: The Mystery of God and Feminist Theological Discourse* (New York: Crossroad, 1992), 86–93.

13 Richard J. Clifford, 'The Hebrew Scriptures and the Theology of Creation', *Theological Studies*, Sept. 1985, 522.

14 See Phyllis Trible, *God and the Rhetoric of Sexuality* (London: SCM Press, 1992, 1978; Minneapolis: Augsburg Fortress Pubs.), 80–81.

15 Jer. 18:1–6; Eccl. 38:32–4; Eph. 2:10.

16 See Anne M. Clifford, art. cit., 202–3.

17 Edward Schillebeeckx, *Interim Report on the Books 'Jesus' and 'Christ'* (London: SCM Press, 1990), 126–8.

18 One of the many strengths of Gabriel Daly's book *Creation and Redemption* (Dublin: Gill and Macmillan, 1988; Collegeville: Liturgical Press), is the way he unifies God's active creation and redemption.

19 K. Rahner, 'Christology within an evolutionary view', *Theological Investigations*, vol. 5 (London: DLT, 1966; New York: The Crossroad Publishing Company), 177–88.

20 Thomas Berry, *The Dream of the Earth* (San Francisco: Sierra Club Books, 1988), 21.

21 Sally McFague, *The Body of God: An Ecological Theology* (London: SCM Press, 1993; Minneapolis: Augsburg Fortress Pubs.), 68.

22 David Tracy, 'God, Dialogue and Solidarity: A Theologian's Refrain', *The Christian Century*, 10th October 1990, 902.

23 Bernard Haring, *Free and Faithful*, vol. 3 (New York: Crossroad, 1981), 16. See also Denis Carroll, *Towards a Story of the Earth: Essays in the Theology of Creation* (Dublin: Dominican Publications, 1987), 173–5.

24 See W. R. Stoeger, 'Contemporary Cosmology and its implications for the Science-Religion Dialogue', *Physics, Philosophy and Theology: A Common Quest for Understanding*, Robert J. Russell, W. R. Stoeger, and George V. Coyne (eds.) (Vatican City: Vatican Observatory, 1988; Notre Dame: University of Notre Dame Press), 221.

25 Edward Harrison, *Cosmology: Understanding the Universe* (Cambridge: Cambridge University Press, 1981), 347.

26 Carl Sagan, *Cosmos* (New York: Ballantine Books, 1980), 286.

27 Arthur Peacocke, *God and the New Biology* (London: J. M. Dent, 1986; Magnolia, Ma.: Peter Smith Pub. Inc.), 91.

28 Thomas Berry, *The Dream of the Earth*, 132.

29 John Polkinghorne, *OneWorld: The Interaction of Science and Theology* (London: SPCK, 1986), 56.

30 Quotation taken from Elizabeth A. Johnson, *Women, Earth and Creator Spirit* (New York: Paulist Press, 1993), 37 and 76 n26.

31 Enda Lyons, *Jesus Self Portrait by God*, (Dublin: Columba Press, 1994), 145.

32 K. Rahner,'The Unity of Spirit and Matter in the Christian Understanding of Faith', *Theological Investigations*, vol. 6 (London: DLT, 1969; New York: The Crossroad Publishing Company).

33 Denis Edwards, *Jesus and the Cosmos* (New York: Paulist Press, 1991), 66.

34 Edward Schillebeeckx, *Christ: The Christian Experience in the Modern World* (London: SCM Press, 1980), 529.

35 Elizabeth A. Johnson, along with others, has been pioneering this particular thesis. See E. A. Johnson 'Jesus the Wisdom of God: A biblical basis for non-androcentric christology', *Ephemerides Theologicae Lovanienses*, LXI, (December 1985), 4, 261–94, and *She Who Is: The Mystery of God in Feminist Theological Discourse*, 150–69.

36 A more detailed development of these links between creation and christology can be found in Dermot A. Lane, *The Reality of Jesus: An Essay in Christology* (Dublin: Veritas Publications, 1975; New York: Paulist Press), 130–7, and *Christ at the Centre: Select Questions in Christology* (Dublin: Veritas Publications, 1990), 130–58.

37 See Mary Midgley, 'Fancies about Human Immortality', *The Month*, (Nov. 1990), 458–66.

38 See Chapter 1, 'From the margins to the centre' (p. 1), Chapter 2, 'The christomorphic character of eschatology' (p. 18), and Chapter 7 (p. 96), above.

39 Karl Rahner, 'Christology within an Evolutionary View of the World', *Theological Investigations*, vol. 5 (London: DLT, 1966; New York: The Crossroad Publishing Company), 160.

40 Karl Rahner, *Foundations of Christian Faith: An Introduction to the Idea of Christianity* (London: DLT, 1978; New York: The Crossroad Publishing Company), 196.

41 Ibid., 196.

42 Ernan McMullin, 'Evolution and Special Creation', *Zygon*, 8 (September 1993), 3, 328.

43 *De Resurrectione Mortuorum*, 6 (PL2, 282).

44 *Gaudium et Spes* (G.S., 32).

45 Vatican II has been criticised as being too anthropocentric; yet it must be pointed out that there are at least traces of a cosmocentric anthropology also within the Council documents. For example *Gaudium et Spes* asserts: 'Though made of body and soul, man is one. Through his bodily composition he gathers to himself the elements of the material world. Thus they reach their crown through him, and through him can raise their voice in free praise of the creator.' (art. 14).

46 See Dermot A. Lane, *Christ at the Centre: Select Issues in Christology*, 85–94.

47 Karl Rahner, 'Resurrection: D. Theology', *Sacramentum Mundi: An Encyclopaedia*, vol. 5 (New York: Herder and Herder, 1970), 333. See also the

helpful article by Edward P. Echlin, 'Does Creation Have a Future?', *New Blackfriars*, February 1996, 98–106.

48 *Modern Eucharistic Agreement* (London:SPCK,1973), 29.
49 Karl Rahner, 'Possible Courses For the Theology of the Future', *Theological Investigations*, vol.13 (London: DLT, 1975; New York: The Crossroad Publishing Company), 33.
50 R. S. Thomas, 'Tell Us', *Mass for Hard Times* (Newcastle-upon-Tyne: Bloodaxe Books, 1992), 46.
51 Theophilus of Antioch, *Ad Autolycum*, no. 2 (Sources Chretiennes, 20, 162–4).
52 Taken from W. J. Burghardt, 'The Eschaton and the Resurrection: Patristic Insights', *The Eschaton Community of Love*, J. Papin (ed.) (Philadelphia: Villanova University Press, 1971), 203–29 at 211.
53 D. Bergent and C. Stuhlmuller, 'Creation According to the Old Testament', *Evolution and Creation*, Ernan McMullin (ed.) (Indiana: University of Notre Dame Press, 1985), 157.

Chapter 12

1 John Reumann, *The Supper of the Lord: New Testament, Ecumenical Dialogues, and Faith and Order on the Eucharist* (Philadelphia: Fortress Press, 1985), 49.
2 Norman Perrin, *Rediscovering the Teaching of Jesus* (London: SCM, 1967), 107.
3 Eugene LaVerdiere, *Dining in the Kingdom of God: The Origins of the Eucharist according to Luke* (Chicago: L.T.P., 1994), 10–14.
4 Ibid., 22.
5 Ibid., 22–4.
6 See Mark: 7:1–23.
7 Marcus Borg, *Jesus, A New Vision: Spirit Culture and the Life of Discipleship* (San Francisco: Harper & Row, 1987), 132.
8 See Isaiah 25:6–12; 65:13.
9 Gerald O'Collins, *Christology: A Biblical, Historical and Systematic Study of Jesus* (Oxford: Oxford University Press, 1995), 70–71.
10 Ibid., 73.
11 Zavier Leon-Dufour, *Sharing the Eucharistic Bread: The Witness of the New Testament* (New York: Paulist Press, 1987), 189–92.
12 The fact that this eschatological saying is placed differently in the Synoptics – in Luke before the double action and in Mark and Matthew after the double action – has suggested to some that the saying does not belong to the so-called original words of institution. While this may have some validity it is difficult, given the eschatological thrust of the life of Jesus, to disassociate the meal tradition and the Last Supper from the messianic banquet of the kingdom of God, especially since Jesus himself makes the connection between meals and the messianic banquet (see Luke 14:1–24; Matt. 8:11; 22:2–14).
13 Ibid., 200.
14 Ibid., 124.
15 A summary of Benjamin's dialogue with Horkheimer is available in Helmut

Peukart, *Science, Action, and Fundamental Theology: Towards a Theology of Communicative Action*, translated by James Bohman (Massachusetts: MIT Press, 1984), 206–10. The translation of Benjamin's position 'On the Concept of History' entitled 'Theses on the Philosophy of History' can be found in W. Benjamin, *Illuminations*, edited by Hannah Arendt, translated by Harry Zohn (New York: Schoken Books, 1969), 253–64. A helpful analysis of Benjamin can be found in Rolf Tiedemann, 'Historical Materialism or Political Messianism? An interpretation of the theses "on the concept of history"', *Philosophical Forum XV* (Fall-Winter 1983–1984), nos. 1 and 2, 71–9.

16 Walter Benjamin, 'Theses on the Philosophy of History', *Illuminations*, 257–8.

17 Quotation taken from Rolf Tiedemann, 'Historical Materialism...' *The Philosophical Forum XV*, (Fall-Winter 1983–1984), 79.

18 This quotation is taken from Herbert Marcuse, *One-Dimensional Man* (Boston: Beacon Press, 1968), 257.

19 Walter Benjamin, 'Theses on the Philosophy of History', *Illuminations*, 254.

20 J. B. Metz, *Faith in History and Society: Towards a Practical Fundamental Theology* (London: Burns & Oates, 1980), 184–5.

21 John Reumann, op. cit. 28, with emphasis given by Reumann.

22 See Alan Verhey, 'Remember-Remembrance' *Anchor Bible Dictionary*, vol. 5, 667–9; 'Memorial, Memory', *The Interpreters Bible*, vol. 3, 1962/1986, 344–6.

23 See Mark Lilla, 'The Riddle of Walter Benjamin', *New York Review of Books*, 25th May 1995 , 37–42 at 38.

24 David Power, *The Eucharistic Mystery: Revitalising the Tradition* (Dublin: Gill and Macmillan, 1992; New York: The Crossroad Publishing Company), 305.

25 Kenneth Leech, *True Prayer: An Introduction to Christian Spirituality* (San Francisco: Harper and Row, 1980), 110.

26 Here we must go beyond what Benjamin says about memory linking us with the suffering and death of the victims of history because in the Eucharist we seek to overcome and transcend the dichotomy between the oppressor and the oppressed through the reconciling love and mercy of Christ.

27 An elaboration of this point can be found in Dermot A. Lane, *Foundations for Social Theology: Praxis, Process and Salvation* (Dublin: Gill and Macmillan, 1984; New York: Paulist Press, 1984), 141–69.

28 See Johann Baptist Metz, 'Faith in History and Society: Towards a Practical Fundamental Theology', 88–99; Jurgen Moltmann, 'The Liberating Feast', Herman Schmidt and David Power (eds.), *Politics and Liturgy, Concilium* 1974; Tissa Balasuriya, *The Eucharist and Human Liberation* (London: SCM Press, 1997).

29 Geoffrey Wainwright, *Eucharist and Eschatology* (New York: Oxford University Press, 1981, 1971), 68.

30 Ibid., 70–4.

31 *S.T.*, III, q.60 ad.3.

32 Council of Trent, Thirteenth Session, Chapter 2 available in *The Christian Faith in the Doctrinal Documents of the Catholic Church*, ed. by J. Neuner and J.

Dupuis. Revised edition (London: Collins, 1983; New York: Alba House), 416.

33 *S.C.*, a.8, *G.S.*, a38, *U.R.*, a.15.

34 *Catechism of the Catholic Church* (Dublin: Veritas, 1994; New York: Paulist Press), a.1402 and 1405.

35 *Baptism, Eucharist and Ministry*, Faith and Order Paper No. 111 (Geneva: World Council of Churches, 1982), a.22, see also a.6 and 18.

36 James P. Mackey, *Modern Theology: a Sense of Direction* (Oxford/New York: Oxford University Press, 1987), 185.

INDEX

Index

hope
  and death, 54
  and Eucharist, 209
  historical, 61–3
  and imagination, 64–5, 162
  in Judaism, 72–8
  in life of Jesus, 78–89
  risen Christ as, 112–31
  search for, 57–71
    anthropological aspects, 63–8
    Christian dimensions, 68–71
    landscape of, 59–61
    mapping out a framework, 61–3
  what can we hope for?, 123–31
Horkheimer, Max, 119–21, 201
Horsley, Richard A., 88
Hosea, 76, 105
human experience, 6. *See also*
    anthropology
  and heaven, 140–41
  and hermeneutics, 14–18
  and hope, 61
  negative experiences, 65
  primacy of, 25
  and Purgatory, 146
  and the resurrection, 117–23
  and salvation, 166–7
  self-awareness, 182–3

imagination
  and hope, 64–5, 162
incarnation, doctrine of, 127–8
  fulfilment of creation, 181, 187–8
individualism, 29, 57, 133, 139
  and reincarnation, 172–3
individuality
  and relationality, 31–4
  through relationship, 38–9
Institution Narratives of the
    Synoptics, 194–5
intermediate state, 150–62
International Theological Commission,
    146, 150, 152, 153, 157
Irenaeus, 180
Isaiah, 76, 85, 93, 99, 163, 196
Israel, Twelve Tribes of, 84

Jeanrond, Werner, 134
Jeremiah, 76, 92, 178, 192
Jesus Christ
  advent of *Eschaton* in, 96–111

apocalyptic eschatology, 89–95
Christomorphic character of
    eschatology, 18–20
  and creation, 180–85
  as 'Cynic Sage', 81
  death of as apocalyptic, 96–100
  descent into hell, 141–2
  Good News of, 85–6
  as hope of the world, 112–31
  humanity of, 183–5
  meals of, 195–7, 207
  mediating role, 154
  and next life, 66–7
  prophetic eschatology of, 78–89
  salvation in the present, 166
  'third quest', 79–83
Jesus seminar, 81
Jewish holocaust, 8, 45, 121
Job, 165, 177, 178
Joel, 93, 98, 99, 104
John, St, 23, 80, 147, 152, 159, 185
  eschatology of, 3, 110–11
  on heaven, 138, 139
  on resurrection, 102
John Paul II, Pope, 12, 58
John the Baptist, 83, 84, 88, 90, 98
  eschatology of, 84–5
Joshua, 105
joy, experience of, 61
Joyce, James, 138
Judaism, 100
  covenant, 198–9
  creation story, 136, 177–80, 184
  darkness in, 85, 98
  eschatology of, 39–40
  experience of God, 87–8
  history of, 68
  hope in, 67, 72–8, 115, 126
  life after death, 66, 138, 141
  perceptions of person, 35
  prophetic eschatology, 170–71
  religious matrix of Jesus, 84
  and resurrection, 122
  table-fellowship, 195–6
  theology of memory, 203–4, 205–7
Judas Maccabeus, 143
Judges, 99
judgment day, 2, 15
  in Judaism, 73–4
Jung, Carl, 22

Kaddish, 86
Kahler, Martin, 97

241